TWELFTH EDITION

MISSOURI

OFF THE BEATEN PATH®

PATTI DeLANO & CATHY JOHNSON

Globe
Pequot

Essex, Connecticut

Globe
Pequot

An imprint of Globe Pequot, the trade division of
The Rowman & Littlefield Publishing Group, Inc.
4501 Forbes Blvd., Ste. 200
Lanham, MD 20706
www.rowman.com

Distributed by NATIONAL BOOK NETWORK

British Library Cataloguing in Publication Information available

ISSN 1539–8129
ISBN 978-1-4930-7822-6 (paper: alk. paper)
ISBN 978-1-4930-7823-3 (electronic)

♾™ The paper used in this publication meets the minimum requirements of American National Standard for Information Sciences—Permanence of Paper for Printed Library Materials, ANSI/NISO Z39.48-1992.

Contents

Introduction viii

Southeast Missouri **1**

Gateway to the West 3

Wine Country 17

Wild Lands 29

River Heritage Area 38

Old Mountain Region 45

Bootheel Region 47

Southwest Missouri **51**

Queen of the Ozarks 53

Outdoor Playground 58

Mining Country 68

Tri-Lakes Area 73

Central Missouri **87**

The Heart of America 89

Historic River Section 113

Missouri's Melting Pot 120

The Ozarks 127

Cheese Country 136

Northwest Missouri **141**

The Northlands 143

Northern Missouri River Valley 145

Amish Settlements 150

Jesse James Country 154

Northeast Missouri **183**

Antiques and Antiquity 185

Mark Twain's River 190

Northern Wineries. 193

Bluffs of the Mighty Mo. 198

Glaciated Plains 203

Missouri's Monarchy. 209

Index 216

About the Authors

Patti DeLano is a travel writer and photographer from the Kansas City area who lived in the Ozarks of Missouri and vacationed across the borders in Arkansas and Kansas for more than 40 years. She has also written **Arkansas Off the Beaten Path** and **Kansas Off the Beaten Path** for Globe Pequot. She now lives on the island of Venice, Florida.

Cathy Johnson and Patti DeLano have been friends since 1970 when Patti moved to Excelsior Springs. Cathy is a fine watercolor artist. She invited Patti to help with the very first **Missouri Off the Beaten Path** and the rest is history. The Off the Beaten Path books were illustrated with Cathy's artistic renderings of Patti's photographs in Missouri, Kansas, and Arkansas as Patti took over the writing. This book is a tribute to the two of them back together again. Cathy Johnson is a lifelong Missourian and has delighted in exploring nearly every corner of her home state, especially reveling in the natural areas and small mom-and-pop businesses. She's written and illustrated 36 books, one about the getaway cabin she built deep in the forest near her home. She lives with her husband Joseph and five cats near Kansas City—but not too near!

One last time . . .

Cathy Johnson and Patti DeLano

together again for Missouri

Acknowledgments

No book comes easily, but a sense of humor helps. It's especially true of a book of this sort, which requires so many hours of research and fine-tuning. And so, the sense of humor and the camaraderie of my Missouri friends were essential to this 12th edition. Cathy Johnson (aka Kate Ruckman) shared the writing of the original book with me in the 1980s; therefore, many of the words were hers. So we did this one together again.

Thank you to William Jewell College in Liberty, Missouri, where as a "reentry student" scholar with some, shall we say, maturity, I learned the art and craft of writing.

The Missouri Tourism Bureau and the Missouri Departments of Conservation and Natural Resources, not to mention all the visitors' bureaus and chambers of commerce I contacted in hundreds of little towns, made it easier.

It's impossible to include all the wonderful, quirky places I discovered while researching this book. Others I simply did not know about; still others have only recently appeared or, sadly, have gone out of business. The pandemic and floods destroyed so many small businesses these last few years. If you know of a special place, or a change to an existing listing, please write me or the publisher so that I can add this information when I next update the book.

We would love to hear from you concerning your experiences with this guide and how you feel it could be improved and be kept up to date. Please send your comments and suggestions to: Globe Pequot, Reader Response/ Editorial Department, 246 Goose Lane, Suite 200, Guilford, CT 06437. Or e-mail: editorial@GlobePequot.com.

NORTHWEST
MISSOURI

St. Joseph

Hannibal

NORTHEAST
MISSOURI

Kansas City

Columbia

CENTRAL
MISSOURI

St. Louis

Jefferson City

SOUTHEAST
MISSOURI

Springfield

SOUTHWEST MISSOURI

Introduction

Think of Missouri and a hundred images tumble forward like candy from a piñata. The Pony Express. The Santa Fe Trail. Lewis and Clark. The Civil War. Frank and Jesse James. Mark Twain (who once said that he was born here because "Missouri was an unknown new state and needed attractions"; we certainly got one in Samuel Clemens).

But all of the images are not from the distant past, flickering like a silent movie through the veil of time. There's Branson, now threatening Nashville as the country music capital of the country, with countless entertainment palaces boasting big-name stars of everything from music to magic. There's even a rodeo restaurant! (I'll tell you how to beat the crowds and traffic and help you find a quiet bed-and-breakfast instead of a computer-located motel.) There's also Kansas City's Country Club Plaza, the world's first outdoor shopping center. Kansas City steaks. Charlie Parker and jazz. General John J. Pershing. Writers Calvin Trillin and Richard Rhodes. The founder of Hallmark Cards, Joyce Hall, built an empire, with the international headquarters in Kansas City. Actors Brad Pitt, Kathleen Turner, Bob Cummings, John Goodman, and Don Johnson, as well as Walt Disney (actually Mickey Mouse was born in KC, too, according to Walt), all have ties to Missouri. And, of course, our own Harry S Truman.

What you may not think of immediately are the things we will show you in *Missouri: Off the Beaten Path*. As you travel the state, we will tell you how to pronounce the names of the towns you pass through, so you won't sound like an outsider: Versailles, New Madrid, Nevada, and El Dorado, to name a few.

harrystruman

Just for the record: Harry S Truman had no middle name. Just the S. Consequently, there is no period after the S in Harry S Truman, because it is not an abbreviation. Only sticklers and people from Missouri notice this, and the author is a stickler from Missouri. However, the controversy goes both ways at the Truman Library, and even Harry himself used a period after the S in his signature—occasionally.

Did you know that J. C. Penney got his start here? And Jacques Cousteau—when you think of the man, you imagine oceanic dives in faraway places, right? Cousteau filmed a "deep-earth dive" right here in Bonne Terre and explored his way up the Mississippi and Missouri Rivers as well. Then there's the Kingdom of Callaway, with its postwar ties to none other than Winston Churchill. There are wineries and breweries and distilleries, and there are elegant restaurants and comfort-food cafes that range from fine French to fire-breathing Cajun, with home-style cooking settled somewhere in between.

What we are not is flat farmland, empty prairie, or wall-to-wall cows (or cowboys for that matter). There's a rich diversity of landscape here.

Missouri is covered with forests and rolling hills. It boasts more than 5,000 caves, and those are only the ones I know about. The rugged white bluffs along the rivers (the rocky remains of a prehistoric inland sea) and the volcanic formations and underground streams and caverns in the Lake of the Ozarks area are among the most beautiful in the country. The rivers that sculpted all this spectacular scenery are magnets for exploration; the Jacks Fork, Eleven Point, and Current Rivers are designated National Scenic Riverways. Remnant prairies still beckon—patchwork bits and pieces left over from presettlement days, when the big bluestem and gayfeather grasses were tall enough to hide someone on horseback, and the wind-driven waves imitated a sea of grass.

In 1673 Marquette and Joliet came down the Mississippi River and saw the land that is now called Missouri. The Jesuit missionaries (the Mission of St. Francis Xavier) established the first white settlement in Missouri near the present site of St. Louis around 1700. The Mississippi River, which forms the eastern boundary of the state, is still one of the busiest shipping lanes in the world and has been flowing here since the dawn of time. The upstart Missouri River, on the other hand, was the gift of a departing glacier a short half million years ago; it simply wasn't there before that time. The division between the glaciated plains to the north (rolling and covered with a generous layer of topsoil, also a legacy of the wall of ice, which stole the soil from points north) and the bony Ozark region to the south (rough and hilly with valleys cut deep into rock) is this river that bisects the state from Kansas City to St. Louis. Missouri is where old prairie runs up against the oldest mountain range in the country—a fitting symbol for one of the most historically divided states in the Union.

It was in Missouri that the Civil War was most brutal, issuing as it did from tension that had been building for decades. This pre–Civil War strife between free-state Kansas and the Southern-leaning Missouri was bloody, especially because many Missourians believed that slavery was wrong and worked with the Underground Railroad to help slaves to freedom.

After the Civil War, Quantrill's Raiders and such legendary outlaws as Cole Younger and the James brothers continued the bloodshed. The state bears the reminders to this day. Civil War battlefields and tiny cemeteries, with their solemn testimony of the losses of the war, embody the lingering dichotomy between Northern and Southern sensibilities.

Before the Civil War and for some years afterward, the two rivers—the Missouri and the Mississippi—were main arteries of commerce. All of Missouri's large cities began as river ports, with a lively competition between them for business and settlers. Kansas City and its popular hot spot, Westport (formerly

Westport Landing); St. Joseph, Lexington, Boonville, and Jefferson City, the capital; and Hermann, Washington, and St. Charles, the first capital, all began as ports on the Missouri. Hannibal, St. Louis, Ste. Genevieve, Cape Girardeau, and New Madrid were ports of call on the Mississippi.

Today the big rivers and their connecting waterway system make a 22,000-mile navigable network. Almost all year the tugs and barges can be seen wherever public and private docks allow commodities to be moved inexpensively by water. Only winter's ice jams stop the flow of traffic.

westward-bound supplyline

To supply settlers moving west, packet boats departed from St. Louis and traveled to Kansas City and westward on the wide Missouri River. More than 20 steamboats a day docked at the wharf facilities in St. Joseph, carrying all types of homesteading materials, beads to trade with the Indians, tools, staple goods—everything the growing nation needed as the westward expansion continued.

Kansas City, Missouri's second-largest city (now outgrowing St. Louis, much to the pride of the western part of the state), had its beginnings as a shipping point on the Kansas (still called the Kaw) River bend of the Muddy Mo, where the river turns sharply east on its trek across the state's midriff. The region known by early explorers as the Big Blue Country was occupied by the Kanza (Kansas), whose name means "people of the south wind." The peaceful Kanza engaged in farming, fishing, and trapping; they were quickly displaced when settlers began to move in.

Missouri was once as far off the beaten path as one could get, the jumping-off point to the trackless West; beyond was the great unknown. You can still see the tracks of the wagon wheels etched deeply into our soil on the Santa Fe, California, and Oregon Trails.

Now everything's up to date in Kansas City, as the lyrics to a song once told us. A beautifully modern metropolis, Kansas City has more fountains than any city except Rome and more miles of tree-lined boulevards than any other American city. The Nelson-Atkins Museum of Art, with its quirky giant badminton shuttlecock on the front lawn, owns one of the finest collections of Asian art in the country.

St. Louis, on the other side of the state, has a world-class botanical garden and a rich cultural heritage that rivals any big city in the East. Not surprisingly, St. Louis is proud of its French legacy, a gift of the early explorers.

The **KATY Trail** (its name is derived from MKT, the Missouri-Kansas-Texas Railroad) begins nearby in Machens, just north of St. Louis. This bicycle and hiking trail follows the old MKT Railroad route to Clinton, 75 miles southeast of Kansas City. It covers more than 237 miles of river bluffs, forests, and farmlands with cafes and shops along its route to cater to trail buffs. The KATY is the longest completed rails-to-trails project in the nation. There are so many fun things to do at the recently resurrected towns of bygone days. The scenery along the trail is breathtaking. Towns near the KATY Trail will be noted for those of you carrying this book in a backpack.

trivia

What's in a symbol? From early civilizations, humans have used symbols to tell the story of what is important in their lives. Missouri has a unique history, and each of the state symbols carries a poignant message of the state and its people. As times change, groups propose symbols to represent products or causes that have evolved and that they believe should be recognized. The newest state symbol is the state grape, which was approved by Governor Bob Holden on July 11, 2003. The state's winemaking industry has grown and prospered, leading to the desire for a new symbol.

The word Missouri first appeared on maps made by French explorers in the 1600s. It was the name of a group of Native Americans living near the mouth of a large river. Pekketanoui, roughly its Native name, means "town of the large canoes," and the Missouri would have required them—it was big, swift, and tricky to navigate before the locks and dams of the US Army Corps of Engineers tamed it, or attempted to.

We don't know how the Native Americans pronounced Missouri, and it is about a 50–50 split between the state's current residents. In a recent survey a little more than half the population, most in western Missouri, pronounced the name "Missour-uh." The eastern half of the state favored "Missour-ee."

The "Show-Me State" carries its nickname proudly. We have a reputation as stubborn individualists, as hardheaded as our own Missouri mules—or so they say—and we won't believe something until you show us. It's not such a bad way to be. Our people, like our agrarian ancestors, want concrete proof—we'll change, all right, but only when we're fully convinced that change is synonymous with progress and that progress is indeed an improvement. The past is definitely worth preserving when it is as colorful as ours.

So we will show you parts of the Show-Me State that are tucked away off the beaten path. Some are in the middle of farmland, some are in national forests, and some are in our largest cities. There will be no Worlds of Fun or Six Flags St. Louis or Kauffman Stadium plugs in this book; such places are definitely on the path, and you can find them on your own. What this book does have is something for everyone, as out of the way—and "far from the madding crowd"—as you could wish.

No matter where you're from, whether you love a fine Bordeaux or a fine bourbon, whether you like to go in a sports car dressed to the nines or in a pickup truck wearing an old pair of jeans, you will feel at home in Missouri.

Missouri Information

State flag: The field is made up of three horizontal bands—red, white, and blue—of equal width. The state coat of arms appears in the center. It is encircled by a band of blue bearing 24 white stars.

Capital: Jefferson City

Statehood: August 10, 1821, the 24th state

State bird: Bluebird

State tree: Flowering dogwood

State flower: Hawthorn

State insect: Honeybee

State tree nut: Black walnut

State animal: Mule

State horse: Missouri Fox Trotter

State fish: Channel catfish

State aquatic animal: Paddlefish

State musical instrument: Fiddle

State American folk dance: Square dance

State mineral: Galena

State rock: Mozarkite

State fossil: Crinoid

State grape: Norton/Cynthiana

Missouri Day: Third Wednesday in October. The day is used to encourage students to study Missouri history and to celebrate the accomplishments of Missouri citizens.

Origin of name: From Native American sounds meaning "town of the large canoes," first applied to the river, then to the land.

Nickname: The Show-Me State

State song: "Missouri Waltz," by J. R. Shannon, music arranged by Frederick Logan from a melody by John Valentine Eppel

State seal: A coat of arms appears on the seal. The shield in the center of the seal is divided into two parts. One half shows a bear and a crescent, representing Missouri. The other half shows the eagle of the United States. The two halves are bound together, or united, by a band ending in a belt buckle. The words in the band—"United we stand; divided we fall"—reflect the need for all the states to be united. Two bears support the shield and stand on a streamer on which the state motto is inscribed. A helmet appears above the shield; the 24 stars above the helmet indicate that Missouri was the 24th state. The date at the bottom in Roman numerals (1820) is the date of the Missouri Compromise.

Southeast Missouri

To call southeast Missouri the most beautiful part of the state wouldn't be fair; beauty is a mysterious commodity based on personal definition, as intangible as smoke. But the region has plenty to offer. There is natural beauty—dappled shade of the national forests, cascades of clear blue springs and rivers, and white river bluffs and volcanic rock formations of the Johnson's Shut-Ins—that meets everyone's definition of beauty. Antebellum and Victorian homes on wide boulevards grace the oldest cities west of the Mississippi. Both beautiful and historic, southeast Missouri will appeal to all your senses with its food, wine, scenery, and rich and varied past.

When the river was the frontier to the American West, thousands crossed it in search of land, freedom, and a new life. Trappers, traders, explorers, and settlers joined Native Americans in the fertile river valleys and rich prairies.

Enter the state from the east, and you will encounter the St. Louis area, the big city/small town that spreads west on I-70 and south on I-55. Sneak off these two freeways, and the many small highways branching off from them, to find some of the most charming towns in the state, towns that date from the beginning of the westward expansion of the country.

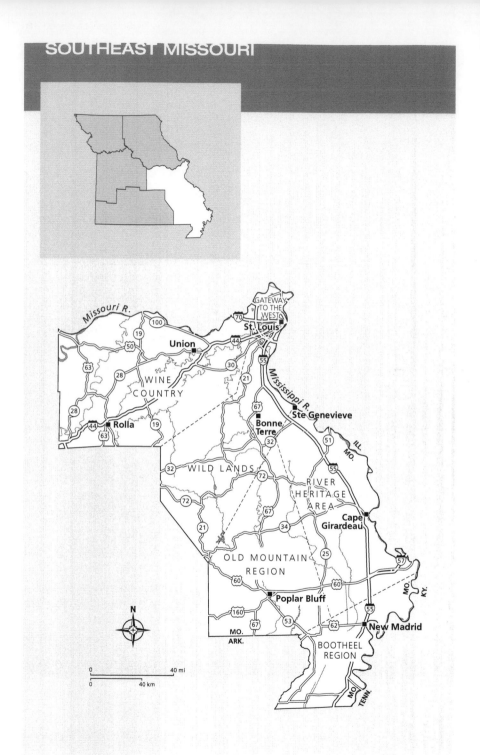

Missouri Spirits Expedition

Since you are probably out driving around the state, you might as well search for some adventure and a prize as well. We have the **Missouri Spirits Expedition,** a statewide distillery trail—inspired by the Lewis & Clark Trail—that searches out 35 different craft distilleries across the entire state. Look for the MSE sign on the wall to identify members. Go to missouricraftdistillersguild.com, give them your email or like them on Facebook, and get a stamp every time you visit a member distillery. Just take the tour and enjoy the tasting and you get a stamp. No purchase necessary. Challenge your group of friends to compete. Visiting 10 wins a $10 voucher, 20 wins a $20 voucher, but finding all of them gets you the grand prize of a special bottle of Missouri Spirits Expedition Blended MO Bourbon Whiskey to place, with pride, on your bar at home. Every single one of these distilleries is in this book; you just have to follow the trail. I wondered how to write about 35 distilleries without repeating the same thing over and over again until I tasted Peanut Butter and Jelly sorghum, Gooey as F**k Rum, Starry Night Absinthe, Bacon Vodka for your Bloody Mary, Blackberry Whiskey, Apple Pie Shine and Pickle Shine (sold in mason jars), Gooey Butter Cake Crème Liqueur, and the list goes on . . . and found it was easy and fun.

Here you have a choice of crowded festivals and busy public campgrounds or the isolation and peace deep in the national forests and wildlife preserves. Missouri in winter is quietly beautiful and secluded; in summer, it is lively and fun. Adventures here range from scuba diving (yes! deep-earth diving in Missouri!) and whitewater canoeing to wine tasting and genealogical searches in the oldest records in the American West. Whether you want to party or to get away from it all, you can wander off the beaten path into southeast Missouri.

Gateway to the West

The bustling *St. Louis* area is still the best place to begin westward exploration. Located on a shelf of riverfront under a bluff, the original city spread to the prairies surrounding it. It was the starting point for the Meriwether Lewis and William Clark expedition in 1804. The history of western expansion begins here, where the Missouri and the Mississippi Rivers meet.

St. Louis, founded in 1764, boasts the oldest park west of the Mississippi (Lafayette Park), the second-oldest symphony orchestra in the nation, the world's largest collection of mosaic art at the Cathedral of St. Louis, and one of the finest botanical gardens in the world. The graceful Italianate mansion *Tower Grove House* at the *Missouri Botanical Garden* (314-577-5100; mobot.org) is a more than 150-year-old wonder that blooms with color each Christmas season. Local garden clubs, the Herb Society of St. Louis, and others

TOP RECOMMENDATIONS IN SOUTHEAST MISSOURI

Bias Vineyards & Winery

Blue Owl Restaurant and Bakery

Bonne Terre Mines

Broussard's Cajun Restaurant

Kimmswick

Rock Eddy Bluff Farm

Southern Hotel

Ste. Genevieve

Washington

bathe the house in wreaths, seasonal flowers, and greens. Candlelight tours and teas and holiday luncheons are the special events. The home and 79-acre garden are open for tours Tues through Sun (closed Christmas) 9 a.m. to 5 p.m. For nonresidents of St. Louis County, admission is $14 for adults; children younger than age 13 free. (In the Children's Garden, kids can climb tree houses and play in water jets.) For residents of St. Louis County, admission is $6.

graduate education

The oldest university west of the Mississippi River is St. Louis University, which began as an academy in 1818.

Also in St. Louis are the futuristic Climatron and the country's tallest man-made monument, the **Gateway Arch,** which is also the world's third-most-popular tourist attraction (but we're talking beaten path here, aren't we?).

It's also a city of firsts. The first Olympiad in the US was held here in 1904; the first hot dog, ice-cream cone, and iced tea were all introduced at the 1904 World's Fair. Remember "Meet me in St. Louie, Louie, meet me at the fair?" For more information about the city, look for the St. Louis website at stlouis-mo.gov.

The Gateway to the West (or to the East, if you are traveling the other way) was fed by train travel beginning in the early 1800s. More than 100,000 passengers have passed through **Union Station** each day since it was built in 1896 at 1820 Market St. (Actually, it sounds more like a revolving door than a gateway.) This is a 2-block-long gray limestone fortress with a red-tile roof that features a clock tower that looms 230 feet in the air. When the last train left the station in 1978, the city had a white elephant of gargantuan proportions on its hands. Union Station is too historic to tear down, too expensive to keep up. Now there are at least 15 shops and arcades to wander through.

TOP ANNUAL EVENTS IN SOUTHEAST MISSOURI

MAY
Annual Jaycee Bootheel Rodeo and Redneck Barbecue Cook-**Off**
Sikeston
A world-championship event with top Nashville recording artists performing nightly.
(800) 455-BULL (2855)
sikestonrodeo.com

Jour De Fete
Ste. Genevieve
A large craft fair.
saintegenevievejourdefete.com

SEPTEMBER
St. James Annual Grape and Fall Festival
St. James
(573) 265-6649

Mosaics
St. Charles
An upscale yet affordable showcase of fine artisans from across the state.
(636) 946-7776 or (800) 366-2427
historicstcharles.com

OCTOBER
Oktoberfest
Hermann (citywide)
First four full weekends in Oct.
hermannmissouri.com

Milo's Annual Risotto Cook-Off
St. Louis
On the Hill at Milo's Bocce Garden.
(314) 770-0400

Oktoberfest
Cape Girardeau
Second full weekend in Oct, with craftspeople in traditional dress and bluegrass music. At Black Forest Village (an 1870s replica village).
(573) 335-0899

DECEMBER
Kimmswick Historical Society's Annual Christmas Tour of Historic Homes
Kimmswick
Each home has a different theme.
visitkimmswick.com

Las Posadas
St. Charles
A lighted Christmas walk with Mary and Joseph, the first Sat night in Dec.
(636) 946-7776
historicstcharles.com

The Grand Hall, once the waiting room, is now the lobby of the St. Louis Union Statin Hotel. Look up at the 65-foot barrel-vaulted ceilings and finely decorated walls. Arches and columns abound. The famous "whispering arch" allows you to whisper to a friend 40 feet away. Sculpted maidens holding gilded torches, floral flourishes, and scrollwork entice the eye. Most impressive is the glowing stained-glass window depicting three women representing New York, San Francisco, and—the one in the middle—St. Louis, the crossroads of America.

And although the trains don't stop here anymore, you can grab the Metro-Link public rail system (metrostlouis.org) right outside for a ride to the Gateway Arch or Busch Stadium. Stop at the sculpture fountain across the street from the station. It's called *Meeting of the Waters* and symbolizes the confluence of the Missouri and Mississippi Rivers.

First, though, get a map of St. Louis. Although its many interesting little neighborhoods make the city charming, they also make it difficult for visitors to find their way.

The **Gateway Arch,** Eero Saarinen's 630-foot architectural marvel that commemorates Thomas Jefferson and the nation's westward expansion, may not be exactly off the beaten path—after all, it's one of the most-visited tourist destinations in the country—but did you know that just south of the Arch, the *Tom Sawyer* and *Becky Thatcher* riverboats provide one-hour cruises of St. Louis Harbor. Visit **Gateway Riverboat Cruises** at gatewayarch.com for times and prices. Gateway descends from Streckfus Steamers, which was established in 1884. Captain John Streckfus ran steamboats from New Orleans to St. Paul, Minnesota, and stopped in towns along the way. There was live music aboard, and Streckfus would comb the clubs in New Orleans looking for good musicians. One day in 1918 he found a musician who was fresh out of reform school. His name was Louis Armstrong, and he would work the riverboats *Sidney* and *Capital* until 1922. Legend has it, believe this or not, that the musicians called the new kind of music they played on the Streckfus riverboats "J.S." (for John Streckfus), and that eventually became the word *jazz.*

While you history-minded folk are in the neighborhood of the Arch, don't miss the **Old Cathedral Museum,** visible just to the west and still in the Gateway Arch Park. Here you'll find some of the finest (and oldest) ecclesiastical art in the country, with works by the Old Masters not uncommon. Documents dating from the beginning of the cathedral as well as photographs on the building of the Arch are all part of the museum. If it's Sunday evening, you can attend Mass at the cathedral at 5 p.m. The Old Cathedral Museum (314-231-3250) at 209 Walnut in St. Louis is open daily from 9:30 a.m. to 3:30 p.m. Donation only.

The Loop Area

The Loop area is fun to visit—the musicians playing on the street, the stars on the sidewalk, and the ambience. Your only regret is that your time here is too short. Even in the middle of the day, the place is alive. What must it have been like at night when Chuck Berry was in town? You can stay at **Moonrise Hotel** (314-721-1111; moonrisehotel.com), a boutique hotel in the heart of the Loop. A big cratered moon spins atop the hotel, and there is a collection of lunar art in the lobby and large rooms.

While you are down on the riverfront, you can even take a 5-minute helicopter tour of downtown. Everything you want to know about the Arch is at (877) 982-1410; gatewayarch.com.

bellefontaine cemetery

Calvary Cemetery and *Bellefontaine Cemetery (bellefontainecemetery.org)* are next to each other in north St. Louis. Here lie the bodies of Civil War General William Tecumseh Sherman; author Kate Chopin; playwright Tennessee Williams; Dred Scott, the slave who sued unsuccessfully for his freedom; and Madame Pelagie Aillotte Rutgers, a woman of color who was one of the wealthiest property owners in the early city. And a monument to the memory of four Nez Perce warriors who died while visiting General William Clark of Lewis and Clark fame. Clark is buried at Bellefontaine, along with Beat Generation author William Burroughs, brewery magnate Adolphus Busch, and Pulitzer Prize–winning poet Sara Teasdale.

If you visit the **St. Louis Cathedral** (cathedralstl.org) on Lindell in the Central West End, built in 1907, look up to the heavens, or the ceiling in this case, and you will see the largest collection of mosaic art in the world. The oak doors lead into a sanctuary decorated in the Byzantine tradition of beautiful domes, arches, and mosaics. The mosaics are made with over 41 million glass tessera tiles with more than 8,000 shades of color; they tell the stories of faith throughout history. You will see Christ's 12 apostles, the Last Supper, and scenes of Old Testament prophesies of Christ's coming. Areas throughout the cathedral contain more mosaic panels. Tiffany's of New York created the panels in the cathedral's Blessed Virgin's Chapel in the Italian style, from Mary's Presentation to her Assumption. Panels also depict the life of Saint Louis IX, king of France and namesake of the city.

Bailey's Chocolate Bar (1915 Park Ave.; 314-241-8100; baileyschocolatebar.com) in St. Louis is the go-to place for chocolate lovers everywhere. David Bailey not only has a full bar with more than 60 different beers, martinis, and champagne, but he also turns out desserts using chocolate from around the world. Truffles, ice-cream desserts, and luscious chocolate drinks for those cool Missouri days. (Ah, yes, try "La Morte"—Death—a blend of chocolate, vanilla, and cream.) If you don't like chocolate but your sweet tooth demands something else, there is always a changing menu of whimsical goodies from which to choose. No sweets for you? Then look at the mix-and-match cheese menu and have several types of cheese with fresh house-made bread, fruit, and nuts. The Chocolate Bar is open Wed, Thurs, and Sun 5 p.m. to midnight, Fri and Sat till 1 a.m.

Still 630 Distillery is in downtown St. Louis at 1000 S. 4th St. (314-513-2275; still630.com) and is ranked third in the nation in craft distilleries by USA Today 10 Best. Stop in for exciting new cocktails every Fri 5 to 9 p.m. and for occasional tastings tours on Sat noon to 4 p.m. by appointment. Enjoy experiencing some of these iconic whiskeys side by side. Or take yourself on a full spirit journey with the variety pack to go. The most interesting thing here is the fascinating Library of Indomitable Spirits, a collection of hundreds of bottles of distilled samples. The Botanical Library has over 400 distilled samples of individual ingredients, the Evolutionary Library has samples from brown spirits—whiskey, rum, brandy—and the Experimental Spirits Program is a catalog of each spirit released. If you are curious about how good whiskey is created, spend some time here before you ask for your first **Missouri Spirits Expedition** stamp.

Also in the downtown area is the ***St. Louis Mercantile Library Association Art Museum*** at 510 Locust (umsl.edu/mercantile). If you admire the works of Missouri artist George Caleb Bingham, who captured our history on canvas; if you're awed by the accomplishments of George Catlin as he traveled among the tribes of Native Americans and painted them one by one; if you've wished you could see a painting by one of the famous Peale family of 19th-century artists (portrait painter Sarah Peale, in this case, who supported herself for many years here in the past century), you won't want to miss this place. Established in 1846, it is the oldest circulating library west of the Mississippi, and in addition to art, you can find rare books: Americana, westward expansion, river transportation, and so on. Admission is free. For a docent-led tour, call (314) 577-5100.

1220 Artisan Spirits at 1220 S. 8th St. is where you can find canned cocktails with names like Paloma (grapefruit juice flavor) and Bramble (vodka with blackberry). Vanilla Cold Brew, a personal favorite eye-opening marriage of cold-brew coffee, vanilla, and chocolate, this perfect-for-the-morning, but delightful anytime canned cocktail with Encrypted Vodka features hints of blueberry and is super smooth and creamy. Get your **Missouri Spirits Expedition** stamp. Now you have two stamps and haven't even left St. Louis yet. This is going to be easy.

The name doesn't tell you the reason for searching out this place, but once you know, you will be a regular at the ***Crown Candy Kitchen*** (1401 St. Louis Ave.; 314-621-9650; crowncandykitchen.net), just 1.25 miles north of the Arch, where wonderful chocolate candy has been made since 1913. The main attraction here, however, is the city's oldest soda fountain. The business was founded by the current owners' grandfather. Their father, George, inherited the business, and the three current owners, Andy, Mike, and Tom Karandzieff, grew up here.

The Mother Road

Getting your kicks on *Route 66* is still possible in Missouri. As the famous highway "winds from Chicago to LA," you "go through St. Louis, and Joplin, Missouri" along the Mother Road. In St. Louis, Drewes Frozen Custard has been a stopping place on old Route 66 since 1929. Farther on you can still see the distinctive art deco tile front from the Coral Court Motel at the Museum of Transportation. Next is Route 66 State Park, where the state is creating a museum devoted to roadside Americana. You can walk among Missouri's wildflowers at the Shaw Arboretum of the Missouri Botanical Garden at Gray Summit and visit Meramec Caverns at Stanton as people have been doing since 1933. Spend the night at the circa 1930 Wagon Wheel Motel, which still stands in Cuba.

Perhaps the most beautiful spot on Missouri's portion of Route 66 is Devil's Elbow along the bluffs over the Big Piney River. The 1940s Munger-Moss Motel is in Lebanon, where you can rest up for the drive through Springfield. Be sure to watch for the Shrine Mosque, an *Arabian Nights*–style edifice that has hosted concerts since the 1950s. Then head to Carthage's magnificent Victorian homes and the Route 66 Drive-In Theatre.

The new highway created some havoc. Spencer is a ghost town now, but some of the original roadway remains from when the town was bypassed. Joplin, the western end of Route 66 in Missouri, is one of the dozen towns named in the famous song immortalizing the more-than-1,000-mile route that winds from Chicago to Los Angeles through the heart of Missouri. Here is a list of cities where you can still get your kicks, in Missouri, on Route 66: St. Louis, Cuba, Rolla, Lebanon, Springfield, Carthage, and Joplin.

Nothing much has changed in their world-class milkshakes: homemade ice cream, milk, and your choice of syrup. If you want a "malted," you can have that, too. Of course, what is a milkshake without a chili dog? Andy and Mike can fix that up for you, no problem. The malted has 1,100 calories in it, so what difference will a little chili dog make in the big scheme of things, right? Oh yes, they still make fresh chocolate candy in the winter. Truth be told, they make chicken salad to die for and a great BLT if you want to be sensible about lunch. Hours are Mon through Thurs 10:30 a.m. to 8 p.m., Fri and Sat 10:30 a.m. to 9 p.m., and Sun 11 a.m. to 5 p.m.

As long as we are talking about ice cream, it's only fair to tell you about another favorite. This is the old 1950s walk-up kind of place with a packed parking lot. See a lot of people in bright yellow T-shirts? Lucky you; you have found **Ted Drewes Frozen Custard** (6726 Chippewa St.; 314-481-2652; ted-drewes.com). This place has been a St. Louis favorite since 1929 when Ted's father started the business. Drewes is known for the thickest shake anywhere (you can hold it upside down and the spoon and straw stay put), so thick

trivia

If you are doing St. Louis on the cheap, you will be glad to find St. Louis's treasured **Forest Park** and the St. Louis Zoo (314-367-2224; forestparkforever.org), where many of the attractions are free. You can see a Broadway-type musical that is locally produced at the outdoor Muny Opera, the oldest and largest outdoor musical theater (constructed in 1917), at no charge. Just show up early and bring a picnic because 1,620 of the 9,000 seats in this urban hillside outdoor theater are set aside as free on a first-come basis. Check the schedule at (314) 361-1900; muny.org. You can take a boat ride around the Grand Basin and have lunch at the Boathouse, a waterside cafe. Trails, bicycling, golf and tennis, hay rides, ice skating, tobogganing, and cross-country skiing are also available. In addition, there's the zoo, an art museum, a science center, and the Missouri History Museum. And if there is a free Live on the Levee concert, you can join the crowd at the riverfront (fairstlouis.org).

("How thick is it?") he calls it a "concrete," because it just won't shake. So thick the server wears a hard hat. These thick—very thick—shakes have mysterious names such as the Cardinal Sin, named for the baseball team (fudge sauce and red cherries), or the All Shook Up (Elvis's favorite snack: peanut-butter cookies and banana). But the strawberry shortcake is the best thing on the menu. Hours are from 11 a.m. until "at least 10:45 p.m." seven days a week. There's a second location at 4224 S. Grand, St. Louis (314-352-7376), if one wasn't enough. This time order the Abaco Mocha, a tropical treat, or a Fox-treat with fudge sauce, raspberries, and macadamia nuts. Drewes closes for about a month from early January to right before Valentine's Day.

A few blocks away is another favorite with the Sweet Tooth in your family. **Gooey Louie's** at 6483 Chippewa (314–352-CAKE (2253); gooeybuttercake.com) is famous for the gooey butter cake everyone loves. Everything is baked from scratch in this family-owned bakery that uses an old family recipe with real farm-fresh butter, eggs, cream cheese . . . well, you get the picture. The Gooey Butter Bites are a good place to start to just try them out, not that there is any chance you won't love them.

Circus Flora (314-827-3830; circusflora.org) is a one-ring circus under the big top in Grand Center. It relives the days before the Civil War when the Floating Palace circus traveled the Mississippi.

The *Loop* area of St. Louis has been evolving into one of the most exciting and entertaining neighborhoods in the metro area. There has been a renaissance in this neighborhood between the 6000 and 6600 blocks of Delmar Boulevard. This area is close to Washington University and is a shining example of urban revitalization, with more than 30 international and American restaurants offering Ethiopian, Lebanese, European, Persian, Italian, Nigerian, Greek, Japanese, Thai, Mexican, Korean, and Chinese cuisine. There are also barbecue, deli, fondue, and contemporary and classic American selections. The renaissance continues in the area of entertainment with sidewalk performers and live music. Almost every genre of music can be found in the many clubs along the boulevard. Make sure that you look down at the sidewalk stars, where the nonprofit **St. Louis Walk of Fame** is a shining tribute of more than 100 stars honoring famous St. Louisians. There are also plaques listing their many achievements, which make this pleasant stroll educational as well as enjoyable. Also impressive and inviting are the many and diverse boutiques.

Pin-Up Bowl (6191 Delmar Blvd.; 314-727-5555; pinupbowl.com) is St. Louis's original bowling and martini lounge. Above eight bowling lanes are four projection screens showing music videos and cartoons. If you are a "pinup connoisseur," you will love this place. Many pinups are from original calendars and *Esquire* magazine centerfolds from the 1940s. The menu features Campbell's soup, fresh pizza, and many appetizers, sandwiches, and desserts. The alley is open until 3 a.m. daily and becomes a party as much as a bowling experience after midnight, with crazy drinks in unusual colors and a mostly yuppie crowd.

St. Louis is the hometown of Chuck Berry, and located at 6504 Delmar in the Loop is **Blueberry Hill** (314-727-4444; blueberryhill.com). Owner Joe Edwards describes this St. Louis landmark as being filled with pop culture memorabilia, including Chuck Berry's guitar and a plethora of vintage 45-rpm jukeboxes. A wide variety of items are available on the menu. There are darts, video games, pinball games, and even a photo booth. The Duck Room features live touring bands, and don't miss the Elvis Room, which features karaoke on Thursday and Friday nights. The restaurant is open from 11 a.m. daily.

Laumeier Sculpture Park (12580 Rott Rd.; 314-615-5278; laumeiersculpturepark.org) is located about 12 miles southwest of downtown St. Louis. The artwork here is grand and huge. Artist Alexander Liberman's *The Way* is made of steel cylinders intended for use as underground storage tanks. He arranged them in bent piles and welded them together. The whole thing was painted bright red. In June and July sculptors work for weeks on detailed sand castles; in winter a fire-and-ice sculpture made of giant ice blocks glows amid roaring bonfires. The 98-acre park has more than 60 pieces. The wooded path hides human-size sheet-metal figures by Ernest Trova. Special events—symphony, dance, ballet, and theater productions—and a gallery full of indoor art are there, too. A cafe and a museum shop are inside, but outdoors is more fun. Take I-44 to Lindbergh Boulevard, go south 0.5 mile, and turn right onto Rott Road; the park entrance is 0.5 mile on the left. It is open daily from 8 a.m. until half an hour after sunset. Call for gallery hours. Admission is free.

You should not go to St. Louis without visiting the Hill, southwest of the city, an Italian neighborhood famous for its restaurants. There is no favorite because it depends on the type of ambience you seek. The best bargain is probably *Cunetto's House of Pasta* (5452 Magnolia Ave.; 314-781-1135; cunetto.com). It's a good place to take the family, prices are moderate, and the atmosphere is Continental—tablecloths, wine, no bright lights, and a full-service bar. Owner Frank Cunetto calls it gourmet Italian with good prices. His dad and uncle opened the doors more than 30 years ago, and it has been a popular spot ever since. Hours are Wed through Sat 4:45 p.m. to close (opens 4 p.m. on Sun).

But more interesting is *Charlie Gitto's on the Hill* (5226 Shaw Ave.; 314-772-8898; charliegittos.com), because this is where one of the best-loved Italian dishes—toasted ravioli—was invented in 1947. It was a lucky accident that Charlie's father was the maître d' at this very spot when it was called Angelo's. He and Angelo were messing around with different ravioli recipes and dropped the little stuffed pillows into oil instead of water. Now they are dusted with fresh Parmesan and served with marinara sauce for the perfect appetizer. If you can't decide what to order, ask for the trio of the day, smaller portions of three menu items selected by the chef. Dessert must be tiramisu, Charlie's mama's family recipe made with cocoa, mascarpone cheese, and homemade cookies soaked in sambuca and espresso.

Then wipe the cannoli cream off your face and be sure to take the time to visit *St. Ambrose Church* (314-771-1228; stambroseonthehill.org), the Hill's centerpiece, about 4 blocks from Cunetto's. It is Lombardy Romanesque and was the first acoustical plaster church in St. Louis. The columns of scagliola plaster look like marble and were made using plaster, ground gypsum, sponges, and polishing. The statues were donated by groups from different villages in Italy. Sunday Mass is at 7, 9, and 11 a.m. Mass in Italian is celebrated on the first Sunday of the month at 11 a.m. Across the street is *Milo's Tavern & Bocce Garden* (5201 Wilson; milosboccegarden.com), where locals gather. When you settle in with one of the restaurant's Italian sausage sandwiches or anchovy pizzas to watch the bocce leagues play, it sounds—and feels—as though you have crossed the Atlantic. Of course, you must try for the annual Columbus Day Bocce Tournament for some serious players as well as Milo's annual Risotto Cook-Off in October. Oh, and for the record, the game is pronounced "bow-chee" not "botch-ee," by the way.

Volpi's (5258 Dagget Ave.; 314-772-8550; volpifoods.com) is a family-owned maker of authentic Italian meats by fourth-generation salumieri. Family recipes have been handed down since 1903 when John Volpi came here from Italy. Lorenza Pasetti and his father, Armando, have continued to prepare

> # 'Sploding Cannoli
>
> Speaking of *cannoli,* that ricotta/whipped cream treat that finishes a good Italian meal, it reminds me of a funny, call it "tradition," that has been in my Italian family for years. Who knows where it started or where it will end, but whenever a newcomer joins the family for a holiday meal for the first time—this means girlfriends, boyfriends, fiancées, visiting in-laws, whatever—we all begin to snicker and giggle when the cannoli are served after dinner. The plates are arranged so that the newcomers get a cannoli with cream filling plugging both ends while the center is filled with powdered sugar. (Don't try this at home.) Then everyone sits around waiting for the unfortunate person to bite into it and cause an explosion of powdered sugar that covers the face of the unsuspecting victim. I really thought the "tradition" would die with my generation, until my son's mother-inlaw joined us for Thanksgiving dinner one year and my little granddaughter, bless her heart, came into the kitchen to whisper in my ear, "Gramma, are we going to do the 'sploding cannoli trick on Grammy?" Some traditions will never die as long as sons whisper into their children's ears . . .

cure-dried Italian meats like prosciutto, pepperoni, rotola, and salami. There are no artificial ingredients, and the product is simple and good. And now, over 120 years after John Volpi opened the little storefront, his great-niece Lorenza has taken over the business.

Naked Spirits, at 1002 Hanley Industrial Ct. off I-64 (314-858-6722; naked-spirits.com), has tastings and tours by appointment if you want your **Missouri Spirits Expedition** stamp. The hours, last check, were Fri 4 to 6 p.m. and Sat noon to 2 p.m. The distillery has one thing you won't find anywhere else: the Naked Spirits' Custom Barrel Program, where you work hand-in-hand with the distiller to create your own spiced or flavored rum. Depending on length of aging, each barrel will produce 200 to 230 bottles of your one-of-a-kind spirit, bottled and labeled with your own custom label. Not just spiced rums but rums like Gooey as F**k Rum, flavored after the favorite childhood dessert your mom made—sweet, gooey butter cake. If that made you roll your eyes, try the more serious Mocha Royale, a high-octane, fully caffeinated, mocha-flavored rum that is more grown-up.

The Lemp Mansion Restaurant & Inn (3322 DeMenil Place; 314-664-8024; lempmansion.com) had humble beginnings when the patriarch of the family emigrated from Germany and began making and selling vinegar and beer. His beer gained notoriety all over the city and soon gained coast-to-coast distribution—one of the first beers to do so—but the family had nothing but grief to go along with its good fortune. Six heirs died—four of them suicides—right there in the mansion. It may well be the most haunted restaurant in the state. And, if you are game to spend the night there, the inn has rooms for you. Be prepared for the ghostly manifestations rumored to happen: knocking sounds, food mysteriously floating about the table, or apparitions in the stairwells. Enjoy your stay.

If you prefer to head south instead, you'll find St. Louis's own French Quarter in historic **Soulard,** 2 miles south of the Arch on Broadway. There's a dandy mix of period architecture and pubs, cafes, and shops for you to browse in. You can buy everything from turnips to live chickens on Saturday mornings in the busy farmers' market in this French/Irish neighborhood, and finish up at a well-stocked spice shop. Soulard is an old brewery neighborhood where rehabilitated row houses line the streets. The Anheuser-Busch brewery is nearby, and when the wind is right you can smell hops and barley cooking. Soulard also has a large collection of jazz and blues clubs.

Antiques stores line both sides of Cherokee Street for 4 blocks in the funky antiques district south of downtown. Prices here are very affordable, and there are dusty treasures in dark corners and beautifully restored pieces as well. You will find rare books, antique linens and lace, and glassware; shop owners will still haggle on the price of more expensive items.

If you want to stay in the St. Louis area but not in the city itself, there is a cluster of suburban cities nearby. Many of them have bed-and-breakfast inns available. Check out the charming cobblestoned street of downtown **St. Charles** (636-946-7776; discoverstcharles.com), once Missouri's state capital and now home to specialty shops and restaurants housed in historic buildings. There are seven B&Bs in St. Charles, located off I-70 west of St. Louis.

Now Kansas City isn't the only Missouri city with a dollhouse museum. The **Miniature Museum of Greater St. Louis** (4746 Gravois; 314-832-7790; miniature-museum.org) has a fine collection of dollhouses and miniatures, many of them painstakingly handcrafted and donated by local miniaturists. The museum is a bit off the beaten path, but well worth the visit. Hours are Wed through Sat 11 a.m. to 4 p.m. and Sun 1 to 4 p.m. There is a small admission charge.

The **Endangered Wolf Center** (636-938-5900; endangeredwolfcenter.org) offers

it'selementary

The first public kindergarten in the country was opened in St. Louis in 1873. Since that time a lot of famous people have started life in St. Louis: Chuck Berry, Maya Angelou, Red Foxx, Yogi Berra, Kevin Kline, Vincent Price, and musicians Akon and SZA. Actor John Goodman is from nearby Affton, and Dick Van Dyke is from Webster Groves. Josephine Baker was born in St. Louis and moved to France, where she was an actress, singer, and dancer, and during World War II a member of the French Resistance. She was awarded the Croix de Guerre after the war for her work as a spy.

an adults-only (that got your attention) Wine and Cheese Twilight Howl. Shall I go on? It begins indoors at 7 p.m. with wine and cheese and a talk by experts on wolf behavior (do they really howl at a full moon?), then moves outdoors near the wolf habitats for the wolf howl. They show you how to initiate a wolf howl and see if the wolves howl back. It doesn't take long to get the howling started, then back inside for dessert and coffee and questions. The program is offered year-round on the third Friday of the month. Advance reservations are required—it fills up fast.

The center is a 50-acre breeding area for red wolves, Mexican gray wolves, and other canids. The goal is the eventual reintroduction of these beautiful dog-like creatures, which are near extinction. The keepers here avoid touching them except for veterinary visits because it is essential to their survival to fear humans. But they do give them names: Rogue and Amigo are two of fewer than 100 Mexican grays left in the world. They are big and strong and watch their puppies closely. Another pair—red wolves—is Paco and Katni, who prance with tails held high to show that this is, indeed, their territory. These canids are the species' last hope for survival. They are kept in fenced enclosures and can be seen from 9 a.m. to 5 p.m. daily. (Call in advance because walk-ins are not permitted. Tours are by appointment only.) In Apr and May, the center is closed for breeding.

Square One Brewing, Distillery and Restaurant, off I-44 at 1727 Park Ave. (314-231-2537; squareonebrewing. com) is in a restored historic building with an outdoor courtyard on Lafayette Square. There are lots of things to try before you get your **Missouri Spirits Expedition** stamp. You can start with brews: Melomel Mead, Bavarian Weizen, Single Malt Scotch Ale, Irish Stout, and Barrel Aged Barley Wine were just some of the brews on tap. Then we move on to spirits: Vermont Night Maple Whiskey, SOS Cucumber Vodka, SOS Jalapeno Vodka, Starry Night Absinthe, Regatta Bay Gin, and Island Time Amber Rum. Kitchen hours are Mon through Thurs

trivia

People streaking along US 40 near the Oakland Avenue exit are likely to hit the brakes when they see massive turtles sunning themselves on the banks of the road. These huge terrapins are not waiting to cross the road but are the creations of sculptor Robert Cassilly. If you look closely, the 40-foot-long snapping turtle, slick-shelled stinkpot, red-eared slider, Mississippi map, and soft-shelled turtle have children crawling inside their cave-like mouths, swinging from their necks, and grasping their eyeballs to climb up top their heads. A path leads to a sunken playground full of turtle eggs, some with freshly hatched crawlers emerging from the shells. Stop and visit the Turtles at Forest Park, Oakland Avenue, just off US 40 East, anytime from sunrise to sunset.

11 a.m. to 9 p.m., Fri 11 a.m. to 10 p.m., Sat 10 a.m. to 1 p.m. (brunch) and 1:30 to 10 p.m. (dinner), and Sun 10 a.m. to 2 p.m. (brunch) and 2:30 to 8 p.m. (dinner). Bar hours run an hour later.

Florissant, just north of downtown St. Louis, is so called because the first inhabitants found it a beautiful, flowering valley. It still is—but that's not all the town has to offer. Jesuit father Pierre Jean DeSmet, champion of the Native nations, founded the **Old St. Ferdinand Shrine** (1 Rue St. Francois; 314-837-2110; oldstferdinandshrine.com), now open to the public. The cornerstone was laid in 1821 to replace the little log church destroyed by fire. Tours are available Apr through Oct, Sun 1 to 4 p.m. without an appointment. The shrine is open for tours any day by appointment.

While you are in the St. Louis area, you can hunt down another stamp for your **Missouri Spirits Expedition.** Look for **Switchgrass Spirits** (6100 Idadle Ave.; 314-203-6539; switchgrassspirits.com), on the north side of St. Louis. When wagons crossed the area not so long ago, the most striking views the pioneers would have taken in were the oceans of deeply rooted switchgrass that stretched as far as the eye could see. Patrick Grosch (head distiller), Nick Colombo (head of operations and finance), and Sarah Miller (head of compliance and outreach) have a distillery named for the view, not just the grass, but their philosophy is that one blade of switchgrass isn't much to see but thousands of acres are a sight to behold. They feel that way about distilling. Together they make a fine product that wouldn't happen alone. They create bourbon and rye, as do the other distilleries we shall visit in this book, but they also make apple brandy with fruit from local orchards. There is a whiskey called Copperhead (it has a bite), and an 80-proof called Rock & Rye, made from rye whiskey and rock candy. But don't let that fool you—they call it "a bottled cocktail with a bite." It is made from Belgian rock candy and citrus. This is one of the many chances in St. Louis to get your 35 Missouri Spirits Expedition stamps and a bottle to take home.

If you just want to get out of St. Louis for a bit, here's a day trip an hour southwest of the city that you might enjoy. Take I-44 and get off on US 50 near *Union.* Two of the distilleries you will be seeking out are nearby, so if you want to begin collecting the stamps, this is the first place to go. The **Old Ozarkian Distillery** tasting room at 203 E. Main Ste A (314-799-1738) has been distilling since 2018 in Union. They use single 15-gallon barrels, and each whiskey and bourbon is unique, done the old-fashioned way. They say "hours subject to change due to distilling and corn-picking," but the tasting room is usually open Sat 10 a.m. to 4 p.m. **Samuel Berton Distilling** (102 Front St., Ste. 102; 314-586-7057; sbdistilling.net), in pretty downtown *Labadie,* can get your day off to a great start with its Bacon Vodka for your Bloody Mary. Bacon

Vodka is made with smoked, peppered bacon and all-natural flavoring. There's also the Rose Hip Liqueur, the Honey Liqueur (old Eastern European drink good for your health), and the Coffee Liqueur to perk you up in your morning cuppa. And get your **Missouri Spirits Expedition** stamp, too. Tasting room hours are Tues through Thurs 1:30 to 5 p.m., Fri through Sat 1 to 7 p.m., and Sun 1 to 5 p.m.

At *Junie Moon Cafe* (300 W. US 50; 636-584-0180; juniemooncafe.com), you can eat down-home comfort food for under 10 bucks. From breakfast to the Blu Cheese Burger with homemade chips, Philly wrap, or pulled pork, it is worth the trip.

Find the **Black Madonna Shrine** at 100 St. Joseph Hill Rd. in Pacific (636-938-5361). In 1927, six Franciscan brothers emigrated to Missouri from Poland. One was Brother Bronislaus Luszcz. The shrine is composed of eight grottoes all crafted by Brother Bronislaus, who built the grottoes by hand, without the use of power tools, from the native Missouri tiff rock, which came from Old Mines, Missouri, a mining community 30 miles southwest of the site. Each grotto is made of mosaics and multicolored rock sculptures. The Shrine Altar is the largest along with the St. Frances and St. Joseph grottoes. Then Our Lady of Perpetual Help and Our Lady of Sorrows lead to the Gethsemane, Assumption Hill, and Nativity grottoes. Black Madonna Shrine and Grottos are part of the 300-acre Franciscan Mission, and walking tours of the area are available.

Wine Country

Wine Country towns cluster along the riverbanks like hardy grapes on vines. The towns of Defiance, Augusta, Washington, Dutzow, Marthasville, New Haven, Berger, and Hermann all have wineries that produce a variety of wines, both dry and sweet. The Seyval makes a crisp medium-bodied wine similar to a Chenin Blanc. The Vidal, a full-bodied wine with fruity characteristics, is somewhat like an Italian dry white wine. The Vignole is more versatile and can range from the style of a German Riesling to a sweet, late-harvest dessert wine. The Norton (Cynthiana) grape produces rich, full-bodied red wines, and the Chambourcin, a medium-bodied red with a fruity aroma. The Concord and Catawba produce sweet wines.

Outside St. Louis on I-44 West is the town of ***Eureka.*** If you are still trying to get your kicks on Route 66, the ***Kozy Kaboose*** is one of the more popular accommodations at the St. Louis West KOA Campground on historic Route 66. There's only one Kaboose at the campground. It's about the same size as your average Airstream and has a full bathroom, queen bed, bunk bed set, and fridge. What more could you ask for? Well, okay, there's a flat-screen TV in this fully heated caboose and Wi-Fi as well. Call (800) 562-6249. The KOA is located at 18475 Old US Hwy. 66 in Eureka and, of course, there are plenty of RV and tent sites and other cabins if you are not lucky enough to grab the Kozy one.

From Eureka take I-44 West to US 109, then head north on US 109 for about 2.5 miles until you reach Alt Road. Turn left onto Alt Road and travel for approximately 1 mile. Turn north at the first right, which will be Hidden Valley Drive. Keep to the right until you arrive at **Hidden Valley Resort,** in Chesterfield, where you can, yes, ski! Find everything from the beginners' Wonder Carpet on Easy Street, so called for obvious reasons—there isn't even a rope to get up the easy hill—to the Polar Plunge tubing area. There is real (man-made) snow, a 310-foot vertical drop, two triple chairlifts, and two rope tows. The Outlaw Terrain Park features rails, jumps, and more for expert boarders and skiers only. There is a rental shop for skis and boards and PSIA-certified instructors. It's fun and easy enough to get you ready someday for your bucket-list trip to Jackson Hole (named America's scariest ski slope). You can check out the live webcam at hiddenvalleyski.com.

Midwesterners seem to have a deeply rooted preference for all things smoked, probably from all those nights our ancestors spent around a campfire. Who can resist a terrific country ham, hickory-smoked bacon, or a tender slab of ribs? You won't have to if you pay a visit to the **Smoke House Market** (16806 Chesterfield Airport Rd., Chesterfield; 636-532-3314; smokehousemarket.com). Everything is smoked the natural way, with no preservatives and real hickory smoke. Smoked pork chops, lamb chops, and Cajun sausage, along with ribs and bacon, are available in the shop. Owners Thom and Jane Sehnert planned it that way, and Jane's got the background for it; her folks had owned the business since 1952. Hours are Tues through Sun 9 a.m. to 8 p.m.

The Sehnerts branched out and opened **Annie Gunn's** (anniegunns. com) next door, a grill with an Irish theme, complete with Irish potato soup and a menu of unusual sandwiches and meat from the smokehouse. The most popular is the Boursin burger, which is covered with highly spiced garlic and herb cheese. And there is the Braunschweiger sandwich, the Cajun sausage sandwich, fabulous smoked lamb chops, ribs, Reubens, French dips . . . and the list goes on. To find the smokehouse, follow your nose, or if your sniffer isn't highly trained, follow US 40 to the Airport Road exit and double back; it's about 30 miles west of St. Louis. Put your name on the restaurant waiting list before you shop at the smokehouse. Annie Gunn's is a popular place for locals and visitors alike.

Highway 100 along the Missouri River is a beautiful drive any time of year because of the white sycamores marking the river's course; in autumn it's spectacular. The Missouri River valley deserves plenty of time; there's a lot to see and experience.

St. Albans is an anachronism, a tiny, planned community founded in the 1930s by the Johnson Shoe Company family. Five thousand acres of rolling hills and meadows reminded Mr. Johnson of an area in England known as St. Albans, and he made it into a working farm. It is some 30 miles west of the city limits of St. Louis on Highway 100, an easy day trip.

Hard-core bicyclists love the St. Albans region. It is full of challenging hills near the Missouri River and great views. This is Missouri's Rhineland, the wine-growing region. Both oenophiles (wine connoisseurs) and devotees of wine coolers will enjoy tasting what the state has to offer. There are two schools of thought about Missouri wines: Some say that because a majority of the grapes grown here are European vines on wild grape or Concord root stock (and some self-rooted French hybrids), the wines will be different from California or French wines. Others, purists to be sure (and the Mount Pleasant Winery falls into this category), say that they will hold Missouri's best wines against California wines in a blind tasting any day and challenge connoisseurs to single them out. They have done so for Les Amis du Vin, or Friends of Wine, a wine-tasting club. Whether you are a member of Les Amis du Vin or just a wine lover, you will notice that the wines of Missouri are as varied as the vintners who make them.

The Frene Creek white wines rival those of the Rhine River Valley. Pop wine drinkers will love Missouri's blends of fruit wines. The peach wine made by Stone Hill and the cherry wine by Hermannhoff are a treat over ice in the hot summer months.

Washington Landing was first settled in the early 1800s. Lewis and Clark passed through the site of the future town of *Washington* (888-7-WASHMO (792–7466); washmo.org) in search of the Northwest Passage and pronounced it promising because of its excellent boat-landing site. Located in the curve where the great river reaches the most southern point in its course, Washington is still a good place to stop when headed west.

Don't miss the *Gary R. Lucy Gallery* (231 W. Main St.; 636-239-6337; garylucy.com). You may recognize Gary's work if you've picked up a South-western Bell telephone book from previous years; his work has graced the cover.

Gary is an extremely thorough man. To get just the right feeling in his series of Missouri River paintings, the artist took his boat as far upriver as was navigable, to Fort Benton, Montana, and explored interesting areas from there back to Washington. No wonder his paintings ring true. Gary's paintings are like those of other famous Missouri artists, such as George Caleb Bingham and

Thomas Hart Benton. He paints river scenes seen only in his mind's eye. Gary mixes research and what he sees from the window of his studio to obtain historical realism. River scenes might include side-wheelers and keelboats, ironclads running Confederate guns, or a card game on a flatboat. The price of an original can be high, and his early works have quadrupled in value. Prints of his oils are for sale in his studio, which is open Mon through Fri 9 a.m. to 5:30 p.m., Sat until 5 p.m.

Pickney Bend Distillery (1101 Miller St.; 573-237-5559), named for a well-known navigational hazard and the final resting place of at least five 19th-century steamboats. Until 1824 Washington was the last town on the upriver journey west. Then the flood came. But that is history; today the distillery makes Hibiscus Gin with that very flavor, one called Navy Strength Gin (after the British Navy), two American corn whiskeys, and a personal fav, Apple Ambush, a blended corn whiskey with apple nectar and cinnamon—smooth and easy going down. By the way, get your stamp for **Missouri Spirits Expedition** here.

The *Iron Spike Interactive Model Train Museum,* at 1481 High St. in Washington (636-283-5166; ironspike.org), isn't just full of old model trains. Train enthusiasts can bring their own engines and hook them up to many different "drags," including passenger trains, oil trains, freight trains, coal trains, and anything else you might want. Then each car has a different destination— mine or factory, for example—and your engine is uncoupled and a switch engine is attached to the cars leaving. Thousands of miles of track go through tunnels and over bridges through Midwestern scenery. There are only two other interactive model train museums in the country—in Oregon and Massachusetts—so you can see and photograph your engine hauling coal or grain in the Midwest. Hours are Wed and Thurs 10 a.m. to 3 p.m., Fri and Sun noon to 5 p.m., and Sat 10 a.m. to 5 p.m.

Believe it or not, Washington also has the world's *only* corncob pipe factory, **Missouri Meerschaum Company,** at 400 W. Front St., begun in 1869. In German, *meerschaum* means "sea foam." It is the color of the clay that surrounds the pipe. In fact, a special hybrid corn was made and developed at the University of Missouri for the sole purpose of these handcrafted pipes. Today, 5,000 pipes a day are packed and shipped all over the country (perhaps to Frosty the Snowman or Popeye) as well as to other nations. The building has the sweet old scent of pipe smoke and a view of the Missouri River passing by. Even people who hate cigarettes must admit that a pipe's sweet scent recalls a grandpa or favorite uncle (think Mark Twain or General Douglas MacArthur). Suddenly, smoking seems good again. You can get a catalog by calling (800) 888-2109 or visit corncobpipe.com.

You are deep into wine country here, and there is no shortage of wineries along the valley. Most offer tastings; you can choose the ones most convenient for your schedule and location. Some offer unusual wines and are well worth the effort to search them out.

Another distillery is in the town of Beaufort. ***Nobletons Distilling House*** (529 Commercial St.; 314-252-8990) is the home of Duckett Rum. You can bring in your own food and enjoy the fire pit on the patio while you taste the rums made here. Be sure to get your **Missouri Spirits Expedition** stamp before you leave.

Bias Vineyards & Winery (3166 Hwy. B; 573-834-5475 or 800-905-2427; biaswinery.com) is in picture-postcard ***Berger*** (pronounced BER-jer, population 214), just off Highway 100. The setting sun at Berger reflects on the river and rugged limestone bluffs, throwing long shadows across the tilled bottom and along the river. Follow the signs to a wooded hillside. As you start up the hill, there is a railroad crossing at the foot of the rise to the vineyards. Carol and Kirk Grass bought the vineyard recently and haven't changed much. It's a nice place to spend a warm afternoon in spring, summer, or fall enjoying a bottle of Missouri wine and a picnic. Winter is quiet, and cross-country skiing is allowed on the property when the snow comes. Bias offers vine cuttings during the January pruning season for creating wreaths or smoking meats. Winery hours are Mon through Sat 10 a.m. to 5 p.m. and Sun 11 a.m. to 5 p.m. Bias now has a microbrewery at the vineyard. ***Gruhlkes*** makes many types of beer—wheat, porter, stout, amber, and pale ale. It is one of just a few wineries anywhere to have a microbrewery.

Next on the road is ***Hermann.*** To orient yourself, begin at the ***Hermann Visitors' Information Center*** (300 Wharf St., at the Hermann Amtrak station; 573-789-0771; visithermann.com). Founded in 1836 by members of the German Settlement Society of Philadelphia, Hermann was intended as a self-supporting refuge for German heritage and traditions, a sort of "second fatherland." George Bayer, who had immigrated in 1830, selected a site in Missouri that resembled his home in the Rhine Valley in terms of climate, soil, and richness of the wild grapevines. Bayer and the other German immigrants dreamed of building one of the largest cities in the US in the Frene Creek valley.

The dream quickly attracted a variety of professionals, artisans, and laborers who began the task of building the city of their dreams. It never did become that giant metropolis of the immigrants' dreams; now it is a city of festivals. There is ***Wurstfest in March, Maifest*** in May, and ***Oktoberfest*** in the fall, each drawing thousands of folks from all over the state. Hermann also boasts seven area wineries. Amtrak helps alleviate traffic on festival weekends.

lookingfor silver,they foundlead

The early French miners came looking for silver that was rumored to lie along the Meramec River but found instead one of the greatest *lead fields* in the world. The Viburnum Trend in the St. Francois Mountains now supplies more than 90 percent of the lead produced in this country, and high-grade zinc is smelted from the slag left from the lead-refining process.

In winter and on non-festival weekends, Hermann is just what it looks like—a quaint German town, quiet, and filled with B&Bs and lodgings, the largest being the huge **White House Hotel** (232 Wharf St.; 573-486-3200; whitehousehotel868.com). You'll find galleries, shops, and brick homes snuggled right up to the street, European-style. During the festivals, though, it becomes crowded and noisy, as busy as Bayer's dream city. Portable toilets appear on street corners, and the revelry spills from wineries downtown. If you want to be off the beaten path around here, you should aim for a weekday in the off-season. Then a traveler has this sleepy hamlet all to themselves.

If antiques are your thing, go to hermannhill.com for a listing of all the shops in town. It will lead you to places like **Red Barn Antiques** (523 W. 9th St.; 573-486-1012), where you can find a pig snooter (what? you don't know what that is?), a calf weaner (hey, what kind of antiques person are you anyway?), and all manner of authentic stuff. Stuff is hanging from the ceiling and piled on tables, and believe it or not, owner John Wilding knows where everything is. The building is worth the trip. They bought a 100-year-old barn, marked all the pieces, toted it to Hermann, and rebuilt it, then filled it with hay knives and ice-maker's tools. This shop is a history book. There is a great selection of traditional kids' toys to get your children off the internet and onto stilts and playing outdoors with woopee sticks and button whizzers. The barn is open year-round Mon through Sat 10 a.m. to 5:30 p.m.

At **Fernweh Distilling,** at 4 Schiller St. in Hermann (573-486-2970; fernwehdistilling.com), distillers make bourbon and rye, of course, but also the Wildflower Single Barrel Spirit, distilled from corn, infused with rose and chamomile, and aged to taste in old sherry casks. Their proprietary mineral water is used in the distillation and proofing processes, resulting in a crisp-tasting vodka. Get your **Missouri Spirits Expedition** stamp here on Thurs 4 to 8 p.m., Fri 4 to 9 p.m., Sat noon to 3 p.m. and 4 to 9 p.m., and Sun noon to 8 p.m.

Swiss Meats and Sausage (2056 S. Hwy. 19; 573-486-2086 or 800–793–SWISS; swissmeats.com) is owned by three-time Hall of Fame winner Mike Sloan and his wife, Lynette. If you didn't even know that there were 40 different kinds of bratwurst, then you are in for a treat. There is also andouille sausage, hams, bacon, bologna, link sausages, and even hickory-smoked turkeys. And to really get exotic: buffalo and elk jerky. Gift baskets can be made up for that guy-who-has-everything boss of yours with the addition of a choice of cheeses as well. Their brats are the Official Bratwurst of Mizzou Athletics and sold at all the games at MU. Mike has also opened *Hermann Wurst Haus* at 234 1st St. if you are in that neighborhood. This is not just your regular hot dog kinda thing. We are talking mushroom and Swiss brats, apple cinnamon sausages, hickory-smoked olde-tyme knackwurst—all mouth-wateringly good. Looking for scrapple? Headcheese? Liverwurst? You found it.

The *Stone Hill Winery* (1110 Stone Hill Hwy., just off 12th Street; 573-486-2221; stonehillwinery.com) was established in 1847, and until Prohibition (when it became a mushroom-growing facility), it was the nation's second-largest winery. Now it is owned by John Held. The world-renowned cellars are carved into the hillside and are reputed to be the country's largest underground vaulted cellars. There's also a breathtaking view of the town. The carriage house and stable have become the *Vintage 1847 Restaurant,* which shares the picturesque hilltop location; a huge window at one end of the restored carriage house looks out on Missouri's blue hills. Visit the restaurant's wine cellar to choose the evening's libation, and do scrutinize the menu carefully—there's a cheesecake to die for.

Copper Mule (2258 Hwy. 100; 573-409-0007; coppermule.com) is owned by Don and Jeanne Gosen and located on the land that their family started farming in 1908. Scenic bluffs outline the former mule farm. Their bourbon is aged in Missouri charred oak barrels. Multiple Missouri bourbon samples are served in the visitor center. Browse the gift shop and enjoy a specialty bourbon cocktail and a snack. Don't forget your **Missouri Spirits Expedition** stamp.

Once in town, be sure to see the *Hermannhof Winery Festhalle* (330 E. 1st St.; 573-486-5959; hermannhof.com), the world's largest wine hall, where you can dance to live German bands every weekend, starting at noon. There is no entrance fee. Enjoy a festival German dinner or a *brat mit krauts* on a bun. Hours are Mon through Sat 10 a.m. to 5 p.m. and Sun 11 a.m. to 5 p.m.

Blackshire Distillery (2206 Hwy. 100 E.; 573-486-3276, blackshiredistillery.com) has some really good bourbon, rye, gin, and vodka, but try the Blackberry Whiskey, a corn whiskey with all-natural blackberry juice that's fun, distinct, and slightly sweet. Get your **Missouri Spirits Expedition** stamp before you leave.

There are so many great little antiques and craft shops that it would be impossible to list them all and, of course, many bed-and-breakfasts in Hermann. Among them is *Herzog Mansion* (700 Goethe St.; 573-340-1825). This

Victorian mansion was built by the owner of the third-largest winery in the world and is furnished in period antiques, including some 6-foot-long tubs with gold eagle-claw feet, brass beds, and 10-foot-tall doors with transoms.

Before we leave Hermann, let's go *Back Home Again* (307 Schiller; 573-486-0581; backhomeagain.net), which is the place to get that fig jam or peach apricot tea you can't find anywhere else—it's also the spot to find a Lithuanian candle house or Russian nesting dolls. Open every day from 9 a.m. to 5 p.m.

Edelbrand Pure Distilling: This tasting room at Übernachten in Hermann (573-488-2010; edelbrandpuredistilling.com) has what you seek if you are looking for a stamp on your **Missouri Spirits Expedition,** even though the distillery is near Marthasville. Hours of operation vary by day, so call and check it out. Edelbrand vinars stand out among the very few fruit brandies distilled in the US.

Take US 50 to Loose Creek. Turn onto Highway A and go north 6 miles to the French river town of *Bonnots Mill.* This tiny town is so picturesque that the Jefferson City Active Sketch Club has come here to work many times. The views of the autumn foliage and the silvery river are glorious. Riverboats and railroads served the town, and railroad enthusiasts still come here. The business district is only 2 blocks long, but if you walk up Church Hill Street and pass the 100-year-old Catholic church, you will be able to see the Osage and Missouri Rivers from the bluff behind the church—a better way to spend time than shopping.

Nestled in a valley between two bluffs at the meeting of the Osage and Missouri Rivers, the *Dauphine Hotel* (100 Iris Ave.; 877-901-4144; dauphine-hotel.com) has found a new life. Part of Bonnots Mill since 1875, the hotel is one of the oldest lodgings in the state (circa 1840s), but until just a few years ago, it was just another old, two-story hotel with a for-sale sign hanging on it. It's been carefully preserved and restored with original antiques. Now it's a bed-and-breakfast inn with seven guest rooms, each with a private bath. In the old days the hotel had one (yes, one) bathroom for all of its guests. A big breakfast is served in the eat-in kitchen or the dining room from 7:30 until 9:30 a.m. every day. The rooms have the original bead-board ceilings and wood floors and are filled with charming antiques—many of them dating from the original hotel—and handmade quilts. After breakfast guests can lounge on the double-decker front porch.

You could also take a quick left on Highway 42 and stop by the *Old Jail Museum Complex,* at 211 West 4th in *Vienna,* which got its start during the town's centennial celebration in 1955, when some concerned citizens purchased the old (circa 1856) stone jail building to prevent it from being destroyed. The jail became a museum; over time two local log cabins were moved to the grounds and a large weatherproof shed was built to house items donated by county residents. The Old Jail Complex is staffed by volunteers from the Maries (pronounced "Mary's") County Historical Society.

While you're in the courthouse, check out the paintings of historic buildings by John Viessman and other local artists. Passing **Visitation Catholic Church** (105 N. Main), take a look at the restored stained-glass windows. This is one of few churches to have glass that is opalescent and painted as well as regular stained glass. Every pane was taken out, shipped off for restoration, and returned without breaking a single piece. Perhaps someone was watching over that operation.

The Corey family returned home to Maries after 30 years and built their dream home in the rock-strewn hills above the Gasconade River near Dixon. They decided to share it, and a country inn was born. The name, **Rock Eddy Bluff Farm** (10245 Maries Rd. 511; 573-759-6081; rockeddy.com), comes from the location of the inn. It sits atop a rugged limestone bluff overlooking the river. Here the water curves and quickens over a shoal, then calms into a deeper pool set against the bluffs. A series of large boulders rises above the water (Thox Rock is the largest), which gave this section of the river the name Rock Eddy. The inn offers private access to the Gasconade River, and canoes are available. You can see 10 miles across the river valley between Vienna and Dixon from here. It is more a country retreat than a bed-and-breakfast, with hiking and a horse-drawn Amish spring wagon. Scenic Clifty Creek has worn a natural arch through the bluff.

The inn's upper story boasts a pretty view of the river; it offers an upstairs suite that gives the sensation of being snuggled into the treetops, hence the name the Treehouse Suite. The handmade quilts and ceiling fans in this suite create a restful atmosphere. You can relax on the deck and eat breakfast or watch the sun set while soaking in the hot tub dubbed the Think Tank.

Turkey Ridge Cottage is away from the Bluff House and has three bedrooms and a fireplace. It is romantic and quiet. The breakfast room has a stocked fridge or you can dine nearby. One guest left a note saying, "I am convinced that time spent at Turkey Ridge does not count against life's allotted length."

The Line Camp Cabin is a new addition to the place, inspired by a herding cabin in Wyoming. Everything here is just like it was in the 1880s: heat from a woodstove, an icebox (with ice), water from a pitcher pump, and light from kerosene lamps. Here you cook, sit in the porch swing, walk to the river, and relive the past. There's even a corral for your horse if you want to bring one along. This is not for everyone, but if you like roughing it a bit, you will love it. It's worth every penny. You will see bald eagles that have been nesting there for years and a great blue heron rookery with about 50 nests in a clutch of trees.

Visit the website to see photos of the area. To find Rock Eddy Bluff Farm on the map, look for a small (nonexistent) town called Hayden off US 63, between Rolla and Jefferson City. The road to the property is gravel.

The **Clifty Creek Natural Area** is on CR 511 off Highway 28 near the quarries. It has a 2.5-mile loop hiking trail that traverses the natural bridge over Clifty Creek.

Rolla is on US 63. Here the famous Rolla School of Mines is situated. If you are interested in mines or minerals, it's worth your while to see the museum. Be sure to take the time to see **Missouri's Stonehenge,** a half-scale version of the English one built 4,000 years ago. Missouri's version was built by the school's specialists in the fields of mining engineering, rock mechanics, explosives research, civil engineering, and computer science. It was built to honor the techno-nerds of long ago who built their version to pinpoint the solstices and changing seasons with moonlight and sunlight falling through precisely positioned stones. The new Stonehenge, however, was built of 160 tons of granite, shaped by cutting torches and high-pressure water jets, and aligned by computer. It also includes an "analemma" solar calendar used by the Ancestral Puebloan people in the American Southwest more than 1,000 years ago and a Polaris window for sighting the North Star. It was dedicated in 1984 on the summer solstice. A member of the Society of Druids offered ancient incantations over this blend of the ancient and ultramodern.

twenty-four andtwo

Missouri was the 24th state admitted into the Union, and the second state (after Louisiana) west of the Mississippi. The Missouri Compromise of 1820 allowed this state to enter the Union on August 10, 1821, as a slave state, but no other concessions were made in states formed from the Louisiana Territory. Missouri was a Confederate state that was held under martial law by the Union army from the very beginning of the war and where families were divided, and brother literally fought brother.

If you are an alumnus of the University of Missouri at Rolla, then the name of this B&B makes perfectly good sense to you. At least that's what Ron Kohsers thought when his wife, Barbara, voiced some doubts about it. **Miner Indulgence Bed and Breakfast** (13750 Martin Spring Dr.; 573-364-0680; minerinn.com) celebrates the Miners—Ron is on the faculty—and hosts plenty of alumni and parents as guests as well. It could be the peach French toast that is often part of the full country breakfast, or the hot cup of coffee on the porch before breakfast, or the swimming pool and hot tub outside the two-story redbrick colonial home that brings people back. Whatever it is, you can surf on over on the Web and make up your own mind or see it in person: Take exit 184 from I-44, turn onto the south outer road (which is Martin Spring), and go 1.5 miles west.

After that have a major indulgence at *A Slice of Pie* (634 S. Bishop Ave.; 573-364-6203; asliceofpie.com), where Ryan and Katherine Warnol serve the best pie you could ever want. Not just fruit pies, which are without a doubt splendid, but potpies, cheesecakes, quiches, and soups for lunch. Bit of trivia here: The shop sits on a pie-wedge-shaped lot.

Because Missouri is world-famous for its barbecue, it is important to point out the best of the best all over this state. Missouri has been the center of the meat industry since its beginnings, and seeing the stands of hickory and oak everywhere, well, you know, the Show-Me State was just made for barbecue. Here in Rolla, *Johnny's Pit* BBQ (201 W. Hwy. 72; 573-364-4838) is the only barbecue in town at this writing that cooks ribs the way they were meant to be cooked, far from flames and in the low and slow, lazy heat of smoke. As tradition demands, the meat is un-sauced and fall-off-the-bone tender right from the pit. Sauce is made here, too, to add to the meat when it is served.

Randy's Roadkill BBQ and Grill (12670 Hwy. E; 573-368-3705; randysroadkillbbq.com) certainly has the most interesting name, one that lures you in just to see if possum, deer, and skunk are actually on the menu (and maybe steal a menu or buy a T-shirt). But it has a 4.5-star rating, so what's not to love? Ribs and pork chops (those pigs are always trying to cross the road) and the usual barbecue fare are on the menu, as well as treats like fried apples. Hope you are not too disappointed to miss the possum and skunk, but you will enjoy the food. Gar-run-teed! Hours are Fri and Sat 11 a.m. to 8 p.m. and Sun 11 a.m. to 7 p.m.

There's a lot happening in *St. James* on Highway 68 east of Rolla if you are an oenophile (that's a wine lover, remember?). First, stop by *St. James Winery* (540 State Rd. B; 800–280-WINE (9463); stjameswinery.com). Jim and Pat Hofherr came here in 1970 with their three children and invested everything they had to begin the winery. After Jim's death in 1994, Pat and her three sons, Andrew, John, and Peter, ran the winery, which won more than 75 awards in local, national, and international wine competitions in 1995. In fact, *Bon Appétit* magazine named St. James's 1993 Seyval one of the top 50 wines in the world. Hours are Mon through Sat 8 a.m. to 6 p.m. and Sun 11 a.m. to 6 p.m.

Heinrichshaus Vineyards and Winery (18500 State Rt. U; 573-265-5000; heinrichshauswinery.com) is a family-owned winery specializing in dry wines, including Vidal Blanc and Chambourcin. Heinrich and Lois Grohe are the owners and wine masters. Heinrich is from southern Germany, and their daughter, Peggy, went to school in Switzerland, where she studied winemaking. The winery offers fresh grapes in season, Missouri cheeses and sausages, hand-thrown pottery, and original watercolors and prints by Missouri artists. Now this is a full-service winery—wine and cheese, a clay carafe, and original art to enjoy while you picnic on the winery grounds. Spring and fall bring festivals and bike tours. A loaf of bread, a jug of wine, and a picnic! Hours are Mon through Sat 10 a.m. to 5 p.m. and Sun noon to 5 p.m.; open an hour later during daylight savings time.

Deep underground in the unchanging atmosphere beloved by spelunkers, a long underground river flows silently through **Onondaga Cave** in **Daniel Boone State Park,** near Leasburg on I-44 east of St. James. This is a place of superlatives: Massive stalagmites rise like peaks from the floor of the Big Room, said to be the largest cave living room in the world. In Daniel Boone's Room the abundance of cave formations is enough to make you shake your head in amazement. Old Dan himself discovered the place in 1798—or rather, he was the first white man to do so. Native Americans had used the area as a hunting sanctuary in earlier times. Organizers of the St. Louis World's Fair in 1904 encouraged the cave's owners to open it to the public—it was a great hit, as visitors came first by railroad and then by surrey and wagon to explore the wonders.

Bourbon, off I-44, was once a whiskey stop on the railroad—could you tell from the name? Now it's the home of **Meramec Farm Cabins and Trail Riding Vacations** (208 Thickety Ford Rd.; 573-732-4765; meramecfarm.com). In the same family since 1811, and now into its seventh generation, this family farm has earned the Missouri Century Farm sign awarded by the University of Missouri to farms that have been in the same family for at least 100 years. This is a real working cattle ranch, with critters and all—kids who don't have a grandma in the country will enjoy petting the horses, feeding the ducks, or playing in a real old-fashioned hayloft. It's great for adults, too. Walk the trail (1.5 miles follow the river's edge) that adjoins the highest bluffs on the Meramec River. Take a dip in a swimming hole, picnic on a gravel bar, or enjoy canoeing on a section of the Meramec that doesn't require a Class V rapids expert.

The farm is just an hour's drive from St. Louis. It lies on a bend in the Meramec River near the Vilander Bluffs. A conveniently located 5-acre gravel bar is there for people who want to fish and swim. Tubing and canoeing are some of the favorite activities, along with hiking and horseback riding. Ask about the many special packages that let you ride the horse that is native to the area, the Missouri Fox Trotter. According to Carol Springer, owner of the spread, these horses really "smooth out the rugged hills." Peruvian Paso and Tennessee Walking Horses have joined the scene, too.

You also can bring your own horse with you, and Meramec Farm will provide a corral for that member of your family. Carol asks that you call ahead for reservations and directions. This is a working farm, and drop-ins tend to arrive at just the wrong time, but Carol has been juggling it all since 1974, so she must be doing something right. For reservations visit the website or call.

While you are in Bourbon, visit ***Half-Crocked Antiques*** (75 Hwy. C; 573-732-4446; halfcrockedantiques.com), off I-44. If you like unique antique decor, this is the place. There is 11,000 square feet of things rusty, chipped, or otherwise valuable. Old signs fill one floor. Open every day from 9 a.m. to 5 p.m. You are gonna love this place, even if just to tell your friends you were Half-Crocked in Bourbon.

East on I-44, ***Meramec State Park*** (mostateparks.com/park/meramec-state-park) in ***Sullivan*** is an excellent spot for canoeing and exploring, though it is often crowded on summer weekends. The scenic Meramec River winds through this park's rough, timbered hills just east of Little Bourbon. Missouri is known as the cave state, with more known caves than any other state—5,200 counted so far. There are some 22 within the park. One, Fisher Cave, is open for guided tours; others are protected as habitat for an endangered bat species. (You didn't really want to go in that badly, did you?)

The folks at ***Stanton,*** farther east on I-44, argue with the people of St. Joseph, who say Jesse James died there. Stanton proponents believe that the murder of Thomas Howard on April 3, 1882, was a clever plot to deceive investigators and authorities—with the backing of then-governor of Missouri Thomas T. Crittendon.

Skeptical? Well, that's the true Show-Me attitude. Take your pick. Believe that Jesse died in 1951, just three weeks shy of his 104th birthday, or that he was gunned down by his cousin more than 130 years ago. Of course, DNA testing on the body buried in Kearney proves them wrong, but old legends die hard.

Jesse was a member of Quantrill's Raiders, who captured a gunpowder mill and used the caverns as hideouts; beneath Stanton's rolling hills lies a complex of caves and finely colored mineral formations, as rare as they are beautiful. The nearby Meramec Caverns has guided tours, restaurants, and lodging.

Wild Lands

South from St. Louis you have the choice of I-55 or old US 61. (You can also take I-270 if you want to bypass the city entirely.) However you get there, don't miss the museum and displays at ***Mastodon State Park*** (636-464-2976; mostateparks.com/mastodon.htm) near ***Imperial;*** the kids will love it and so will you.

The museum features life-size dioramas, reconstructed mastodon skeletons, ice age fossils, and artifacts more than 10,000 years old. Ancient Indians hunted mastodons with stone-tipped spears. This was the first place that archaeologists found definite evidence of them, and it was an important discovery. Four women fought back when developers tried to buy the significant archaeological site. They organized fund-raising to match the bid. We in the Show-Me State thank them for their persistence. There is a small admission charge for adults. Museum hours are Mon through Sat 9 a.m. to 4:30 p.m. and Sun noon to 4:30 p.m. (Winter hours are in effect during Jan and Feb: open Mon, Thurs, Fri, and Sat 11 a.m. to 4 p.m. and Sun noon to 4 p.m.)

This area contained mineral springs, which made for swampy conditions perfect for preservation. Large mammals became trapped in the mineral-rich mud, which preserved their remains perfectly as the mud hardened to stone. You can still see the **Kimmswick Bone Bed,** which is one of the most extensive Pleistocene beds in the country and of worldwide interest to archaeologists and paleontologists. Explore the visitor center, too. It offers a life-size replica of a mastodon skeleton, Clovis points, and other remnants of early human occupation. Access to the Bone Bed begins at 1050 Charles J. Becker Dr., Imperial.

Now aim just south for the town of **Kimmswick** (636-464-6464; visitkimmswick.com), laid out in 1859 by a German named Theodore Kimm. In the early 1880s, Kimmswick's beautiful Montesano Park attracted people from St. Louis by excursion boat, and riverboats and railroads stopped here. But the horseless carriage changed the destiny of Kimmswick; the new highway system bypassed the town and left it to become a sleepy little backwater. Even the trains and boats no longer stopped to trade. Kimmswick's shops and restaurants are some of the best along the riverfront. *But most shops and restaurants are closed on Monday.* Did I make myself clear? Don't want you to find out the hard way.

You can still get to Kimmswick by riverboat, yes, you can. The **Tom Sawyer Riverboat** goes to and from the town to the Gateway Arch Riverfront in St. Louis. Choose from the 2-hour Express Cruise or the 4-hour Leisure Cruise. Both let you go onshore and explore the town by foot and include lunch at the Blue Owl. Book reservations at (877) 982-1410. Low river levels will cause cancellations, so check dates ahead.

The **Blue Owl Restaurant and Bakery** at 2nd and Mill Streets (636-464-3128; theblueowl.com) shows that Kimmswick refuses to be gobbled up by St. Louis and works to maintain its individuality as the town that time forgot.

The building was erected in 1900 and was called Ma Green's Tavern until the 1950s. It was restored in the 1970s and now has warm wood floors that are charmingly out of level, and lace curtains in the windows. Railroad-car siding covers the walls, and waitresses dressed in long pinafores serve lunch on delicate blue-and-white china. Miss Mary's Veranda is open for outdoor dining (May through Oct), along with a dining room, too, so now there are five dining options. There is live German music with accordion.

The Blue Owl is open year-round Tues through Fri 10 a.m. to 3 p.m. and Sat and Sun 10 a.m. to 5 p.m. Enjoy country breakfasts and homemade soups on weekdays and the wonderful Sunday special of homemade chicken and dumplings, and be sure to see the pastry case as you come in the door. Take a good look at the temple of temptation. The Levee High Apple Pie was created to celebrate the Great Flood of 1993, when the river crested at 39.9 feet against the 40-foot levee.

Walk around Kimmswick; there is a lot to see here, from historic homes and businesses to some fine little restaurants and shops. But keep in mind (I repeat) that most everything is closed on Monday.

Highway 21 south out of St. Louis has a few interesting places worth a visit. From Highway 21, go east on Goldman Road, then south on Old Lemay Ferry Road to **Sandy Creek Covered Bridge** (9001 Old Lemay Ferry Rd.; 636-464-2976), near Goldman. Built in 1887 to connect the county seat of Hillsboro County with St. Louis, it has the appearance of an old red barn and is 72 feet long.

A few miles from Sandy Creek Covered Bridge is the **Villa Antonio Winery** (3660 Lindhorst Rd.; villaantoniowinery.com) in Hillsboro. It is open from 11 a.m. to 5 p.m. every day. Dinner is served Thurs, Fri, and Sat by reservation only. Cordon Bleu chef Bruce Piateck creates everything from scratch—the sausages as well as the sauces they flavor—and a wood-fired pizza oven ensures the best pizza around. Cannoli? You got it. Bon appetito!

Now the **Sandy Valley Brewery** (636-475-5008) has joined the party. It is a small-batch experimental brewery run by farmers, artists, and wine makers aging its products in wine barrels (of course), creating artisan ales and lagers. They call it winemaking and brewing "colliding and cross pollinating," which certainly makes you want to taste it.

Another winery worth visiting is **Persimmon Ridge Winery** (7277 Sheppard Dr.; 636-948-2082; persimmonridgewinery.com). This family-owned winery near **Barnhart** is a beautiful, quiet spot tucked in the woods (perfect for a wedding or just lunch). It has a wood-fired pizza oven for pizzas made with fresh ingredients. You have to bring your own wine glass or buy one in the gift shop, which is strange, and you cannot bring in outside beverages (even water), which is stranger. And fair warning, the winery is not pet-friendly. Even service dogs must be called in ahead. But it is such a pretty place set in the woods at the end of a winding road that these small inconveniences can be overlooked.

From the new Highway 21, take the Schenk Road exit south to Old Highway 21, where you will see the sign and Sheppard Drive. Turn right and follow the road about 0.5 mile to the gate and vineyards.

Or swing southwest on US 67 at Crystal City to the city of **Bonne Terre,** a year-round resort, as interesting in December in the middle of a blizzard as it is in the heat of a 100-degree summer day. There isn't all that much to see—aboveground, that is—but if you choose **Mansion Hill** (651 Oak St.; 573-358-5311) as your first stop and meet owners Doug and Cathy Goergens, the town will come alive for you. In this setting it would have to: The mansion occupies the highest point in Bonne Terre, on 132 acres of timber in the Ozark foothills. Each room has its own view of the estate (which has a 45-mile view of the surrounding area), and four huge fireplaces warm the great rooms.

The mansion was built in 1909 by the lead-mining baron responsible for **Bonne Terre Mines** (185 Park Ave.; 314-209-7200; bonneterremine.com), which are the world's largest man-made caverns and honeycomb the earth under the city. Hand-dug with pick and shovel, the mines are now flooded. They are the pride of the Goergenses, who also own West End Diving in St. Louis. The mines can be explored two ways in any weather: by scuba diving, as do hundreds of divers who make the trek to Bonne Terre winter and summer, or by walking along the above-water trails. The dive experience in the mine has been named one of America's Top Ten Adventures by *National Geographic* magazine.

Your first view of the mine is breathtaking: Under the crystal-clear water, illuminated from above by electric lights, divers can see all the remnants of the mining days, including ore carts, elevator shafts, buildings—even tools and drills left when the mine was abandoned in 1961. No less a personage than Jacques Cousteau was a guest at the mansion and filmed a dive here. The place is gorgeous.

From the entrance to the mines, turn right onto Park Street and go to Allen Street. Follow it until you see the old St. Joe Lead Company Headquarters on the right and the 1909 depot on the left. **The Depot** at 39 Allen St. is built in the Queen Anne and Stick architectural styles and is on the National Register of Historic Places. The English-style phone booth outside, a caboose, boxcars, and rail lamps and posts give it a 19th-century flair. Inside the depot, the Whistle Stop Saloon is filled with train memorabilia and open for banquets only. The second and third floors are part of a turn-of-the-20th-century bed-and-breakfast. The mansion and depot are filled almost every weekend, year-round, by clubs who travel here to scuba dive. All rooms have twin beds to accommodate the divers. Call (888) 843-3483, which is the main office and reservations center for everything at the Bonne Terre Mines.

Located in an area of the eastern Ozarks known as the Old Lead Belt, *Missouri Mines State Historic Site* (4000 Hwy. 32; 573-431-6226) showcases the mining industry in a 19,000-square-foot former mine-mill powerhouse. In 1975 the St. Joseph Lead Company donated 25 buildings and the surrounding land to the Missouri Department of Natural Resources. There is also an excellent mineral collection at the museum, as well as a gift shop that sells very reasonably priced specimens. The Missouri Mines State Historic Site is open Mon through Sat 10 a.m. until 4 p.m. and Sun noon until 5 p.m. Sunday hours are extended in summer until 6 p.m. The museum is located on Highway 32 just outside Park Hills.

History buffs shouldn't miss the Civil War battlefield at *Fort Davidson State Historic Site* at *Pilot Knob* (118 E. Maple; 573-546-3454). You can still see the outlines of the hexagonal fort built in 1863 by Union forces. Flanked on three sides by high hills, the fort was vulnerable to attack from above, which must have been apparent to General Thomas Ewing. After losing 75 men in the Battle of Pilot Knob, he had his soldiers muffle their horses' hooves with burlap and evacuate during the night. At the park you can get dates and times of battle reenactments.

If you happen to be on Highway 32 headed westbound for Dillard Mill, canoeing in Salem, or hiking in the Indian Trail State Forest, you might enjoy shopping in *Bixby* at the *Good Ole Days Country Store* (573-626-4868) on Highway 32. You will notice the bright red 1946 Missouri Pacific caboose tucked against one side of the store. The store has modern gas pumps and Model A vintage pumps (also painted bright red) out front, and inside is the same blend of old and new. Twenty-five cents buys a cup of coffee (on the honor system), while above your head an O scale model train runs on a track suspended from the ceiling, complete with flashing lights and whistles. There's more to see: Antiques fill almost every available inch of space on the hardwood floors. Out back is an old log cabin–turned–antiques store, which also houses a collection of minerals from surrounding hills.

Bixby's general store has never closed since it was first opened in 1906 when the railroad put a railroad siding right next to the store. The store sold everything from casket materials to plows to groceries; locals didn't have to go anywhere else (not that there was anyplace else to go anyway). The store still has a lot of convenience items and a good deli for lunch and ice cream (get a real malt to eat in the caboose). Hours are Mon through Sat 4 a.m. to 6:30 p.m. and Sun 10 a.m. to 6 p.m.

One of Missouri's best-kept secrets is the *Arcadia Valley*—and its villages of Arcadia, Pilot Knob, and Ironton—where there are quite a few antiques shops and scenic hiking opportunities. The mountain town of *Arcadia* is part of the ancient St. Francois Mountain formation. This mountain range (the highest point in the state) was formed roughly 1.485 billion years ago, making them much older than the Appalachian or the Rocky Mountains. North of Arcadia sits **Royal Gorge.** It's been there on the order of 1.5 billion years. It is made of old volcanic rock and, more recently, with a giant stone and mortar wall—which supports the roadway—built during the Great Depression. Designated a natural area in 1973, the Shut-Ins and towering rhyolite outcroppings above Minor Creek are magnificent. The gorge cuts through Ketcherside Mountain. You can travel along that path if you follow Highways 21 or 72. You can drive through the gorge or follow the **Royal Gorge Natural Area Trail** for sensational views of it. The easy trail spans 2.2 miles. There is a visitor center in the old train station, and nearby is the **Arcadia Valley Academy and Thee Abbey Kitchen** (211 S. College St.; 573-546-4249; arcadiavalleyacademy.com). The former Ursuline Academy is now a destination with a comfy B&B, a great kitchen, ice-cream parlor, antiques mall, and entertainment. Murder mystery weekends are fun, and entertainers (comedians, ventriloquists, musicians) are often there as well. The academy has economical European-style rooms with shared baths.

Two blocks up the road are nine 1915-built vintage stone and stucco homes that have been renovated and converted into vacation houses complete with an outdoor pool, pavilion, and outdoor fire pit. Check out **Arcadia Valley Bungalows** (210 E. Walnut St.). Take a long scenic drive along the winding mountain roads or hike to Missouri's highest point on the Taum Sauk Mountain Trail and explore the natural beauty of the St. Francois Mountains.

Wilderness Lodge (573-637-2295; wildernesslodgeresortltd.com), is at 2331 Country Rd. 342, also called Peola Road, on the crystal-clear Black River in **Lesterville;** this great old-fashioned Ozarks experience includes Black River canoe and inner-tube floats in its package. The lodge is made of logs, and the cottages are quintessential rounded Ozark-river stone, each with a fireplace. The lodge is open the first weekend in Apr through Thanksgiving weekend. Rates include breakfast as well as dinner. Float trips are an additional charge.

There is a romantic B&B near **Ironton,** just 80 miles south of St. Louis. Thinking of a destination outdoor wedding? This could be the spot. Brenda Merello's **Plain & Fancy B&B** (11178 Hwy. 72; 314-640-2564; plainfancybb. com) is in the heart of the beautiful Arcadia Valley in a scenic region of the Ozarks. Lie in an outdoor hot tub overlooking peaceful Stouts Creek, roam the gardens, relax in the quiet gazebo, hit the swimming pool, or lounge around the fire pit on a cool evening. The B&B is close to three of Missouri's best state parks, where you can enjoy trail rides and float trips, as well as shopping for antiques or exploring a historic Civil War battlefield. Take Highway 21 south about 2 miles from Pilot Knob to the Highway 72 junction, then take Highway 72 east past Highway JJ for a couple of miles.

This little beauty is not on the Missouri map. The town of **Celedonia** is an old Ozark town that is now a part of a national historical district. Come and visit the **Golden Rule General Store** to buy forgotten necessities, and **Twelve Mile Creek Emporium** (218 S. Hwy. 21; 573-854-1074; twelvemilecreekemporium.com) to check out the shabby chic and primitive home decor, then finish up where you can eat, drink, and stay in an old Civil War hospital.

Ready for some action? **Bluff View Marina** (93 Hwy. AA; 573-223-4849; bluffviewmarina.net) in nearby Piedmont has boats and pontoons for rent. From May 13 to Aug 13, the marina is open seven days a week from 9 a.m. until 6 p.m.; Aug 14 to Sept 10, Mon through Thurs 9 a.m. to noon and Fri through Sun 9 a.m. to 6 p.m. Even off-season you can stop by the trailer and talk to someone about renting watercraft.

The nearby **Johnson's Shut-Ins** (north of Lesterville on Highway N) will surprise you with their rugged beauty, which is like terrain you'd expect to find in Maine or Colorado. These worn and convoluted forms have a story behind them: Would you believe Missouri once had its own Mount St. Helens? Prehistoric volcanic eruptions spewed tons of magma, towering clouds of ash, and acid debris, flattening vegetation and covering whole areas with newly formed igneous rock. Some 250 million years passed and shallow inland seas encroached, covering the already ancient volcanic mountains with layers of sedimentary rock. Over the course of many millions of years, these layers built up until they were hundreds of feet thick. There were more violent uplifts across the Ozarks; the seas retreated; rain, wind, and moving water eroded the softer sedimentary rock layers, cutting the river valley ever deeper. Swirling over and between the buried igneous hills, the river scoured and carved potholes, chutes, and spectacular gorges. It is amazing that something as penetrable as water can cut the hardest stone—here's proof.

The Johnson's Shut-Ins are pocketed away in the scenic St. Francois Mountains; when you see them, you will understand the name. You feel isolated, hidden, shut in—but without a trace of claustrophobia. The Black River flows through the park and winds past some of the oldest exposed rock in the country. There are little waterfalls and swirling water everywhere. Adding to the unique nature of the area are the drought-adapted plants commonly found in the deserts of the Southwest. Scorpions and the rare eastern collared lizard (which rises to an upright position to run on its hind legs and is a treat to see) also find a home in the glades. (Never put on your boots in the morning without first shaking them out—scorpions love hiding places.) Call (800)

334-6946. The website mostateparks.com can give you more information about the park and other parks in the state.

East of the park, the Taum Sauk section of the Ozark Trail leads to **Mina Sauk Falls** (the highest falls in Missouri) and **Taum Sauk Mountain,** the highest point in the state at 1,772 feet above sea level. (Okay, no snickering—this is not Colorado.) According to Native American legend, the mountain's rugged face shows the grief of Mina Sauk, daughter of Taum Sauk, chief of the Piankishaws. Because of her improper marriage, her new husband (of the Osage tribe) was thrown off the mountain. In her despair, she leapt from the peak. The spot where she landed is considered the origin of Mina Sauk Falls, which cascade 200 feet over the granite ledges.

highestwater fallinmissouri

Mina Sauk Falls is the highest waterfall in the state. During the wet season the waterfall cascades 132 feet down a series of volcanic ledges into a sparkling clear pool with a rock bottom.

The **Ozark Trail** winds through the heart of Missouri. Miles and miles of rocky terrain ramble from Steelville and West Plains along glades, forests, and prairies. Here you can hear the wind and feel a snowflake on your face. The more than 300 miles of pathways are serene and quiet, with scarcely another person along the trail. The solitude can be overwhelming and the views breathtaking. Some of the best views in the Ozarks can be found at Onondaga, Taum Sauk, and Johnson's Shut-Ins. (Construction has begun to expand the trail to 500 miles of Missouri wilderness and continue it into Arkansas for an additional 500 miles on the Ozark Highlands Trail.) The northernmost part of the trail—the Courtois Creek Section near Steelville—offers a blend of bottomland and hardwood trees.

The area of the **Mark Twain National Forest** boasts some of the Ozarks' tallest standing pines, and of course there are creeks, bluffs, and small waterfalls. The Berryman Trail for mountain bikers has a trailhead 17 miles east of Steelville and intersects the Ozark Trail at Harmon Springs. A fine spot to camp waits here with a spring and small pond. Many of these trails teemed with deer, elk, and herds of bison when they were traveled by Native Americans in the 1800s. The red wolf lived here, although none has been seen in years. Guides say black bears and wild horses may be seen. The trail offers views of the current river valley, old graveyards, caves, and bluffs. Rigorous hiking and more moderate hiking spots near the state parks are here as well. Primitive camping (at least 100 feet from the trail, water, and scenic areas) is allowed along most sections of the trail. Some areas are open to horses and mountain bikes. Although the trail is open year-round, the best times to visit are in the spring when the dogwoods bloom or in the fall under a canopy of russet leaves. The winters are mild in the Ozarks, though, and winter hiking can be fun. Summers in Missouri are not the best for hiking—they tend to be humid and buggy. But whatever the season, be prepared. Have a map, appropriate rainwear gear, and water—and let somebody know where you are going.

In the town of **Davisville** there is a small, haunted cemetery, the locals tell us. The **Woodlock Cemetery** at 43 Crabtree Rd. seems like your average cemetery, and it's pretty normal for a cemetery to be haunted, you might say, but this one is slightly different. There is a stone staircase going up the hillside, and this is where the ghost—and his ghost horse—have been seen. This is private property, so be careful about trespassing.

North of the Shut-Ins, through some of the prettiest hills this side of the Great Smoky Mountains, are **Dillard** and the **Dillard Mill State Historic Site.** Like a Currier & Ives scene beside its mill run, it is one of the state's best-preserved water-powered gristmills. This picturesque red building sits squarely at the juncture of two of the clearest-flowing Ozark streams, Huzzah and Indian Creeks. The original mill machinery is still in operation, grinding away.

When you've finished with industrial history, check out the natural history. Dillard has a 1.5-mile hiking trail through oak and hickory forests that ends at a pine-topped plateau.

Backtrack a bit on Highway 49 and turn east onto Highway 32 to **Elephant Rocks State Park** (573-546-3454) near **Graniteville.** It is the first park in the state to have a trail designed especially for the visually and physically impaired. Signs along the trail, written in Braille and in regular text, describe the origin of the elephant rocks and guide visitors along a paved 1-mile path.

Elephant Rocks is one of the oddest geological formations—more than a billion years old—you're likely to find in Missouri. Here monolithic boulders stand end-to-end like a train of circus elephants, dwarfing mere mortals who stand beside them. Made of billion-year-old granite, the rocks were formed during the Precambrian era when molten rock forced its way to the surface, pushing the earth's crust aside. The magma cooled and hardened slowly as this area became less volcanically active; it broke in vertical cracks, which weathered and

strangeasit sounds

In the Mark Twain National Forest, you will see what are called *"blossom rocks,"* moss- and lichen-speckled sandstone rocks that appear to have just "blossomed" from the ground. The massive rocks project from the gentle slope of a wooded hillside and appear where other rocks are present. One blossom rock—125 feet in diameter and 50 feet high—is covered with flowers in early spring.

rounded to form the huge "elephants." This weathering eventually breaks even the largest rocks down into pebbles and gravel, but not to worry: More stone elephants are in the making all the time. The pink patriarch of the pachyderm herd is Dumbo, at 27 feet tall and 35 feet long and weighing in at a sylphlike 680 tons. Winding trails, colorful lichen and wildflowers, cool oak-shaded grottoes, and a picnic area in the shadow of the rocks add to the attractions here.

River Heritage Area

If you didn't head off into the wilderness back on US 67 at Crystal City but stayed on I-55 or US 61, you will now enter the River Heritage area. From river bluffs and hills to lowlands, from historic towns to waterways, the River Heritage region boasts enough destinations for several vacations. The French influence is visible everywhere you look in *Ste. Genevieve,* from the name itself to the many buildings à la française. The earliest records of the Missouri Territory invariably mention Ste. Genevieve. French colonial-era homes are tucked in all along the Great River Road from St. Louis south to Cape Girardeau on the Mississippi River's banks. Wide porches and steep roofs have cooled these homes for more than 200 years. The homes predate the Louisiana Purchase, dating from when the French were coming up the Mississippi River from New Orleans and bringing style, food, and traditions with them.

Ste. Genevieve has been clinging to the riverbank here since the 1730s, when French trappers sought valuable beaver pelts. The 5,000 people who call Sainte Gen home still celebrate Bastille Day and are justifiably proud of their French Creole–style buildings. The Great Flood of 1993 threatened the town, but it managed to stay dry with a lot of sandbagging by citizens and history-minded volunteers from across the nation.

Many visitors to Ste. Genevieve are research scholars and genealogists from around the world. The records at the library, courthouse, and churches are the oldest in the West. St. Genevieve calls itself the oldest town west of the Mississippi (more than one Missouri town makes this claim, though) and says, "All history of the West begins here."

It was voted #25 in the 50 most beautiful small towns in America. Stop by the information center on 3rd Street. Many of the town's homes date from the 1700s and are preserved as historic sites and open for tours. Start with the *Ste. Genevieve Museum* (360 Market St.; 573-883-3466), which houses one of the first bird mounts by John James Audubon himself, who did business—albeit briefly—here in the early 1800s. You'll see French-style sabots (wooden shoes), early songbooks, a flute belonging to Audubon's partner Rozier, and much more.

The Bolduc House, circa 1788, and *LeMeilleur House,* circa 1820, can be toured at *French Colonial America* (198 Market St.; 573-883-3105; french-colonialamerica.org). The two-room French colonial Bolduc House is one of the best examples of its type of architecture along the Mississippi. Tour guides in period costume lead visitors through the building, where the yellow glow of tallow lamps dimly light the flintlock rifles above the mantel and the bison rug on the floor. Outside an herb garden, a well, and an orchard are inside a typical French-style palisade enclosure.

Then choose among the homes, churches, shops, and country inns dotting the town. Search out places for little treats, such as *Sara's Ice Cream and Antiques* (124 Merchant St.; 573-883-5890), where you can enjoy hand-dipped ice cream and fountain sodas. Sara's is closed from Oktoberfest through Mar. Hours are noon to 6 p.m. daily.

You can't help but notice the *Old Brick House,* built in 1780, which faces the courthouse square, at 3rd and Market Streets in Ste. Genevieve (90 S. 3rd St. for your GPS; 573-883-2724; thisoldbrickhouse.com). The favorite entree is liver knaefly, a liver dumpling. Before you liver-haters turn up your noses, this German cook urges you to try the dish. It wouldn't be a regularly scheduled favorite if it weren't great, right? Okay, you want something you know—how about a sizzling steak or secret-recipe fried chicken? Whatever you eat, enjoy the surroundings while waiting. They say that the bricks that built this wealthy merchant's home in 1785 arrived as ballast on French ships, and it is thought to be the first brick building west of the Mississippi. The building spent years as a courthouse, a school, and a tavern. In 1816 a duel was fought on its steps and a man was killed. Today the polished wood floors and lace curtains offer a more peaceful environment, and the most dangerous thing here is the coconut cream pie. Open Mon through Wed 11 a.m. to 8 p.m., Fri and Sat till 9 p.m., and Sun till 7 p.m. Breakfast is served Mon through Fri; lunch is available every day.

vivebastilleday!

In Ste. Genevieve the annual **Bastille Day** celebration on July 14, which celebrates the town's proud French heritage, rivals our own Independence Day.

Just a couple of doors down the street from the Old Brick House is *The Anvil* (46 S. 3rd St.; 573-883-7323), a bar and restaurant that serves great fried chicken and other real down-home food. It was built in 1850 to house a hardware store and then became the Anvil Saloon in 1855 (a gentlemen's saloon and barbershop, actually). Interesting story: The bar and back bar were moved to the saloon in 1855 by oxcart from a steamboat that had run aground on a sandbar and needed to lighten up. Weekday hours are 11 a.m. to 8 p.m., until 9 p.m. on weekends.

Down the block at 146 S. 3rd St. is the circa 1790 **Southern Hotel** (573-883-3493; southernhotelbb.com). Mike Hankins saw the old wreck, which had been abandoned since 1980, and fell in love with the redbrick, Federal-style three-story hotel. It is believed to be the oldest operating hotel west of the Mississippi River. The hotel is full of antiques and claw-foot tubs. Meals feature fresh herbs from the garden behind the hotel, and flowers from the garden fill the rooms. The garden itself is magical. An arbor leads to a wide cedar swing at the center; Mike has wired the whole area with thousands of tiny white lights. When he hits the switch at dusk, the garden is a romantic fairyland. Tucked away in a corner of the garden is a great little shop with dried flowers, herbal soaps, and hand-painted goodies—don't miss it! You can buy the *Pepper and Roses* cookbook or enroll in the "Cooking Experience" class. It has been open since 1987 with eight guest rooms, each with its own bath. Rooms include such wondrous French breakfast items as strawberry soup, artichoke-heart strata (a layered egg-and-bread dish), croissants, homemade lemon bread, juice, and coffee. Mike and Cathy will make you feel at home.

trivia

The Mississippi River is the reason St. Louis exists. It was the original highway for every civilization that thrived in the middle of the country, but it is also the most diverse inland river in the world. More than 500 species of wildlife use the river and its floodplains.

Inn St. Gemme Beauvais B&B (573-608-0581 or 573-390-5133; innstgemme.com) and **Dr. Hertich's House** are at 78 and 99 N. Main St., respectively, in Ste. Genevieve. Both are on the National Register of Historic Places. Built in 1848 and 1850, the inn is the state's oldest continually operated bed-and-breakfast. This lovely old Victorian will spoil you. All the rooms are suites, with big easy chairs in the sitting room and canopy beds and rockers in the bedrooms. Teatime is every day at 2 p.m., and wine and hors d'oeuvres are offered every day at 4 p.m. A full gourmet breakfast, of course, is served in the morning at 8 and coffee is ready even earlier in the second-floor lounge for you early birds. There is also a restaurant that can seat up to 26 people. The cuisine is French. Outside is a lovely herb and flower garden to enjoy. The hotel is on Main Street, so it is within walking distance to everything. Dr. Hertich's House was the residence and clinic of the first town doctor. It has four suites, all with gas fireplaces and whirlpool baths.

The information presented here only begins to touch on what is available in Ste. Genevieve. Looking for wine? Check out the **Brix Urban Winery & Market** (245 Merchant St.; 573-883-2800). How about candy? The **Sweet Things** confection shop (242 Market St.; 573-883-7990) features fine chocolates (try the famous fudge Creole). Hours are Mon through Sat 10 a.m. to

5 p.m. and Sun 12:30 to 3:30 p.m. There's also all manner of antiques shops and restaurants, and a whole list of bed-and-breakfasts. The town's website is stegenevievemissouri.com.

Cave Vineyard Winery & Distillery (21124 Cave Rd.; 573-543-5284; cavevineyard.com) is where you can enjoy wine in a natural cave. The natural saltpeter cave is located directly underneath the winery and tasting room. The opening to the cave is approximately 100 feet across and 35 feet tall. No claustrophobia here. It can comfortably seat about 100 people. While most caves maintain a constant temperature, this one changes with the weather. However, it is still quite comfortable on the hottest of summer days. The cave is open year-round, weather permitting, and can even be enjoyed during the winter months. There's even fresh-baked biscotti to dip in the wine made from grapes grown right here in the vineyard. Brandy was the next step from winemaking, and the distillery is making small-batch, copper-distilled brandy from grapes grown here at the vineyard, and grappa as well. You can get your **Missouri Spirits Expedition** stamp, too.

The *Pickle Springs Natural Wildlife Area* is a 180-acre natural landmark that has been described as magical. It is worth the 30-minute drive from Ste. Genevieve. Aficionados of the park call it a geological and botanical wonder. The *Trail Through Time Path* has a waterfall, a natural spring, and the amazing double Lamotte sandstone natural bridge formed from the sandy beaches that used to exist here. Only 500 million years ago, there were oceans in Missouri. It makes you feel like you are counting in dog years, but these giant sandstone bluffs have magnificent views. You step back in time along boardwalk-type steps to make the climb easier. From Ste. Genevieve take Highway 32 west, turn left on Highway AA and then left again onto Dorlac Road.

At *Perryville,* off US 61, is the *St. Mary of the Barrens Church* (1811 W. St. Joseph St.; 573-547-2508), dating from 1827. The grounds are open to walk through; be sure to visit the church's museums. This is also the National Shrine of Our Lady of the Miraculous Medal. Regular guided tours are offered Mon through Fri at 10 a.m. and 1 p.m., and Sat and Sun at 1 and 3 p.m. There is no charge to visit St. Mary's Barrens.

For more history (and fun), detour east a bit on the Great River Road and watch for *Tower Rock* jutting up 85 feet out of the Mississippi. Don't miss the little German towns of Altenberg, Whittenberg, and Frohna.

Villainous Grounds on the square in Perryville (26 N. Jackson St.; 573-605-1333) is the spot to find comics and coffee and food. Tickle your sweet tooth as well as your funny bone while you rummage through a large collection of old comic books with a cuppa. The bazaar is a collection of work by local artisans and crafters and is located on the second floor above the coffee shop. Open Mon 6 to 10 a.m. and Tues through Sat 6 a.m. to 5 p.m.

Stay on US 61, and the next stop is *Jackson.* The oldest Protestant church west of the Mississippi, the circa 1819 *Old McKendree Chapel* (4080 Bainbridge Rd.), a national Methodist shrine, is here. But the best attraction for you railroad fans is the *St. Louis Iron Mountain & Southern Railway* (252 E. Jackson Blvd.; 573-243-1688 for schedule and prices; slimrr.com/sitemap.html). Ride a piece of history. Sights and sounds will carry you back to the late 1800s and early 1900s, when this was the preferred method of travel. This was the "mother line" of nearly all the smaller rail lines that eventually became the historic Missouri Pacific Railroad. Darren the Magician roams the train to entertain the child in you. There's the Dinner Train, or you might relive the 1880s train robbery by the James Gang or experience the intrigue of murder on a Murder Mystery Train. Take I-55 to exit 99 and go 4 miles west on US 61 to the intersection of US 61 and Highway 25.

If you want to experience the elegance of the 1800s, stop by the *Oliver House* (224 E. Adams St., Jackson; 573-579-3807). The lady of the house is known as Missouri's Betsy Ross. Marie Oliver and a friend designed and made the first and only official state flag. The house is decorated with authentic furniture of the period, and music plays on the Edison Victrola. Visiting hours are on the first Sunday of the month from 1 to 4:30 p.m. May, July, and Oct, and the three Sundays before Christmas for the candlelight tour.

While you're near Jackson, take a side trip to *Burfordville* on Highway 34 East. The *Bollinger Mill* has been in continuous operation since 1825—these people really kept their noses to the grindstone, didn't they? Located on the Whitewater River, the four-story, stone-and-brick structure shares the setting with the *Burfordville Covered Bridge,* one of three covered bridges remaining in the state. The building of the bridge began in 1858 and, like much of Missouri's everyday life, was put on hold by the Civil War. The Burfordville Bridge was completed in 1868. It is a 140-foot span of incredibly long yellow poplar timbers, which grow near the river. It's another excellent setting for artists and photographers, not to mention history and nostalgia buffs.

Gothic Splendor

An outstanding example of Renaissance architecture in the gothic style is the Old St. Vincent's Church in Cape Girardeau. It was built in 1853 and contains more than 100 medieval-design plaster masks and intricate interior work. It is listed on the National Register of Historic Places.

You're deep in southern Missouri now and headed for "The Cape." On I-55, *Cape Girardeau* (cityofcapegirardeau.org) is the biggest city in the area, with a population of almost 35,000. But Cape Girardeau has also preserved its heritage carefully, and it's a beautiful city in spite of—and in the midst of—phenomenal growth.

Cape Girardeau is radio and television talk-show host **Rush Limbaugh**'s hometown, and the city offers a self-directed (very conservative) tour (with nothing but right turns?). Pick up a brochure at the visitor bureau at 1707 Mount Auburn Rd. (800-777-0068; rosecity.net/rush/rushtour.html).

Drive through the city and note the many 19th-century buildings. The beautiful *Glenn House,* circa 1880, is a good example. Civil War fortifications still remain in the area.

Although Cape is modern and expanding too fast, all is not lost. Proceed directly down to Water Street, which, as you may have guessed by the name, is along the mighty Mississippi. Unfortunately, a rather tall, ugly wall has been built to protect the area from floods, so the view lacks something—water, to be exact. There is an opening and a deck you can drive onto to enjoy the sights, though, if you are fond of rivers—and who isn't? There's just something about the power of that big river.

Get a feel for the history of the area with Cape's unique **Great Murals Tour.** It all began at the *Southeast Missourian* newspaper building where *The Art of Printing* and *The Art of Making a Newspaper* were done in 1947. Tourists enjoyed finding famous faces in the ceramic murals, which were the first of their kind in the country. They were joined by the Jake Wells Mural, representing the people whose dreams carved the region's progress. This is one of the largest murals in the state. In the city's downtown area five more murals celebrate the Mississippi River (in Waterfront Park): the *Riverfest*, the *Riverfront*, the *Bicentennial*, and the *Silver Coronet Band* mural about Cape's musical legacy. The *Missouri Wall of Fame* has 45 panels featuring famous Missourians, from Burt Bacharach to Tennessee Williams.

One more claim to fame: The movie *Gone Girl* was filmed here on Spanish Street, which also has a nice little Italian restaurant, **Bella Italia Ristorante** (20 N. Spanish St.; 573-332-7800; bellaitaliacape.com). It's open Mon through Thurs 11 a.m. to 9 p.m., Fri until 10 p.m., and Sun until 8 p.m. Along the same street are some nice shops to browse.

The **Glenn House** (325 S. Spanish St.; 573-587-4248; glennhouse.org) is a circa 1883 two-story Victorian that is open for tours and contains period furnishings, 12-foot stenciled ceilings, and some good displays devoted to the steamboat era on the Mississippi. It is haunted by a young girl who fell to her death on the staircase (I am not making this up), but she is only heard when the home is decorated for Christmas. Have a spirited holiday! It is open May through Oct and Dec, Sat and Sun 1 to 4 p.m. or by appointment.

About a block away is what will probably be your favorite place if you have any Cajun instincts at all. ***Broussard's Cajun Restaurant*** (120 N. Main St.; 573-334-7235; broussardscajuncuisine.com) even has a test on the back of the menu to see if there is a trace of Cajun blood in your veins. The "how to tell a full-blooded, dipped-in-the-bayou Cajun from someone who just wishes he was" test begins with the question "Did your grandmother regularly eat *couche* for breakfast?" and ends with "If someone stepped on your toe would you yell '*ho yii*' instead of 'ouch'?" If any of you good ol' boys are missing home, this is the place for you.

The food here is authentic, fire-breathing Cajun. The menu has a glossary of terms and a key to spicy foods for those of you who don't like surprises. It is an inexpensive, casual place, but bring enough money to try a Cajun Combo, which includes a little bit of everything. Also, if you have room, the special includes a salad and French bread. Other entrees are the traditional red beans and rice with sausage and fried crawfish tails. Polish it off with a draft. A live band plays blues and dance music Fri and Sat from 8 p.m. until closing time. Eating hours are Sun and Tues through Thurs 11 a.m. to 8 p.m. and Fri and Sat till 9 p.m. Broussard's motto is *"Laissez les bons temps rouler!"*—"Let the good times roll."

trivia

Cape Girardeau was named after Jean Baptiste Girardot, who established a trading post here in 1733. When Spain offered inexpensive, tax-exempt land, Spanish immigrants were drawn to the area. Cape Rock (2 miles northeast via Highway 177 and East Rock Drive) is the site of Girardot's trading post. Although nothing remains of the original settlement, views of the Mississippi River are wonderful from the bluff. Good spot for a picnic.

River Ridge Winery (CR 321, Commerce; 573-264-3712; riverridgewinery.com) is in a century-old farmhouse nestled in the hills where Crowley's Ridge meets the Mississippi River, 2 miles north of **Commerce,** south of Cape on Highway N. The hand-tended French hybrid grapes are grown on the hills behind the winery. You may sample the fine dry and semi-dry table wines crafted by winemaker Jerry Smith. He and his wife, Joannie, also have a showroom of unique wine-related items. You can picnic by the river or in the vineyards or relax by a warm fire at the house and enjoy some wurst and bread. Open Mon through Thurs 11 a.m. to 6 p.m. and Sat and Sun till 6:30 p.m.

Near Cape Girardeau grits begin to sneak onto the breakfast menu, and the accent begins to sound slightly more Southern than Midwestern.

The Evil That Men Do

During the forced removal in 1838, 12 detachments of **Cherokee** were ordered by General Winfield Scott to move to Oklahoma. All entered Missouri in Cape Girardeau County. Rain, snow, freezing cold, hunger, and disease took their toll on the emigrants as the ice prevented both boat and horse from moving. More than 4,000 Cherokee—nearly one-fifth of the Cherokee population—died in camps by the river waiting for the journey to resume. To learn more about this march, you can visit the office of the Northern Cherokee Nation of the Old Louisiana Territory on Independence Street (Tues through Sat). You can also visit Trail of Tears State Park, located approximately 10 miles north of Cape Girardeau on Highway 177.

On US 61 South watch the signs for **Lambert's Cafe** (2305 E. Malone, Sikeston; 573-471-4261; throwedrolls.com), home of "throwed rolls." Lambert's is a most unusual place. Yes, they do throw rolls there.

It all began on a busy day in May 1976 when passing rolls real nice-like got too slow and a customer hollered, "Just throw me the *x*#_ thing!" Before you could say "thank you kindly," others cried out for service, and they have been throwing rolls at Lambert's ever since.

The folks here take control of your dinner needs—and control is the right word (got to have it when you're lobbing a long one). Want another roll? Sing out and look alive, because one will come whizzing by. To complement the rolls thrown your way, another ladleful of sorghum (Missouri's answer to Vermont maple syrup) will be slopped onto your roll, which is already dripping butter. This will require a trip to the restroom to unstick your fingers. Lambert's is fun—if you like noise, confusion, and a lot of food and attention from the waiters. If your plate begins to look empty, someone comes by with a ladle of beans, fried okra, or applesauce and plops it in the middle of your plate; when you finish dinner, you will be full. Very, very full. Then you will discover that Lambert's is famous for the size of their slices of homemade pie and cobbler. The drinks are served in gallon mason jars, and the atmosphere is a madhouse on a good day, but it's a spot you can talk about for years. Hours are Mon through Thurs 10:30 a.m. to 8 p.m. and Fri through Sun till 9 p.m.

Old Mountain Region

Now you have a choice—go south to the Bootheel region or loop back up toward St. Louie. West on US 60 toward Dexter, the flat, Kansas-like real estate will begin to curve again in the distance.

A short trip will take you through **Paxico** to **Mingo National Wildlife Refuge,** a vital 21,676-acre link in the chain of refuges along the Mississippi flyway. The hills flatten into wetlands and plant varieties change visibly. Mingo Swamp was formed some 18,000 years ago when the Mississippi abandoned its bed, leaving an oxbow that filled in with dense swamp species. Abundant artifacts point to the area's use by Native Americans, drawn here by swamp-loving wildlife. (No artifacts can be removed from Mingo, however, so arrow-head hunters, take note.)

The area offers a boardwalk nature trail with seven interpretive stations and a chance to see wildlife in its natural habitat. There is a resident waterfowl flock as well as thousands of seasonal migrants, and two active bald eagle nests are located on the refuge. Be sure to stop by the refuge visitor center before heading into the swamp (especially during the winter months), not only to let someone know where you are going, but also to enjoy the interpretive displays. The trails are accessible for all, including those with disabilities. It's pretty impressive. Together with the adjacent Duck Creek Wildlife Area, a state wildlife management area, this is the largest hardwood swamp remaining in the state. Lake Wappapello is also nearby; watch for signs.

If you didn't expect to find a museum of fine art in the Ozarks, you're in for a surprise. The **Margaret Harwell Art Museum** (421 N. Main St.; 573-686-8002; mham.org) in **Poplar Bluff** boasts a growing collection of works by contemporary Missouri artists. Housed in a beautiful 1883 home, the museum has mounted one-man shows by important artists such as sculptor Ernest Trova, Swedish artist Anders Zorn, and Missourian Thomas Hart Benton. There is no charge to view the exhibits. The museum focuses on themes ranging from contemporary photography to fiber art and recognizes the importance of the native arts of the Ozark region. It has held exhibits of folk art, including quilting and basket making. It is the only art center within a 90-mile radius and the only art museum within 150 miles of Poplar Bluff. Docents conduct regular tours of the exhibits. Hours are Tues through Fri noon to 4 p.m. and Sat and Sun 1 to 4 p.m. Tours are by appointment only.

The **Lake Wappapello Outdoor Theatre,** next door to the Fisherman's Net, comes alive on Fri and Sat nights at 6:30 May through Oct with live blue-grass and gospel music. There is no admission fee but donations are appreciated. Bring your lawn chair and settle in to enjoy the music. When it rains, everyone moves to the music barn.

For just a quick barbecue fix, **Myrtle's Place Backalley** BBQ (109 N. Broadway; 573-785-9203; myrtlesplace.com) has carry-out as well as the restaurant there in town. Myrtle's has it all, including breakfast. If you call in advance they will cook you a ham, turkey, pork butt, ribs, or chicken for your next get-together. Hours are Mon through Fri 5 a.m. (yes, that's a.m.!) to 3 p.m. and Sat until 2 p.m.

Poplar Bluff isn't all fried and barbecue, though. You can *mangiare benne* at **Castello's Ristorante** (2775 N. Westwood Blvd.; 573-712-9010; castellosrestaurant.com), which serves old-country Italian food just like Nana Ginni Castello taught the family to make. Being Italian myself, I can recommend the sauce. You can do Castello's for breakfast Mon through Thurs 5:30 to 9 a.m., Sat 7 to 11 a.m., and Sun 7 to 11:30 a.m. Or go for dinner Mon through Thurs 5 to 9 p.m., Fri and Sat 5 to 10 p.m, and Sun 4 to 8:30 p.m. **Tony's,** the bar at Castello's, is open Mon through Sat from 5 p.m. (happy hour 5 to 7 p.m.).

There's Mexican, too. **El Acapulco** (2260 N. Westwood Blvd.; 573-776-7000; elacapulcomo.com) has a huge menu (the sizzling fajitas come to the table on very hot skillets) and is open Sun through Thurs 11 a.m. to 9 p.m. and Fri and Sat till 10 p.m.

Bootheel Region

You are in Missouri's Bootheel now—not really the Midwest anymore, more like the South.

Southeast of Sikeston you'll find hills that really roll. **Big Oak Tree State Park** (13640 S. Hwy. 102, East Prairie, 573-649-3149) tells the story of the 1811 New Madrid earthquake, which altered the topography of the southeast lowlands. All the land from Cape Girardeau south to Helena, Arkansas, sank from 10 to 50 feet, flooding most of what is now New Madrid, Pemiscot, and Dunklin Counties. Rich Bootheel forests were converted to swampland, providing temporary protection for the giant oak that gave the park its name. You may see trees 120 to 130 feet tall. Enjoy a bayou setting for picnics or fishing. Big Oak Tree is east off Highway 102.

Nearby **Towosahgy State Historic Site** (off Hwy. 77, CR 502, East Prairie; 573-748-5340) is 64 acres of prehistory. Archaeologists believe the site was inhabited between AD 1000 and AD 1400. Although other groups had lived in this area before that time, their societies did not reach such a highly organized level as that of the Natives at Towosahgy. Experts believe their use of the Mississippi for trade and transportation contributed to this advancement. The river was the link between Towosahgy and the ceremonial center near the present site of Cahokia, Illinois.

Cotton fields join wheat fields as you approach **New Madrid** (that's pronounced MAD-rid, much more Midwestern than Spanish) on I-55. The Mississippi River Observation Deck offers a panoramic view of the New Madrid oxbow; 8 miles of river are visible from the top of the most perfect oxbow on the Mississippi.

The oldest city west of the Mississippi (see, there's that claim again) has something for everyone. Begin at 1 Main St. This building, on the banks of the Mississippi near the observation deck, was once the First and Last Chance Saloon. There were no roads to New Madrid; all the traffic came off the mighty river. Here was the first—and last—chance to get a drink back in 1783. It is now the **New Madrid Historical Museum** (1 Main St.; newmadridmuseum.com).

New Madrid looks sleepy, dreaming away beside the river. It looks safe. It looks as if nothing much could happen here—indeed, as if nothing much ever has. If that's what you think when you see the place, you're wrong.

In Missouri's early days, the lowlands around the Bootheel were known as the "Big Swamp" because they were covered with stagnant waters of marshes, swamps, and bayous. There were mosquitoes everywhere, which were the deadly enemies of settlers. A series of earthquakes in 1811 and 1812 further discouraged settlers. Today "Swamp-east Missouri" has been changed—through drainage projects—to some of the most productive land in the state.

The area balances precariously on one of the most active earthquake faults on the continent, the **New Madrid Fault.** In 1811 the balance shifted. The earth shrugged. The mighty Mississippi was suddenly dammed and ran backward, boats broke up and sank at their moorings, homes disintegrated before their owners' horrified eyes. John James Audubon recounted a hilarious—if frightening—tale of a wedding party broken up by the quake, and the naturalist John Bradbury described it in harrowing scientific detail as he calmly watched the earth come apart. The quake was so violent that it rang church bells in Boston.

All is not peace and quiet, even now. There is a measurable tremor on the seismographs almost every day that can be felt by local folks. The Center for Earthquake Studies at Southeast Missouri State University informs us that a major quake is not just possible, but inevitable; stresses within the earth slowly mount until something has to give. When it does, the area of damage will be more than 20 times that affected by a California quake because of the underlying geologic conditions—the ground will literally liquefy.

Residents have developed a wonderful gallows humor—you'd have to! T-shirts read, with a certain quirky pride, "It's our fault" and "Visit New

Madrid—while it's still here." So, you want real excitement? Head for New Madrid. (Of course, the author files a disclaimer here. If there's a quake while you're in town, it's "not my fault.")

trivia

The city of Kennett here in the Bootheel is proud of its daughter, singer Sheryl Crow, who attended Mizzou before launching her career.

While in New Madrid, visit the ***Hunter-Dawson Home and Historic Site.*** Built in 1859 by William Washington Hunter, this crisp white house with its ornate trim and contrasting shutters recalls a more genteel era. The costumed guides who answer all your questions treat you with that special Southern charm and add to the atmosphere. A small admission fee is charged.

As you continue south from Sikeston and New Madrid, the land becomes flat bottomland. Southern-style cotton, soybeans, and peaches are the important crops here. From Kennett and Malden on the west to Hayti and Caruthersville on the east, hospitality is just what you would expect in this area of Southern heritage, and Missouri begins to feel like Dixie. Welcome, y'all.

Places to Stay in Southeast Missouri

ST. LOUIS

Drury Inn St. Louis at Union Station
201 S. 20th St.
(314) 231–3900
Inexpensive

Hyatt Regency Downtown
315 Chestnut St.
(314) 231–1234
Moderate

Red Roof Inn
11837 Lackland Rd.,
Westport
(314) 843–7663
Inexpensive

Ritz-Carlton, St. Louis
100 Carondelet Plaza,
Clayton
(314) 863–6300
Expensive

CUBA

Motel 6
97 Ozark Dr.
(573) 885-0100
Inexpensive

Super 8 Motel
I-44 and Highway 19
(573) 885-2087
Inexpensive

PILOT KNOB

Ft. Davidson Motel
310 S. McCune St.
(855) 680-3239
Inexpensive

VIENNA

Scenic 63 RV Park and Motel
12141 Hwy. 63 S.
(573) 4223907
Inexpensive

FARMINGTON

Days Inn
1400 Liberty St.
(888) 276-1233
Inexpensive

LESTERVILLE

Black River Family Restaurant & Motel
Highway 21
(573) 637-2550
Inexpensive

PERRYVILLE

Days Inn
1500 Liberty St.
(573) 547-1091
Inexpensive

CAPE GIRARDEAU

Holiday Inn Express
3253 William St. SW
(573) 334-4491
Inexpensive

STE. GENEVIEVE

Family Budget Inn
17030 New Berman Rd.
(573) 543-2272
Inexpensive

JACKSON

Drury Inn
225 Drury Ln.
(573) 243-9200
Inexpensive

POPLAR BLUFF

Super 8 Motel
2831 N. Westwood Blvd.
(855) 516-1090
Inexpensive

SIKESTON

Holiday Inn
120 S. Interstate Dr.
(888) 787-8846
Inexpensive

NEW MADRID

Hunter Lodge Motel
501 SE Outer Rd.
I-55, exit 40, Marston
(573) 643-9888
Inexpensive

Places to Eat in Southeast Missouri

ST. LOUIS

LoRusso's Cucina
3121 Watson (on the Hill)
(314) 647-6222
lorussos.com
Moderate

WASHINGTON

Cowan's Restaurant
114 Elm St.
(636) 239-3213

cowansrestaurant.com
Inexpensive

FARMINGTON

Spokes Pub & Grill
1627 W. Columbia St.
(573) 756-6220
spokespub.com
Inexpensive

CAPE GIRARDEAU

Port Cape
19 N. Water
(573) 334-0954
Inexpensive

NEW MADRID

Rosie's Colonial Restaurant & Tavern
Highway 61 North
(573) 748-7665
Inexpensive

ROLLA

Alex's Pizza
122 W. 8th St.
(573) 364-2669
alexspizza.com
Inexpensive

Southwest Missouri

Mark Twain National Forest covers thousands of acres of southwest Missouri. Hundreds of miles of hiking and horseback trails free you from even the small, state-maintained highways. If you wander too far off the beaten path here, you will find yourself lost in the woods (and Missouri's bright bluebirds and crimson cardinals will clean up your trail of bread crumbs).

Many of the lovely, quick-running streams are designated National Scenic Riverways, and the "Tri-Lakes" area has water, water everywhere. Resort towns are crowded in the summer and deserted in winter. Spring and fall (while school's in session) are just right for exploration. Campgrounds and canoe rentals are everywhere, and there are both gentle rivers for floating and whitewater for adventure.

Driving the *Glade Top Trail* is another way to see the forest. Google Maps does not show it. State and county maps do not show it. The free county maps are confusing, as are state maps. It is a good idea to spring for the $10 Forest Service map. Entering Glade Top from the south end in Theodosia, head west on Highway 160. From the west end, look for the town of Rueter. The north end is probably the best from the

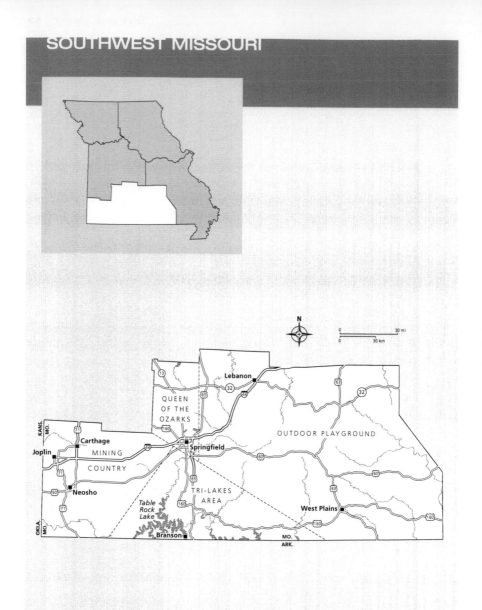

intersection of Highway 5 and Highway 76 in Ava. Regardless of which way you are coming, look for a brown metal sign with white letters saying "Mark Twain National Forest Glade Top Trail." There is one of these signs for each direction. But the best idea is to go to ozarkmtns.com for directions. You are seriously *off the beaten path* here.

If caves fascinate you, if you like spectacular rock formations, or if you collect rocks or minerals, southwest Missouri will keep you busy. Truitt's Cave at Lanagan, Ozark Wonder Cave at Noel, the Tiff Mines near Seneca, and the Carthage Marble Quarry at Carthage are a few spots you'll want to check out, along with Fantastic Caverns at 4872 N. FR 125, Springfield.

Queen of the Ozarks

The hub of southwest Missouri is **Springfield,** the state's third-largest city, on I-44. Its location on the spacious, grassy uplands of Grand Prairie and Kickapoo Prairie, the rural landscape of the Springfield Plain, is one of the most beautiful in Missouri. Here's a happy combination of forests, running water, and magnificent rock outcrops dotting a farmland that resembles the bluegrass area of Kentucky. Herefords, Black Angus, Charolais, and Simmental graze in the cleared uplands. Lespedezas, orchard grass, and fescue glaze the gently rolling pastures with green. The city website is springfieldmissouri.org.

If you are an antiques hunter, Springfield's 6-block, turn-of-the-20th-century historic Commercial Street District is a good place to wander around. The South Campbell Street and Boonville Avenue shops just north of Park Central Square and the stores just below the square on South Street are all filled with antiques, too.

C Street, as Commercial Street is known, is much more than just antiques— it is home to so many interesting and unique shops that the list would go on and on. Just to name a few:

420 W. C St. is home to the **Moon City Pub** (417-315-8142), serving locally crafted beers and cocktails, with great live bands and music every Mon through Sat; hours are 1 p.m. to 1:30 a.m. Thursday is open mic night with an easygoing atmosphere that makes it fun for the talent to give this venue a whirl. **Chabom Tea and Spices** (indieteaspice.com) is at 209 E. Commercial. Looking for White Strawberry Basil or Ceremonial Matcha Powder? This place has tea and herbs (by the scoop) and body products like Dead Sea Salts and Beeswax Beads, just about anything, all wonderfully scented. Hours are Mon through Sat 10 a.m. to 6 p.m. and Sun noon to 5 p.m.

Okay, **Bass Pro Shops Outdoor World** at 1935 S. Campbell—a major intersection in Springfield—is rather on the beaten path. It is also found in other states around the country, but if you have never been to a Bass Pro Shop, you just must stop (and will probably end up spending the day). It bills itself as the world's greatest sporting-goods store, then lives up to that boast. How many sports shops have a two-story log cabin right in the store? Or a sumptuous restaurant like Hemingway's, serving lobster dinner and a glass of fine wine in front of a room-size aquarium (with white-bellied sharks smiling through the glass and a 15-foot eel hiding in the filter system)? You just gotta love this place and you can spend hours here (all free!).

Across the aerial walkway from Hemingway's is the old-fashioned Tall Tales Barbershop. There is original wildlife art, a museum of the outdoors, trophy animals by the hundreds, and the biggest live bass in captivity. You can buy a hand-knit sweater, get wet beside an indoor waterfall, practice with your new shotgun in the shooting range downstairs, and buy a pair of gym shoes or a fishing rod. Just plan on spending a couple hours when you go in, and take a camera—there are photo opportunities indicated everywhere; you can pose with 10-foot black bears or tiny fawns. Call (417) 887-7334 or visit the website at basspro.com for hours.

From Bass Pro, go to *Nearly Famous Deli & Pasta House* (2708 S. Glenstone; 417-883-3403; nearlyfamous.net). This family-owned restaurant turns out the most scrumptious of soups (try the chunky tomato, a daily house specialty), salads, sandwiches, dinner items, and heavenly desserts that will make you wonder why this restaurant is not called the Famous Deli. My favorite combo is tomato soup and an egg salad sandwich; both are memorable. Hours are Tues through Sat 11 a.m. to 2:30 p.m. and 4:30 to 8 p.m.

battleplunges missouriinto war

Located 10 miles southwest of Springfield is the site of the *Battle of Wilson's Creek,* which occurred August 10, 1861, and marked the beginning of the Civil War in Missouri. The park has an interactive visitor center featuring a movie and a battle map. You can take a self-tour or a guided tour or bring your horse and ride the trails of Wilson's Creek.

You will notice a Chinese restaurant on almost every corner in Springfield. This town is known as "the home of cashew chicken." This specialty is on every menu, so just pick a restaurant and try this Ozarks invention (yes, seriously).

Casper's (601 W. Walnut St.; 417-866-9750) is strangely interesting. Don't let the unassuming exterior fool you. It opened in 1909, holds the title of the oldest diner on Route 66, and is one of those places you will tell people about for years. When you step inside, look up at the quirky round ceilings covered in posters and enjoy the genuine ambience of a Route 66 diner. It features classic fast food at its best: real hamburgers made of ground beef, a world-famous original recipe chili, and, of course, shakes and malts and fried pickles (you knew that was coming, didn't you?). You will see Casper himself peeking at you from different places, too. Hours are Mon through Sat 10:30 a.m. to 4 p.m.

Springfield is a major city, but as in most big cities, there are hidden treasures. Gary and Paula Blankenship's **Walnut Street Inn Bed and Breakfast** (900 E. Walnut; 417-864-6346; walnutstreetinn.com) has a quiet ambience to counter the big-city feel. Each of the 12 rooms includes a private bath, some with original porcelain antique fixtures, hardwood floors, and antique furnishings. Ozark specialties such as persimmon muffins and walnut bread are featured along with a full breakfast. The inn now offers something even more tempting: in-room massage from a certified masseuse! There's also a two-person steam bath. What a fine weekend retreat this has turned out to be.

trivia

Actor Brad Pitt graduated from Kickapoo High School in Springfield. He starred in the movie *The Assassination of Jesse James,* about Missouri's Robin Hood outlaw who, folklore has it, gave money he stole from railroad barons and Yankee banks to farmers. Actress Kathleen Turner is from Springfield too.

The inn caters to business travelers with an additional phone line in each suite for computers. In the main house and in the carriage house, Wi-Fi is available. The new AA baseball stadium is located just 2 blocks north of the inn on John Q. Hammons Parkway, now the home park of the Springfield Cardinals, a minor-league team affiliated with the St. Louis Cardinals.

The circa 1856 **Gray/Campbell Farmstead** in Nathanael Greene Park (2400 S. Scenic Ave.; 417 725 4921; graycampbellfarmstead.org) is the oldest house in Springfield. Guides present the history of the farmstead and conduct tours of the log kitchen, granary, two-crib barn, and family cemetery. It is open Apr and Oct on Sun 1:30 to 4:30 p.m., May through Sept on Sat and Sun 1:30 to 4:30 p.m., or by appointment.

In America, it's all about cars, right? Has been since Henry Ford started cranking them out for us, and instead of just a dream, they became a "one-in-every-garage" fact. The **Route 66 Car Museum** (1634 W. College St.; 417-459-2452; 66carmuseum.com) begins with the Brass Era (1890 to 1915) when the beautiful new American automobiles had brass fittings, then moves to the Sports Car section, displaying cars bred for speed and handling. The Classics are all rare and valuable (collectors want these), but a personal favorite is the Celebrity section with cars owned by famous people or featured in TV shows and movies. Open 9 a.m. to 5 p.m. seven days a week.

TOP RECOMMENDATIONS IN SOUTHWEST MISSOURI

Bass Pro Shops Outdoor World

Candlestick Inn

Coldwater Ranch

Japanese Stroll Garden

Jolly Mill

Ozark National Scenic Riverways

Also in Nathanael Greene Park is the ***Mizumoto Japanese Stroll Garden*** (friendsofthegarden.org), a 7.5-acre stroll around three small lakes with extensive landscaping. There is a teahouse, a moon bridge, and other features unique to a Japanese garden. It is open Apr through Oct, Fri through Sun 5 to 8:30 p.m.

Springfield is home to—are you ready for this?—the ***World's Largest Fork.*** It's just stuck in the ground there at 2215 W. Chesterfield Blvd., south of the stroll garden, and it should be in a book like this one, shouldn't it? Photo-op here to send to friends back home.

An outstanding nature center, designed by the Missouri Department of Conservation, is at 4600 S. Chrisman (417-888-4237). Want to know how to tell a hawk from a heron when they're far overhead? One of the volunteers at the ***Springfield Conservation Nature Center*** will show you silhouettes suspended from the ceiling that correspond to identifying shapes on the floor. Another room invites you into the dark with displays that light up—or sing out—as you press a button or break a light beam. See a barred owl, hear a whip-poor-will, watch a flying squirrel—it's all here. Three miles of nature trails take you through Ozark woodlands—80 acres of hilly wilderness—and a small bog; cross genuine suspension bridges and learn while you take in the fresh air.

Civilwarstrife

Missouri gave 109,000 men to the Union cause and about 30,000 men to the Confederacy. Vicious guerrilla action terrorized the state, especially near the Kansas border. The Battle of Wilson's Creek near Springfield was one of the bloodiest of the Civil War.

Springfield is a mecca for watercolorists. For more than 50 years, the ***Springfield Art Museum*** (417-837-5700; sgfmuseum.org) has been the locus for Watercolor USA, one of the most prestigious shows in the nation. Every June through August the museum displays the best and the brightest; you may browse or buy at 1111 Brookside Dr. (You'll know you're close when you see the large yellow sculpture called *Sun Target*; local kids call it the *French Fries.*) The museum also owns a fine permanent collection of original works. Visit at any time of the year. Museum hours are Wed through Fri noon to 8 p.m., Sat 10 a.m. to 6 p.m., and Sun 1 to 5 p.m.

The **Landers,** at 311 E. Walnut, is the home of the Springfield Little Theatre, which features talented actors from around the Ozarks. Kathleen Turner and Brad Pitt got their starts here. In 1909 theater architect Carl Boller designed the theater to look like a jewel box and a cartouche. It has a high, curved ceiling resembling a crown. The theater has been refurbished to its original splendor. The seats include the original wooden armrests and floral ironwork. The ribs going up the cartouche are like a crown inset with jewels, where the lights sparkle surrounded by 14-karat gold leaf and sterling painted moldings. The baroque decor and heavy draperies give it an elegantly royal feel. The $400,000 renovation of this magnificent theater alone is worth seeing, but the fact that it also offers a six-show main season (each show running three weeks), the Springfield Opera, the Springfield Ballet, and the Mid-America Singers makes it all the more worthy of a visit. Call the box office at (417) 869-1334 for current productions, or visit springfieldlittletheatre.org.

Ty Lechyd Da Distillery (pronounced Tea-Yah-Key-Dah, which is Welsh for "*House of Cheers*") is at 305 Market Ave. (417-832-8277, springfieldbrewingco.com). It makes several bourbons and ryes, but some are special. Hinterland Bourbon Whiskey is finished in maple syrup barrels for just a hint of maple on your tongue; Songbird Gin and Goldfinch House Gin are rested in Sauternes wine barrels. These gins have notes of bright citrus, crisp botanicals, oak, and just a hint of cinnamon. The Double Barrel 5-Year Rum is 5-year, double-oaked, blackstrap molasses rum and a 2022 ADI silver medal winner. The Oba Pearl Fine Grappa is made in collaboration with Lindwedel Winery in Branson using its locally grown Vidal Blanc grapes. Don't forget to get your **Missouri Spirits Expedition** stamp before you leave.

Culture Boutique Hotel at 445 E. Commercial St. (417-720-1949; culturecstreet.com/boutique-hotel) is worth the trip to Springfield. This six-room inn

"Whistle Stop" Trail

The **Frisco Highline Trail** is the KATY Trail of southwest Missouri. The 36-mile trail is now open from Springfield to Bolivar. The most beautiful part is the 18-mile stretch from Walnut Grove to Bolivar; it winds its way through pasture and forest, over 16 trestles, and right through La Petite Gemme Prairie Natural Area. This is the second-longest hiking, biking, and equestrian trail in the state. But here's a trivia note you might enjoy: It is the route once traveled by Harry S Truman as a precursor to his "Whistle Stop Campaign" in 1948. For more information about the trail, go to friscohighlinetrail.org.

and cafe is in a historic building. It was once a drug store, an opera house, and a mattress factory, as well as other businesses. The themed rooms are inspired by a different city in Eurasia, including Nepal, Morocco, Turkey, and India. What is really cool is that the furnishings in the hotel have been made from reclaimed materials that were once a part of the historic building. The cafe features all local ingredients and Eurasian coffee.

Outdoor Playground

Just outside Springfield on US 65 is another kind of mecca—tiny *Galloway* is wall-to-wall antiques. It's as if the town had been invaded by aliens selling oldies; nearly every building and home is now a shop. Find everything from a vine- and thorn-wrapped birdhouse (to discourage cats, of course) to European china, but don't stop before you get to the flea market a half-mile or so north of the other shops. Here you'll find two floors of great bargain flea-market antiques. If you travel northwest from Springfield on Highway 13 to *Bolivar* and the *Pomme de Terre* and *Stockton State Park* lakes, you will see some Missouri countryside that will invite you to stay longer than you planned. Both lakes have plenty of boating, fishing, and water sports of all kinds. If you want to get up close and personal with the area and have your bikes for the KATY Trail, stop near Bolivar and try the *Frisco Highline Trail,* the best and most scenic rail trail in the Ozarks region of southwest Missouri. The trail covers about 35 miles and travels through woodlands and fields, passing 16 bridges across two counties. The trail is partially paved with asphalt and gravel and links Bolivar and Springfield. The road has about a 3 percent inclination, which might challenge you between Bolivar and Springfield.

If you are hungry and thirsty, in the little town of *Urbana* is the perfect old-fashioned drive-in place called *Mr. Ed's* (3192 Hwy. 65; 417-993-5316), with good burgers and ice cream as you would expect from a place that's been there since 1963. Hours are Apr through Oct, Sun through Thurs 11 a.m. to 10 p.m. and Fri and Sat till 11 p.m.; Nov through Mar, Sun through Thurs 11 a.m. to 9 p.m.

If you head north on I-44 to *Lebanon,* you will find a town loaded with surprises. The *Route 66 Museum* in the Lebanon Laclede County Library is still quite active and has a gift shop. The city has turned a section of Boswell Park into a tribute to Route 66 with three large murals and some trivia. The park is located right on the location of the old Route 66. If you plan to spend the night here, you can enjoy the feel of old Route 66 at the *Munger Moss Motel* (1336 E. Rte. 66; 417-532-3111; mungermoss.com). Built in 1946, it's an old-fashioned mom-and-pop motel that has been managed by the same mom

TOP ANNUAL EVENTS IN SOUTHWEST MISSOURI

MAY
Plumb Nellie Days
Branson
(417) 334-1648
downtownbranson.org

AUGUST
Ozark Empire Fair
Springfield
With live music
(417) 833-2660

Old Soldiers and Settlers Reunion
Cassville
(417) 847-2814

Marian Days
Carthage
Annual religious events for Vietnamese
Catholics
(417) 358-7787
carthage-mo.gov

SEPTEMBER
Laura Ingalls Wilder Festival
Mansfield
(877) 924-7126

Annual Autumn Daze Craft Festival
Branson
With more than 150 crafters
(417) 334-4084
explorebranson.com

DECEMBER
Old Time Country Christmas
Silver Dollar City
With lights, music, and special Christmas
attractions for adults and children
(417) 336-7100

Trail of Lights at Shepherd of the Hills
Branson
A spectacular drive-through display of
lights
(417) 334-4191
explorebranson.com

and pop since 1971. The rooms are Route 66 themed with great photos, yet up to date with Wi-Fi. Even the iconic sign out front was refurbished with a cost-share grant from the Neon Heritage Preservation Committee, the Route 66 Association of Missouri, and the National Park Service. The gift shop is filled with Route 66 memorabilia, and a historical vintage auto court is fun to see.

Flea markets and antiques shops are all over the place in Lebanon, more than 23 at last count. The ***Heartland Antique Mall*** (2500 Evergreen Pkwy.; 417-532-9350; heartlandantiquemalllebanon.com) is a 40,000-square-foot, 250-dealer antiques mall voted #2 in the state as "Best Antiques Mall." Open every day from 8 a.m. to 8 p.m. And here's a good deal: The Russell Stover Candy store is next door!

While you are in the Lebanon area you might want to visit ***Whirlwind Ranch,*** where the alpacas are part of the family. The ranch's Whirlwind Ranch Store, at 24649 Snowberry Dr., has a beautiful selection of products made from 100 percent baby alpaca fiber and blends of 70 percent alpaca and 30 percent acrylic. There are ponchos, sweaters, and blankets along with alpaca toys and teddy bears. You can even buy a pet bed stuffed with alpaca fiber for your dog or cat. In winter, there is nothing warmer than hats, scarves, ear warmers, or hiking socks made of alpaca. If you enjoy knitting, crocheting, spinning, or weaving, there is a colorful assortment of sport-weight and fingering-weight yarns, hand-dyed and made right at the ranch. Liz, Linda, and Walter Mitchko will welcome you. The website whirlwindranch.com will tell you all about the ranch. From I-44 take exit 129 and turn right to the first traffic light. Turn left onto Highway 32 East. Go about 7 miles to Snowberry Drive (the second dirt road on the left after B Highway), turn left onto Snowberry, and go 2 miles—the driveway entrance is on the left at the top of the long, steep hill. Stop at the first house. Please call ahead (417-533-5280) to schedule your visit.

If you are into horses and you have your horse along, a small side trip south of I-44 on Highway J will quickly take you to **Waynesville** and the **4J Big Piney Horse Camp** (573-774-6879; 4jhorsecamp.com). This is a chance to get off the road and into the woods, so bring your horses and ride over mountains, through beautiful valleys, along the edge of bluffs, through quiet forests, and along the famous Big Piney River. There are all types of fun activities for when you are enjoying time off the horse, as well. The campsites have water and electricity, and Betty Laughlin does the cooking in a dining hall that seats up to 300 people. Modern restrooms, showers, and electricity are available, too, and horses are comfortable in their box stalls. Brothers Jimmy, Jay, Jeff, and Joey are partners in the operation. Sunday church services are held in the dining hall and on the trail. Camping arrangements must be made in advance, so call for camping and riding dates for May through Oct. Enjoy the thrill of feeling the wind in your hair as you ride through this Missouri paradise.

On the square in **Waynesville** is the **Old Stagecoach Stop,** which has been totally renovated and is exactly as it was when the stage stopped here at the courthouse. It is listed on the National Register of Historic Places and is open Apr through Sept on Sat 10 a.m. to 4 p.m. Guided tours are available. For more info, call (573) 336-3561 or go to oldstagecoachstop.com.

Fort Leonard Wood is the home of the US Army Corps of Engineers. It is also the home of the Army Engineering Center and the **US Army Engineer Museum.** The fort covers about 63,000 acres in the Ozarks about 130 miles southwest of St. Louis on I-44 near Waynesville. A recipe for creamed chipped beef on toast, called SOS by the soldiers who had to eat it, is tacked on the wall of a restored mess hall, one of several "temporary" wooden buildings built during World War II. A field kitchen lists the fort's daily food requirements in 1943, including 4,750 pounds of bacon, 47 gallons of vinegar, and 105 gallons of syrup.

The museum's oldest treasure is a signet ring that belonged to Lysimachus, an engineer general who served Alexander the Great in about 330 BC. The museum walks people through a chronological history of the corps. There are several specialized galleries. Many of the temporary mobilization buildings, two-story wooden barracks familiar to soldiers at every post in the world and built to last about 10 years, have been restored to create typical company areas. A supply room with a wood-burning stove, racks for M1 rifles and .45-caliber pistols, and entrenching tools would bring a tear to a supply sergeant's eye.

The history of the corps, however, dates from the Revolutionary War. There's a 1741 muzzle-loading cannon that the French lent to the Continental army, and a shovel and axe dating from the 1781 Battle of Yorktown, the first engineering victory of the army engineers who built fortifications and trenches into British positions. The oldest unit in the US Army is the 101st Engineer Battalion of the Massachusetts National Guard, established in 1636 as the East Regiment. Another display demonstrates low tide at Omaha Beach during the D-Day invasion of June 6, 1944, with an engineer disposing of German mines that would have been a danger to Allied ships.

walking on air

Eminence is the home of astronaut **Tom Akers** and his family. Akers, who has had four space flights to date, holds the record for the number of hours of EVAs (extravehicular activities, or space walks), most of that time accrued while helping repair the Hubble Space Telescope. Colonel Akers has experienced more than 800 hours of space flight, bringing his total EVA time to 29 hours and 40 minutes. He was a member of the first three-person EVA and the longest EVA—8.5 hours—in history.

Children can take the wheel of a restored pilothouse, US *Snag Boat No. 13*, which kept the Mississippi River clear for more than 50 years. Other hands-on activities include a land-mine detector. Gun enthusiasts will enjoy the 19th-century Gatling gun, an 1819 Flintlock rifle, an 1816 Springfield .69-caliber musket, and many small arms from more recent wars.

The museum is at 495 S. Dakota Ave. Hours are Mon through Sat 10 a.m. to 4 p.m. Admission is free but donations are accepted. Call (573) 596-0780 for more information.

St. Roberts is a popular tourist area for visiting military and families attending basic-training graduations at Fort Leonard Wood, which is the home of the Maneuver Support Center of the US Army.

Wander down Highway VV from Licking and enjoy the rugged countryside, which contains some of the largest springs in the world. The Jacks Fork River and the Current River near **Eminence** provide year-round canoeing. If they're lucky, canoeists on the Current and Jacks Fork Rivers just might get to see the beautiful wild horses of Shannon County, which have been roaming freely for more than 100 years. It's lucky the Broadfoot Herd, Grassy Herd, and Shawnee Creek Herd exist in the wild; 2016 marks the 20th anniversary of a federal law that protects the horses and prevents the National Park Service from removing them from Ozark National Scenic Riverways land. Find **Windy's Canoe Rental** (windyscanoe.com) for canoes, tubes, kayaks, and rafts to take out on the rivers to see this rare sight.

Highway 19 is a rustic stretch of the Ozark Plateau. The hills are steep and the road curvy, so your only choice is a slow drive across narrow bridges over gleaming waterways. You can't pass anyone on Highway 19, so you may as well relax and enjoy the view. This scenic highway has its share of people there just to see the towering pines that create a lush green canopy that shades the roadway. The highway snakes from near Hannibal to the Arkansas state line. You can drive from Hermann to Eminence while stopping at little shops for ice cream, sandwiches, and shopping. The views are enchanting, so take your time and slowpoke along.

Missouri's southwestern rivers—quick-running, spring-fed, and bone-chillingly cold—are so beautiful they bring a lump to your throat. In fact, the Current, the Eleven Point, and the Jacks Fork have been designated **Ozark National Scenic Riverways.** It is Missouri's largest national park.

Generations of canoeists and trout fishermen know these secluded waters. You can spend the day without seeing another soul, then camp on a quiet sandbar at day's end and listen to the chuck-will's-widows and owls call while your fire lights the riffles with bronze. Pick fresh watercress from these icy waters to garnish the trout that sizzles in lemon butter on your grill and know that life gets no better than this. There are plenty of rental outfits; pick up brochures anywhere. Ask about **Bluff Hole,** a hidden swimming hole where the Jacks Fork River widens. There is deep water at the base of the rock shelf and gravelly shallows near the bank. The hole is hidden away at the end of a tree-shaded path and has been a favorite of swimmers for generations.

Springs gush from beneath solid rock, slowly carving themselves a cave. Early residents built mills here to produce flour, cornmeal, and sawn lumber. There's as much natural history as human history along these bright rivers.

The crystal-clear waters of the spring-fed Current River drift past rocky bluffs and shorelines thick with wildflowers. Schools of darters flash by in the cold water (water temperatures range from 53 to 57 degrees Fahrenheit year-round). This gentle wilderness is a favorite canoeing and tubing area for Midwesterners. Even beginners can navigate the waters without getting too wet except by choice. Paddle hard around the occasional rootwad, an area of ripped-up tree roots that may create some whitewater—or simply get out and push the canoe past it. Most stretches of the river are rated Class I, as easy as it gets. The gravel bars are fine places to pull out and have lunch or even to camp for the night. Only owls and the leaf rustle of small creatures break the silence. The tranquil moss-covered hillsides are a peaceful escape from the busy world back home. At some points along the river, the water turns a rich blue-green as it gets wider and deeper, sometimes as deep as 25 feet.

The half-day trip from Weymeyer put-in to Van Buren is an easy and beautiful route. A few miles before the Van Buren Bridge is **Watercress Park,** the site of a single Civil War battle—with trenches and grave sites—where the Union army held the Confederates at bay across the river one cold night. At the pull-out spot, just past the Van Buren Bridge, you can leave your canoe on the beach and let the outfitters know you are back.

Alley Spring feeds the Jacks Fork River and is called the most picturesque spot in the state. Some 80 million gallons of water a day flow through here, and the Old Red Mill has been restored to working order. The springwater is a consistent 58 degrees Fahrenheit year-round.

Big Spring is the largest concentration of springs in the world—a mystery to hydrologists, who do not understand the large volume of water. Beautiful rivers gush right out of the ground from the base of spectacular rock bluffs and create the most consistent spring-fed, crystal-clear rivers in the country. Round Spring Cave is just off Highway 19.

If you have horses, **Cross Country Trail Rides,** 17142 CR 203 on Highway 19 East, has a week planned for you. You can take the whole family on a cross-country trail ride from Apr through Dec. You will camp for the week on the Jacks Fork River. The ride returns to base camp every night, where all your meals (18 total) are served and entertainment is royal. Well-known country music performers entertain at a dance every night but Sunday. There are horse shows, team roping events, and other sports to show off your steed. Jane says they fill up months in advance; to ensure a spot for you and your mount, call (573) 226-3492. This is a "BYOH" affair; no rental horses are available. Visit the website at crosscountrytrailrides.com.

If you don't have your own horse, head for **Coldwater Ranch** (17154 Coldwater Ranch Rd.; 573-226-3723; coldwaterranch.com) on Highway 19 north of Eminence and turn right onto CR 208. Jim and Kathy Thomas have horses at their place and will arrange anything from an hour-long ride to a six-day pack trip. For the overnight trips, tents, sleeping bags, food, and beverages are provided, and your steed has a saddlebag for your personal stuff. Quarter horses and a few gaited horses range from mounts for the novice to those for the experienced rider. The ranch accepts all ages; they have had 4-year-olds and 80-year-olds. Horses are rented by the hour; overnight trips include three meals and about 10 hours of riding. Recent expansion on the ranch includes cabins and RV/camping. You can also bring your own horse and rent a stall.

A winding drive along US 160 takes you to the beautiful Eleven Point River, with its many natural springs and lovely spots for picnics. You will be surprised at the excellent roads through these wooded hills.

The Between the Rivers section of the ***Ozark Trail*** covers about 30 miles. The northern entry point to this section is on US 60, approximately 3.5 miles west of Van Buren. Trailhead parking is provided for users at US 60 and at Sinking Creek Lookout Tower, about a mile west of Highway J. The trail winds south for the first 13 miles across small tributaries that feed the Current River. Creeks with names such as Wildhorse Hollow, Devil's Run, and Big Barren flow through the area. Designed for both hikers and horses, the trail crosses a ridge that divides the Current River from the Eleven Point River along Gold Mine Hollow. The trail offers panoramic mountain views and deeply wooded areas to filter the summer sun. Deer gaze from the shadows, too. If you are a hiking enthusiast, this area is for you. Pick up a book with a listing of all the hiking trails on federal property, complete with maps, at the US Forest Service office in Winona, grab your backpack, and head out.

Wooded Ozark roads stretch out before you now, with oak trees shouldering evergreens; the Doniphan Lookout Tower watches the national forest for fires here. Tune your AM radio to 1610 for Ozark Riverway information if you are headed for canoeing or camping at one of the many parks or rivers nearby.

If you have a carload of children and want a resort, the ***River's Edge Resort*** (16392 Tom Akers Rd.; 573-226-3233; riversedge.com) is also near Eminence and offers not only rooms and cabins but also hot tubs, inner tubes, firewood, and lodging on the Ozark National Scenic Riverways at the Jacks Fork of the Current River. All the rooms and cabins offer direct river access for floating, canoeing, fishing, tubing, swimming—whatever you want to do wet—as well as hiking, riding, cycling, picnicking, hunting, and even golfing. The River's Edge has a private beach, and under the shady canopy of old trees you will find a gallery of interesting iron sculptures that you won't soon forget. Relax is the key word, even if relaxing means doing something exciting.

Eminence Canoes, Cottages & Camp (573-226-3500 or 800-723-1387; eminencecanoescottagescamp.com) has everything you need for wilderness adventure. Rent a canoe and float on the 135 miles of spring-fed, clear waters of the Jacks Fork and Current Rivers, and unwind in the informal cottages on 30 acres. These mini-homes have one to three bedrooms and fully equipped kitchens (and gas grills, free movies, and cable TV). Or you can camp out along the Jack's Fork River Valley in the family- and pet-friendly campgrounds.

Because of the number of campers who take this route to the wilderness, the little town of **Van Buren** on US 60 is the home of several neat shops and museums.

The **Hidden Log Cabin Museum** (305 W. John St.; 573-323-4563) is the darling of Ozark historian Wanda Newton. For many years she knew that a log cabin lay at the heart of the neat, ordinary frame house next door. She waited for the house to go on the market and spent the time buying antiques and refurbishing them. She also studied the history of the Ozarks and dreamed. Then in 1990, it happened. The old Bowen place was for sale, and she bought it and began removing decades of "improvements" from its interior.

A one-of-a-kind "yawning" fireplace of hand-cut sandstone with a huge arch rock was professionally rebuilt and the hearth made ready for cooking with a collection of early ironware. Layers of sheetrock, insulation, and ceiling tiles were removed to expose the original construction. Furniture and household goods from the 1800s were placed in the painstakingly restored home. By the spring of 1993, her work was complete. In addition to the original log cabin room, the museum also has a dining room, bedroom, kitchen, and summer kitchen, each room filled with artifacts and furnishings. But most important is the woman who has lovingly created its homelike atmosphere. Wanda knows every jewel in this jewel box. Many of the pieces of furniture are from families who lived here. The treasures span two centuries, from tools of the early 1800s, pre–Civil War books and toys, and willow furniture made by gypsies to a 1930s Zenith radio from the Depression years. Many of the items are dated—a rope bed is from 1838, and an immigrant trunk dates from 1869. Located in downtown Van Buren, the museum is a block west of the courthouse on the south side of the Float Stream Cafe at the corner of John and Ash. Hours are Mon through Sat 9 a.m. to 5 p.m. and Sun 1 to 5 p.m. Apr through Nov. There is a small admission fee.

The **Float Stream Cafe** (101 Dollie Ln.; 573-323-0606) has been a tradition here for over 50 years. The original building was destroyed by flood in 2017, but the new place is well worth a visit. Good food is served here, including a special every day, seven days a week. Friday is fried catfish day, and Sunday has chicken and dumplings. The cafe is open Sun through Thurs 6 a.m. to 7 p.m. and Fri and Sat 6 a.m. to 8 p.m.

The beginnings of **Grand Gulf State Park** (Missouri's answer to the Grand Canyon) in Thayer go back 450 million years to a time when sediment was deposited by ancient seas, forming dolomitic rock. As the area uplifted and the sea receded, water percolated down through cracks in the rock and began to dissolve passageways underneath. Streams cut their own beds on the surface of the soft rock. As air-filled caves formed and cave roofs collapsed, streams were diverted underground. The collapse of the Grand Gulf occurred within the past 10,000 years—fairly recent by a geologist's reckoning.

West Plains is a starting point for canoeing on the North Fork River. Or you can strike off on foot into the wilderness of the **Mark Twain National Forest.** There's the **Old-Time Music Ozark Heritage Festival** (417-256-8835; oldtimemusic.org) in June, so come to this historic downtown to celebrate the Ozark Highlands culture with music, hoedown dancing, and a jig dance competition. Hear authentic mountain string band music by local artists. The music of the Ozark hills has its roots in Ireland, Scotland, England, and Africa. It is made up of strings for plucking and strumming—and dancing. Of course, there are the usual food booths and local crafts.

The **Dawt Mill** was established in 1897, and its water-powered buhr stone mill is still grinding grain. More than a century ago, teams of mules and horses would pull wagons filled with corn and wheat to the mill, which sits on a high bank of the North Fork of the White River, and farmers would wait for their turn at the mill. The cotton gin would be pumping out cleaned cotton ready to be sold or spun. While waiting for their grinding, the families would shop at the general store or use the blacksmith's skills repairing farm implements and shoeing animals. People gathered on the porch of the mill to play music by the clear, cold water in the evening and would fall asleep under their wagons while the mill ground into the wee hours of the morning.

The Dawt Dam creates what is known as a "canoe buster" that is intimidating to novice canoeists. The gift shop sells quite a few T-shirts with "I Shot the Dam at Old Dawt Mill" emblazoned on the front. The Ozarks draw feelings of times long past. There are still a few mills along the water to give you a glimpse of what life was like in the 1800s. If you enjoyed seeing the Dawt Mill, head for the **Hodgson Water Mill,** circa 1861, only a few minutes away. (Return to Highway PP, then turn left onto Highway H and go north to Highway 181.) Watercress still thrives in Bryant Creek, and all the old milling machinery is still inside. Interesting: There is an opening to a cave inside that creates natural air-conditioning.

Continue south on Highway 181 for about 5 miles and watch for **Zanoni Mill** on your right. It is not open to the public, but worth slowing down to see a well-preserved and rare example of an overshot millwheel.

If you continue south on Highway 181, then right on Highway N, just north of the junction with Highway 95, you can follow the signs to the town of **Rockbridge** and the **Rockbridge Mill** on the banks of Spring Creek. The original town was burned during the Civil War, but a new village grew up around the mill in 1865.

The **Rainbow Trout and Game Ranch** (4297 CR 142, Rockbridge; 417-679-3619; rockbridgemo.com) offers trout fishing in Spring Creek. The creek is stocked with large rainbows that don't seem to know they are there to be your dinner. The 3,000-acre ranch has a gun club for hunting the white-tailed deer and wild turkeys living in the woods. This is an Ozark dream-come-true where you can hike or saddle up and ride the logging trails crisscrossing the ranch where no car can go, maybe find the forgotten quarry, then relax in the 19th-century Grist Mill Club's antiques-filled saloon and have a drink or enjoy the first-class restaurant. Rooms start at $125 per night; the houses and cabins will sleep a whole family, the secluded Oak Ridge Place accommodates 10, and the New House sleeps 6.

Deep in the Ozark hills near **Ava,** a bell chimes in the early morning quiet. Trappist monks in white robes and cowls move quietly into the darkness of the chapel for morning prayers and meditation. A day begins at **Assumption Abbey** (417-683-5110; assumptionabbey.org), one of only 18 monasteries of the Trappist order in the country. The abbey is surrounded by 3,400 wooded acres. The monks seldom leave the abbey, and by their simple lives of prayer, labor, study, and solitude seek a deeper personal relationship with God.

So why mention a monastery in a travel guide, you might ask? Well, although man cannot live by bread alone, a visit to the Assumption Abbey bakery is in order. To be self-supporting, as monasteries must, the monks discovered a market for fruitcakes. Now they produce more than 30,000 fruitcakes annually. Since the fruitcakes proved so popular, a new and larger bakery was added. Fresh fruit jellies and jams are also sold in the bakery store. Call the bakery at (417) 683-2258. Each fruitcake weighs two pounds and is generously filled with raisins, cherries, and pineapple marinated in Burgundy and is bathed with an ounce of dark rum for moistness and flavor. They bear no resemblance to the ready-made kind you get from your aunt at Christmas. They are sold by direct mail to customers throughout the US and are carried at prestigious stores such as Williams-Sonoma.

The abbey extends hospitality to men and women of all faiths. If you need a restful weekend, or counseling from the monks, you are welcome. Guests get home-cooked meals served family style by the brothers. A love offering helps defray the costs. Reservations for overnight stays are requested and donations help with the expenses. The simple quarters contain wash basins, twin beds, a shared bath/shower, and a small homemade desk. Monks bring fresh soap and towels. It is a simple life. If you would like to spend a few days at this retreat, call or write Highway 5 Box 1056, Ava, MO 65608. The abbey is always closed during January for the monks' retreat and reflection.

North on Highway 5 is tiny **Mansfield,** home of the **Laura Ingalls Wilder–Rose Wilder Lane Museum and Home** (3060 Hwy. A; 877-924-7126; lauraingallswilderhome.com). Laura's home is just as she left it, and the museum contains four handwritten manuscripts. Author of the now-famous (courtesy of television) *Little House on the Prairie,* among other books, Laura was encouraged to write by her daughter, Rose Wilder Lane, a well-known author in her own right from the early 1900s. They are buried in the Mansfield cemetery. Admission is $18 for adults, $8 for children up to 18 years old.

Head on to **Mountain Grove** for a great steak and baked sweet potato at the unusual **Club 60** (6773 US 60; 417-926-9954; club60steakhouse.com). The license-plate fence in front of this old 1946 tavern will catch your eye. Although drinks are served and there is a pool table, this is very much a family place. Co-owner Jim Alessi is confident to say "we offer the best steak you will ever have in Missouri." Of course, he has also created over 500 specials (and still counting). Hours are Tues through Sat 4 to 9 p.m.

Go west on US 60 to swing back into Springfield.

Mining Country

Head west on I-44 to Halltown, then slip onto Highway 96 west for **Carthage,** where the majestic 1895 Jasper County Court House stands proudly on the square, turreted like a medieval castle. Settled in the 1840s, Carthage was burned to the ground in guerrilla raids during the Civil War. The Battle of Carthage was fought July 5, 1861—16 days before the Battle of Manassas in Virginia—making it the first land battle of the Civil War. More than 8,000 men fought here, 1,000 of them German American Union troops from St. Louis led by Colonel Franz Siegel. The rest of the soldiers were Southern sympathizers led by Missouri governor Claiborne Jackson. Destruction of the town was total. The 1849 home named Kendrick Place, built by slaves, was one of the few homes left standing after the war. In the late 19th century, all-new homes were built here; there is an abundance of Victorian homes, and more than 100 of them have been restored.

This interesting piece of history can be researched more thoroughly at the **Civil War Museum** (205 Grant St.; 417-237-7060), open Tues through Sat 8:30 a.m. to 5 p.m. and Sun 1 to 5 p.m. Lead and zinc mines were developed after the war, and wealthy owners built magnificent homes away from the mining camps. Marble quarries provided Carthage gray marble for many large state and federal buildings. The fine old homes here bespeak prosperity. It's still a beautiful city—the courthouse, high school, and many of the churches and homes are built of the stone quarried here. (The stone is not technically marble, but a limestone that takes a high polish.) Both the courthouse and high school contain murals by Lowell Davis, one of America's best-known nature artists and a native of Carthage. Follow the historic-drive markers for a tour of Carthage's magnificent old mansions that have been kept so beautifully throughout the years.

Carthage has more than its share of well-known native sons and is becoming a center for artists in the area. About 18 resident artists call the city home. Internationally known zoologist and naturalist Marlin Perkins (remember *Wild Kingdom?*) was born here; you'll find a bronze sculpture of Perkins by artists Bob Tommey and Bill Snow in Central Park on Garrison Avenue.

howtomake aspy

In her teens, *Myra Belle Shirley* saw her town leveled by war. The Battle of Carthage was the first major Civil War battle, fought July 5, 1861. She became the infamous Confederate spy and outlaw Belle Starr.

If you fancy colonial reproduction furniture, visit **Colonial House Historic Reproductions** (348 Grant St.; 417-358-8454; colonialhousedecor.com) on historic Carthage Square, where every piece is authentic reproduction. This shop is unique to southwest Missouri. Look at the handmade Windsor chairs and reproduction pewter; many objects are made by the Amish. Hours are Mon through Sat 10 a.m. to 5 p.m.

One of the very last drive-in movie theaters on Route 66 is in Carthage. The **66 Drive-in Theatre** is at 17231 Old 66 Blvd. (417-359-5959). Showtime is 8:15 p.m. Apr through mid-Sept.

As long as we are being nostalgic, and maybe hungry, find **Iggy's Diner** (2400 S. Grand Ave.; 417-237-0212). It's the real thing: an American diner complete with shakes, malts, and red barstools, and from all reports the food is great—not your regular fast food. Of course, the biscuits and gravy is the true test of a shiny 1950s diner and Iggy's passed with flying colors. The diner opens at 6 a.m. and closes at 9 p.m. daily, so you can eat breakfast and lunch there as well as dinner if you plan it right.

trivia

The town of *Noel* gets popular every year at Christmas—at least its post office gets popular—as people send letters and cards here for postmarks. It's actually pronounced "Nole." South of Noel is Bluff Dwellers Cave, a well-known tourist attraction that was 250 million years, give or take a million, in the making. It has drawn cave seekers since 1927.

The town of **Avilla** along Route 66 near Carthage is an abandoned village said to be haunted. Interesting story: Ghostly townsfolk walk around the town and can only be glimpsed out of the corner of your eye, they say, never full on. And what makes the story even more interesting is that the Avilla Death Tree (sounds scary but no one in town seems to know exactly which tree it is) is haunted by the headless ghost Bushwhacker Rotten Johnny Reb, a guerrilla fighter from the Civil War seeking revenge against the Yankees who hanged him. Missouri was held under martial law by the Union throughout the entire war and its men were drafted into the Union army. Yet this torn state had a star on the Confederate flag. So you can see there were very mixed feelings here—that persist to this day.

Joplin is the end of the Missouri portion of old Route 66 and has been a stopping point on cross-country travel for many decades—in fact, since 1889, when Joplin City was named for the Reverend Harris G. Joplin, a Tennessean settler. The abandoned tailing piles and mine shafts scattered about the town and the elegant homes just west of the downtown area are reminders of the city's mining era. There is a pretty waterfall cascading off a 163-foot-wide ledge at 5400 Riverside Dr. You can enjoy the water at *Grand Falls* or just hike around and savor the beauty and sound of the water. Good place for family fun (even though there was a shriek when someone spotted a harmless snake). The natural beauty makes for grand photo-ops. Call (800) 657-2534 for more information.

The Joplin Museum Complex in Schifferdecker Park is also home to the *Joplin Historical and Mineral Museum* at 504 S. Schifferdecker Ave. (417-623-1180; joplin-museum.org). These two mining-industry museums tell the story of the town and the minerals mined there.

The Joplin Historical Society preserves much of the city's history at the *Dorothea B. Hoover Historical Museum* (417-623-1180; joplin-museum.org), located at the intersection of 7th Street and Schifferdecker Park. It has some fascinating exhibits one would not expect in any old museum: The House of Lords shows us what a house of ill repute was like—liquor, gambling, ladies of the night—and how the gentlemen of Joplin spent their evenings. Bonnie and Clyde spent time in Joplin, and a section is devoted to them. You can spend the day here: Peruse a miniature circus with fun-house mirrors and the sounds of the Big Top, a doll collection filled with delicate porcelain dolls in handmade clothing and jewelry, and a cookie-cutter exhibit (yep, you read that right), then hit the turn-of-the-20th-century soda fountain for a black cow. Hours are Tues through Sat 10 a.m. to 5 p.m.

On May 22, 2011, Joplin was hit by a powerful tornado that wiped out a large portion of the city, including the medical center. There were more than 900 injuries and 161 lost their lives. Joplin has made a good recovery and is now in business again. To learn more about the city of Joplin, visit its website at joplinmo.org.

Peace Church Cemetery here in Joplin is home to the ghost of Billy Cook, a serial killer who left six people dead on a 27-day killing spree in the 1950s. He was buried in an unmarked grave after spending a short time in the San Quentin gas chamber, but he is still trying to hurt people. Locals swear things have been thrown at them, leaving scratches to prove it. Wander over at your own risk.

trivia

Two major Civil War battles were fought in **Newtonia**—with total forces numbering in the thousands. The 1862 battle was one of very few encounters in which Native Americans fought on both sides. Southern forces had Choctaw, Cherokee, and Chickasaw soldiers, while other Cherokees fought with the Union forces. This was the first battle of Colonel J. O. (Jo) Shelby's famous Iron Brigade. The 1864 battle, also involving Shelby, was the last battle in the Civil War fought west of the Mississippi. A Civil War cemetery here houses the remains of 13 soldiers, including the famous (or infamous to the Confederates) Robert Christian. Many slaves and their descendants are also buried here. The earliest stone is from 1858.

Joplin is also the home of the *Spiva Center for the Arts* (222 W. 3rd, corner of 3rd and Wall; 417-623-0183; spivaarts.org). Spiva Center has three galleries. The first is international art, the second is home to regional high-quality works. The third, upstairs, is rented to local artists. Classes are offered to children from grade school through college. Hours are Tues through Sat 10 a.m. to 5 p.m.

Outside Joplin go east on Highway V to Diamond. From Diamond drive 2 miles on Highway V and then south about a mile to find the *George Washington Carver National Monument,* which commemorates a man who was more than an educator, botanist, agronomist, and "cookstove chemist." He was a man who wanted "to be of the greatest good to the greatest number of people," a man who refused to accept boundaries, who drew from science, art, and religion to become a teacher and director of a department at Tuskegee Institute in Alabama. He taught botany and agriculture to the children of ex-slaves and tried to devise farming methods to improve the land exhausted by cotton. Known as the "Peanut Man," Carver led poor, one-horse farmers to grow protein-rich and soil-regenerating soybeans and peanuts. The Carver Nature Trail leads from the birthplace site past two springs and ends at the Carver family cemetery.

Just down US 71 is the *Real Hatfield Smokehouse* (7329 Gateway Dr., Neosho; 417-624-3765; hatfieldssmokedmeats.com). Owner Chad Neece has a sparkle in his blue eyes as he talks about his "home-grown" hogs. "We smoke anything you can get from a hog," he says. Bacon, hams—you name it, he smokes it. He will mail hams anywhere in the US and even has a regular customer in London. The small smokehouse uses a special sugar cure and hickory logs to give meats a golden-brown finish and good flavor without as much salt as other smokehouses. Hours are Mon through Sat 8 a.m. to 6 p.m.

Myrtle's Distilled Spirits (1013 Neosho Blvd.; 417-223-7463) has apple pie shine, butterscotch shine, pickle shine, and butter pecan shine, all bottled in mason jars, as shine should be. There is outdoor seating to enjoy the fine Missouri weather and get a stamp on your **Missouri Spirits Expedition** log as well.

Langston Hughes—born in Joplin in 1901—was a poet, novelist, playwright, social activist, and one of the early innovators of the art form known as jazz poetry. He was a journalist and one of the leaders in the Harlem Renaissance.

If you love ghost-storied and mysterious sights, visit *"Spooksville,"* 11 miles southwest of Joplin. It is here that an eerie light has been appearing in the middle of a lonely road most nights since 1886. This almost supernatural spook light created panic in the small village of Hornet and is often referred to as the Hornet Ghost Light. Early settlers actually left the area in terror because of the giant ball of light bouncing over the hills and across the fields. Today the light seems to concentrate on one gravel road known as Devil's Promenade or Spook Light Road. The light has even been rumored to come right up to your car and land on the hood, then bounce off or go out and appear later behind you. It disappears whenever approached. If you have the nerve, take I-44 west from Joplin to Highway 43, then drive south on Highway 43 approximately 6 miles to Highway BB. Turn right and drive approximately 3 miles to road's end. Turn right and drive another mile to a second dirt road to the left. If you haven't chickened out yet, you will now be headed west on Spook Light Road. The road is long. Park anywhere along the side of the road and wait. Try to find the darkest spot about 2 miles down the road. You can even venture down some of the very dark side roads. There is no charge for this thrill except the years of therapy it will take to get over it.

The town of *Pineville* is pretty small but home to the *Tall Pines Distillery* (3316 Goodin Hollow Rd.; 417-223-7463; tallpinesdistillerymo.com). The distillery is nestled in the bluffs of southwest Missouri within minutes of the scenic Elk River right off I-49. The natural springs and limestone create the perfect environment to make unique spirits—handcrafted moonshine—like Bananas Foster and Huckleberry that you will love. There is whiskey and brandy as well as moonshine and Rebellion, a 100-proof aged bourbon. It is a grain-to-glass distillery using local ingredients. The owners call themselves "a different class of hillbilly." Well, its shine is in jugs, not mason jars, so that's pretty classy. There is a large event center for parties and occasional live music jams. Get your **Missouri Spirits Expedition** stamp.

Pierce City on Highway 37 has a couple of neat little places to stop for a rest. But this is only a rest stop, because what you really want to see is the

Jolly Mill. You will be rewarded with a lovely wooded drive after you leave Highway 97 and turn onto US 60. Go 1.9 miles to a sign on FR 1010, then 1.9 miles across a creek with a bridge with no sides to FR 2025, past an old white church and churchyard, then 0.7 mile to the park.

This park is sort of a secret spot that the locals enjoy. Its history is fascinating. In 1848 George Isbell built a water-powered mill to serve settlers with gristmill products (and spirits). The new village that grew up around him was called Jollification, and it was a rest stop and resupply point for wagon trains headed west to Kansas and Indian Territory. When the Civil War came, the area was ravaged, and two cavalry battles raged here. Bushwhackers terrorized and burned the village but, here's a surprise, the distillery was spared.

A new village rose from the ashes and the distillery resumed operation. In 1872 a railroad was built to Indian Territory, eliminating wagons. At the same time, George Isbell refused to pay the new tax on spirits, stopped making whiskey (much to the regret of travelers), and turned his attention to milling flour. The village faded, and by 1894 the mill stood alone with the schoolhouse. But the mill prospered; flour was milled here until the 1920s, and gristmill products were ground for 50 more years.

A community effort was made to have the mill placed on the National Register of Historic Places, and it was rehabilitated. It is once again a working mill. The water still rushes by picnic tables, the covered bridge, and another wooden bridge. It is worth the drive to see.

Webb City*'s* claim to fame, the ***"Praying Hands,"*** is in ***King Jack Park.*** This 32-foot concrete-and-steel structure is atop a 40-foot-high hill. The park is named for the ore called "jack" that made the city rich in the 1870s. There are no signs inviting visitors to stop to see the huge sculpture; it just suddenly appears. The hands were created by Jack Dawson, an art instructor at the Webb City schools, and he intended it to be just a quiet reminder for people to turn to God. Webb City is off US 71.

When you get enough of the indoors, you outdoorsy folks can go west on US 59 at Anderson to enter canoe heaven. US 59 runs along the Elk River, and the sudden appearance of the famous overhanging bluffs makes you want to duck as you drive under them.

Tri-Lakes Area

The last town on Highway 76 before you enter the Mark Twain National Forest is ***Cassville.*** Highway 76 is a long and winding road through the forest, so if you arrive at this point after dark, you might as well spend the night.

The **Devil's Kitchen Trail** winds from the valley to the top and down again, giving a close-up look at the geology and history of the area. Eleven of the national forest's 14 caves are found along the rocky bench here. Shelters like these were used by Ozark bluff-dwelling Indians who lived here about 10,000 years ago. Artifacts such as food and fragments of clothing have been found to date this culture. The Devil's Kitchen was named for the stone formation that provided a hideout for Civil War guerrillas. As you head south on Highway 112, softly winding roads, tree-lined hills, and spectacular views pop up as you crest hilltops in this lovely national forest.

Roaring River State Park is the fountainhead of the Roaring River. There is a hidden spring in a cave filled with crystal-clear aqua-blue water that stays a constant 58 degrees Fahrenheit year-round. More than 20 million gallons a day are pumped into the river. Here the state maintains a trout hatchery and stocks the river daily in season.

The biggest day of the year happens on March 1, when the whistle blows early in the morning to open trout season. Anglers stand shoulder to shoulder in hopes of catching a lunker or their limit. Friendly competition abounds to catch the biggest trout. If you skip work to make opening day, try to avoid all the press who are waiting to snap pictures of the annual event. If you catch a big fish, you might just end up on the front page of the local newspaper . . . and then you will have some explaining to do when you get back to work.

trivia

Unlike Huckleberry Finn, you don't have to play hooky to go fishing in Cassville because school is officially closed on March 1 every year so residents can grab a fishing pole and open trout season. It has been a school holiday in this Ozarks town near Roaring River State Park for as long as anyone can remember. Many spend the night along the stream to secure a good spot. There can be as many as 4,000 anglers vying for spots. In 2005 Missouri Secretary of State Robin Carnahan fired a pistol at 6:30 a.m. to officially open the 6-month season.

The park runs the **Roaring River Inn** (417-847-2330; roaringriverstatepark.com). The inn, made largely of wood and stone, has 26 rooms and a view of the river valley below. Along with rooms, there are kitchenette suites, sleeper cabins (4-plex and duplex); children under 4 are free. No roughing it here: Refrigerators, satellite television, heat and a/c and, thank heavens, coffeemakers are all provided. (Well, there is a campground, too, for those of you wanting to rough it.) There is also a park store and pool. Other accommodations are available outside the park and in the town of Cassville.

Parkcliff Cabins (24600 Parkview Dr.; 417-236-5902; parkcliff.com) offers log cabins beginning at $120; others have a loft, deck, fireplace, full kitchen, and two bedrooms. This is the perfect romantic winter getaway if escape is what you are looking for, but the nearness of Branson, Table Rock Lake, and Eureka Springs, Arkansas, makes it a perfect family getaway as well. There are also several campgrounds in the Mark Twain National Forest.

Roaring River State Park is part of the White River basin. From a geologist's point of view, the basin tells a fascinating story. The White River has cut into the flat Springfield plateau, creating deep, steep-walled valleys and exposing varied layers of rock—shale, limestone, dolomite, and chert.

missouri
divided

By the time the Civil War was approaching, Missouri was warring within itself. The governor and many legislators favored secession but were outvoted at the convention called to decide the matter. The governor's faction fled south to Cassville, where they signed an ordinance of secession and affiliation with the Confederate States of America.

Pastures fringed with woods are found along Highway 76 East through the Piney Creek Wildlife Area. Mile after mile of ridge roads and startling views unfold until finally, over the crest of the last hill, beautiful Table Rock Lake appears before you. It feels like the top of a Ferris wheel from this vantage. The occasional small farm or Ozark stone cottage dots the roadside. Valleys with pastures, ponds, or a lone barn sitting starkly against the sky are the only traces of civilization.

At the town of Cape Fair you can turn right on Highway 76 to Table Rock Lake or turn left to **Reeds Spring.** Because of the proximity of Silver Dollar City, quite a few artists are in residence here.

Table Rock State Park is one of the most popular (meaning crowded) state parks in Missouri. Off the beaten path here means wilderness, on the path means bumper-to-bumper in summertime. As in most resort areas in the state, early spring and late fall are perfect times to roam without the huge crowds summer brings.

Author Harold Bell Wright came to these hills for his health in the early part of the 20th century and was so taken by the beauty of the area that he settled in to write. *The Shepherd of the Hills* is his best-known and most-beloved book; it captured the imagination of generations and even became one of John Wayne's early movies.

US 65 is an old-fashioned, uncrowded Ozark highway. You can still see the view as you crest hills here, but the **Shepherd of the Hills Inspiration Tower** (417-334-4191; theshepherdofthehills.com) offers an incredible one. The tower's first observation level is at 145 feet; the tower is 230 feet, 10 inches tall, with two elevators or 279 stairs to the top. But rest assured, it is stable. It is designed to withstand 172 mph winds (gusts of 224 mph), and it cost $1.5 million to build; this is not surprising since it contains 92,064 pounds of steel and is set in 43 truckloads of concrete. It also contains 4,400 square feet of glass, for a breathtaking view from the highest point around the Tri-Lakes area. The address for your GPS is 5586 W. 76 Country Blvd.

trivia

The **Shepherd of the Hills Theater** is the longest-running theater in the country. It began with a stage with its audience on blankets on the hillside, upgraded to folding chairs, and now is an outdoor amphitheater that seats around 2,500 people. The theater has been in nonstop operation for more than 60 years. In 1998 there was a big fire in the dressing rooms and it was announced that there would be no show that year. People poured in with stage props (antique guns, for example) to help, and the theater was up and running in time for the annual performance.

If you've heard of Silver Dollar City (and you will if you stay in Missouri for long), you've heard of **Branson.** Once a quiet little town pocketed in the weathered Ozark Mountains near the Arkansas border, it has seen business pick up considerably of late. It is certainly *not* off the beaten path; it is Missouri's Las Vegas, sorta. Branson has changed in the past several years from the strip of country music "opries" and related foofaraw crowded cheek-by-jowl along Highway 76 (known as "the strip") to the country-music capital of the Midwest, giving Nashville a run for its money. More than 50 theaters in town now feature such stars as Elvis Presley. No, really. Elvis is alive and well and living in Branson. This Elvis does an uncanny impersonation of the King. Tickets run about $40.

Branson is trying to keep up with the demand of more than 4 million tourists a year, but as you would suspect, about an hour before the matinee or evening shows begin, the traffic is much like a long, narrow parking lot. The secret to getting around is learning the back roads. Just knowing that the quickest route is not 76 Country Boulevard (a road to avoid if at all possible) can save you enough time for dinner.

There are other little secrets, too. The chamber of commerce will give you a free, easy-to-read map showing the shortcuts from one end of the 5-mile strip to the other. The recently repaved back roads can make life a little easier, even though you can't avoid the traffic altogether. The city now has a trolley system on the strip, and that helps a bit.

Do flea markets interest you? You're in the right place; downtown Branson has five of them. If you don't find something in this lineup, you aren't looking very hard, or you have a good deal more self-discipline than most of us.

Okay, this is not for the faint of heart—which means your kids will love it—but *Branson Zipline and Canopy Tours* (2339 US 65, Walnut Shade; 417-561-0699; wolfemountainbranson.com) is a once-in-a-lifetime bucket-list kind of thing you might want to try just to tell your friends you did it. You begin the experience by checking into Wolfe Creek Station and riding to your destination in one of their Pinzgauer Swiss Army Troop Carriers. The guides are well trained, so you can be sure your experience at one of the only themed zipline courses in the world will be safe as well as fun. Tour options include the Flying Prospector, the Ozarks Explorer, and the Canopy Adventure Combo, each between 1.5 and 3.5 hours long (there's no going back). Or, and this will surely be your first choice, the Blue Streak Fast Line & Free Fall Xpress. It starts with a Pinzgauer ride to the top of Wolfe Mountain, where you will zipline above the tree canopy and land on top of the tallest tower on the property. Then an exhilarating 100-foot vertical free fall follows. Trust me, you will love it. Well, your bigger kids (if they weigh between 70 and 275 pounds) will love it and love listening to you scream.

You probably had breakfast at your B&B, so think brunch now and order a three-egg omelet at *Mel's Hard Luck Diner* in Branson's Grand Village Shops (2800 W. 76 Country Blvd., Ste. 103; 417-332-0150; melshardluckdiner.com) and have someone sing a country song. The singing waitstaff makes sure your day begins with a song. This is a real 1950s diner—before health food was a thing—and huge, delicious desserts and burgers (maybe that should be burgers and desserts, in the proper order for some people) will take you back in time. Sigh. Hours are Thurs through Sat 11:30 a.m. to 7:30 p.m. Another great place for "off-the-beaten-path" dining is *Sugar Leaf Bakery Café* (2800 W. 76 Country Blvd., Ste. 211; 417-336-6618; sugarleafbakerycafe.com), also in the Grand Village. There are handmade cakes, cookies, and other goodies, along with soups, salads, quiches, specialty coffees, and more. Hours are Mon through Sat 10 a.m. to 4 p.m.

Because Branson is in the throes of a building boom and the traffic can be a genuine pain, the best thing to do is to find a bed-and-breakfast somewhere away from Branson and then just go in when you are psyched up to do it. (Avoiding the whole place might be more to your liking.) But you've come this far, so the first order of business is to get that map (the chamber of commerce and many hotels have them) and use all the side-road traffic shortcuts you can to reduce travel time and frustration. If you are not attending a show, stay off the streets around the 7 and 8 p.m. curtain times, when about 1,500 people per theater are all on Highway 76 and the local police are issuing tickets for driving in the center turn lane. Branson traffic lulls roughly before 8:30 a.m., between 10 and 10:30 a.m., and from around 2 to 2:30 p.m. Branson drivers are very courteous, though, and it won't be long before someone lets you pull out in front of them onto the strip.

One of the most interesting things to do when you hit Branson is to head to the old downtown area, which sits on the banks of the Taneycomo River. Here you can visualize what the town was like before it became an entertainment center. The riverfront and downtown area is going through a renaissance, and many changes are under way. To acquaint yourself with some of the improvements planned, visit branson.com, which is the website of the Downtown Branson Main Street Association (417-334-1548).

To take the pulse of the town, you must visit the **Branson Cafe** (120 W. Main St.; 417-334-3021; downtownbransoncafe.com), established in 1810 and the oldest restaurant in town. It started when Branson was just Branson, a nice little town. A big country breakfast with all the trimmings and friendly, charming waitresses await you when you slide into a red upholstered booth and kick back to enjoy. The waitresses are a wealth of information about where to go and what to see that is "hot" in Branson. The cafe has a daily luncheon special posted in the window. All the homemade favorites appear there on a weekly basis. For dinner you might try some of the freshly caught trout from the Taneycomo River. Be sure to save room for some homemade cobbler or pie. Hours are Mon through Fri 6 a.m. to 3 p.m. and Sat and Sun. 6 a.m. to 8 p.m.

There are many gift shops on Main Street, but one of the "don't miss" ones is **Dick's 5&10 Cent Store** (103 W. Main St.; 417-334-2410; dicksoldtime-5and10.com). You truly do take a walk back in time to the good old days when you could have a quarter and shop to find just the right toy to delight your child's heart. You can find such things as those gadgets that "moo" when you turn them over or paper dolls, the kind we used to play with for hours. There's also an assortment of old-time dime-store items.

The ladies who like lovely things will not want to miss **Victorian House** (101 W. Main St.; 417-335-8000), an exquisite shop packed with frilly, lacey, sheer, flowered, floaty, crocheted (I have run out of adjectives) beautiful blouses, dresses, vests, or whatever else you are looking in very feminine clothing. You will love everything—seriously, everything—in the shop. It is truly a "fantasy" shop of beautiful things. Hours are 9 a.m. to 6 p.m. every day.

Keep going another block east, across the railroad tracks, and you will find the **Branson Scenic Railroad** (206 E. Main St.; 800–2TRAINS (287–2467); bransontrain.com). You and the kids will absolutely love this ride through the Ozarks, over tall trestles and bridges, through tunnels of solid rock, with grand views from the glass dome on top. This romantic vintage passenger train known as the *Ozark Zephyr* has a dining car where a four-course candlelight dinner is served. The dinner train leaves at 5 o'clock every Saturday night. All train trips leave from the historic Branson Depot. You might want to call ahead for schedules and packages; the train doesn't run from Dec to the first week in Mar.

If you are in a mood to do some trout fishing on Lake Taneycomo, check with **Scotty's Trout Dock** (500 Boxcar Willie Dr.; 417-334-4288; scottystrout-dock.com). Staff can supply you with boats, kayaks, fishing guides, and all the necessary items and good advice on how and where to catch "the big one." They rent tackle, boats, and even pontoons, and they will supply a guide if you want one. Or maybe all you need is a driver, so you can stretch out and catch some rays on the back of the pontoon—definitely a "little slice of heaven." Hours are 7 a.m. to 5 p.m. daily.

Head west on 76 ("the strip"). You can stroll along the strip or take the trolley, leaving the driving to someone else so you can have fun with your friends. You and the kids can "Ride the Ducks," vintage World War II amphibious vehicles that go along the strip, through an outdoor military history museum, and then splash into the lake.

The Branson/Lakes Area Chamber of Commerce will send you information packets. The one to ask for is the *Branson Roads Scholar: Mastering the Back Roads of Branson*. It contains a map of alternative routes and traffic tips. Call (417) 334-4084 or visit bransonchamber.com.

The most exciting part of visiting Branson is how easy it is to get up close to the stars—the music legends who are playing golf (10 a.m. Wed at Pointe Royale Golf Course on Highway 165 often has seen stars like Mel Tillis and Moe Bandy teeing off together) or shopping at the grocery store. That constellation of stars is only the beginning. Other stars are scheduled to shoot through Branson for performances, too.

Don't leave town without having biscuits and gravy at **Billy Gail's Cafe** (5291 Hwy. 265; 417-338-8883). Blue gas pumps stand in front of this former gas station/log cabin. Inside, owners Billy and Gail Blong serve up really good food in a comfy-casual, 10-seat dining room with red-checkered tablecloths. The cafe is famous for its gi-normous 14-inch "hubcap pancakes," which overflow the plate and hang almost to the table. The pancakes are almost crepe-like, with a very light consistency, but you can load them up with blueberries, peanut butter, chocolate chips, pecans, or bacon. If you like to try new things, try the French Cake. It's a combination French toast and their regular pancake, dipped in egg batter and cooked on the griddle. It can also be covered with the healthy toppings of your choice. Another Billy Gail's has opened in the Branson Mill on Gretna Road. It is all the same, including the 14-inch pancakes.

Missouri Ridge Distillery (7000 Hwy. 248; 417-699-4095; missouriridge-distillery.com) is where M. Gregory Pope, master distiller and brewmaster at the distillery and brewery and his wife, Jolie, founded their distillery in 2015. It is truly a mom-and-pop, family-owned, small-batch, artisan distillery and is nestled in the beautiful Ozark Mountains. They are third-generation distillers. Guests can enjoy tasting throughout the day; tours are impromptu. You can watch the sunset and enjoy good barbecue on Fri and Sat with pulled pork and brisket at 11 a.m. and ribs after 4 p.m. (by reservation only). Get your **Missouri Spirits Expedition** stamp.

Slow down 2 miles outside town and turn west onto Highway V. There's something here you won't want to miss: ***The College of the Ozarks*** (100 Opportunity Ave.; 417-334-6411; cofo.edu) in ***Point Lookout.*** It's a college campus, all right, but wait. What's going on here? Everybody looks so . . . busy. This is a different kind of college—a fully accredited, four-year school where each full-time boarding student works at one of 65 campus jobs or industries to pay in part for their tuition. It calls itself "the campus that works." The rest is provided through scholarships. The campus fruitcake and jelly kitchen is open during business hours weekdays. Student workers bake some 20,000 fruitcakes a year and produce delicious apple butter and many flavors of jelly.

Students built the college itself—it's a pretty one—and run the Ralph Foster Museum and the Edwards Mill (a working replica of an old-time gristmill) as part of their tuition. If you're hungry while you're here, stop at the student-run ***Dobyns Restaurant*** on Point Lookout. It is more than just a restaurant. The dining hall seats 275 people in an elegant and relaxed rustic lodge design with handmade furnishings and magnificent landscaping—and all the cooking is done by the students. There is even a gourmet bakery with fresh pastries and desserts. A gift shop—with student-made stained glass, jellies, fruitcakes, pottery, and freshly milled grain products—is inside. What more could you want? Well, okay, there's a hotel facility as well. Prices for these luxury rooms (which have king- and queen-size beds and fireplaces with balconies overlooking the campus) are moderate and many of them sleep six, with two bedrooms and pull-out couches. The School of the Ozarks campus is beautiful, perched on its hill; don't miss the view from Point Lookout. Stand here at dusk when the bells of the carillon roll out over the mist-shrouded river below, if you want goose bumps up and down your arms. When the sun slides down the sky, that sound of bells on the crisp evening air is unforgettable. Williams Memorial Chapel is a fine place to stop for a moment; the tourist bustle slows to a halt here and there's room to breathe.

Say you want to get out of Branson for a while: find ***Copper Run Distillery*** (14720 Bus. 13, Walnut Shade; 417-587-3456; copperrundistillery.com).

It relocated here in April 2022. The distillery makes whiskey, rum, vodka, and moonshine. Yep, moonshine—something that has been made in these Ozark hills for generations. But now you don't have to be a bootlegger and worry about the Volstead Act, because these are "hand-crafted spirits" (to use their words, which sound better than "hooch" or "white lightning"), and this is the first legal distillery opened in the Ozarks since Prohibition in 1933. And to be honest, distilling whiskey and rum is much more complex than one would think. (Moonshine is just unaged whiskey, consumed before it is placed in barrels to mature.)

Owner Jim Blansit studied brewing and distilling for many years before returning home and embarking on this adventure at the family farm. He and his father built this bar out of old barrels and barn beams. There is an antique stove that belonged to his grandfather, and materials for the ceiling came out of a 105-year-old barn. He has been making small-batch spirits since 2009. There are free tours on the hour of the distillery, including a sample of the spirits. The

On a Very Personal Note

My husband and I had driven to the Branson area to see Willie Nelson and Wayne Newton. I pointed out a tattoo shop to him and told him I wanted to go back the next day to interview the owner for the book. He went off to play golf that day, and when he came home I proudly showed him a new tattoo of a butterfly on my, uh, hip.

He was not amused. In fact, he was not pleased at all. He began to get surly about it. Then he smiled and accused me of getting a "stick-on" tattoo. He led me into the bathroom to rub it with soap and water. It did not come off. I expected him to tell his golf buddies about it the next day, but he never mentioned it to anyone. He was truly embarrassed for me. Every night when I undressed, he glared at me. Now mind you, I had just turned 50 years old and we had been married nearly 25 years. To say he did not like surprises is putting it mildly. He is very conservative.

Of course, so am I. The waterproof tattoo was not done by a shop but purchased in the five-and-dime downtown. But I was having so much fun I decided to carry on with the fiction. Before the butterfly began to wear off, I used alcohol to remove it and applied a new one—on the other side this time—and waited for him to figure it out. He didn't. This went on for four weeks—first on the right, then on the left—the butterflies remained on my backside, and impossibly, he did not notice their change of address. But the good news was that on the fifth week when I replaced the butterfly with a dragon, he did notice.

It was probably the best practical joke I have ever managed. My husband believed me; my best friends and my mother believed me. Only my dad (who never saw it) never believed it. He said he simply knew me too well to believe I would have a butterfly permanently placed on my derriere. Now, the dragon maybe . . .

lounge area has great live music with local musicians. Get a **Missouri Spirits Expedition** stamp. Copper Run is open Mon through Sat 10 a.m. to 7 p.m. and Sun 11 a.m. to 7 p.m.

Big Cedar Lodge (612 Devil's Pool Rd.; 800-BCLODGE (225–6343); big-cedar.com) in *Ridgedale,* 9 miles south of Branson, is off the beaten path literally, but is very well known by people throughout the country. You can stay in the lodge itself or in private cabins, and there is a Jack Nicklaus–designed executive golf course called *Top of the Rock.* It is an Audubon Signature Course, the first in the state and only the sixth in the country. The distinction means the course meets Audubon's environmental guidelines on natural habitat and water life. Big Cedar also has a fine trout stream and waterfalls all over the place. Devil's Pool Restaurant offers a level of dining not found easily in the Ozarks—maple-glazed quail with white bean ragout, prime rib, and a champagne brunch on Sunday.

Top of the Rock Chapel is a three-story native limestone chapel with arched windows and a steeple and is right next door to the lodge. Built by Ozark artisan craftsmen, it features antique pine-wood doors, 23-foot vaulted ceilings, and floor-to-ceiling bay windows that offer a sweeping view of Table Rock Lake. This is a must-see any time of year. The chapel is at 150 Top of the Rock Rd. in *Hollister.*

January is spawning season at *Shepherd of the Hills Fish Hatchery* (483 Hatchery Rd.; 417-334-4865), 6 miles southwest of Branson on Highway 165 in the White River valley, just below Table Rock Dam. The Missouri Department of Conservation produces 1.2 million fish annually, 80 percent of which go into nearby Lake Taneycomo. There is a visitor center filled with exhibits and aquariums, and four trails ranging from 0.3 mile to about 1.5 miles. It's open year-round (except state holidays), seven days a week from 9 a.m. to 5 p.m., and until 6 p.m. Memorial Day to Labor Day. Visit on the last Saturday in February for "Vulture Venture" (noon to 6 p.m.) and see hundreds of vultures enjoying their winter roosting spots. There are fun activities for the kids, too. Visit mdc.mo.gov and type in "Shepherd of the Hills Fish Hatchery" for more information.

If you want luxury in the European style, the *Chateau on the Lake* (415 N. Hwy. 265, Branson; 855-251-3141; chateauonthelakebranson.com) is high-dollar elegant. This 10-story hotel sits on a hill right next to Table Rock Lake and has 302 rooms and suites. A standard room with a mountain view begins at $99 and goes higher if you want to see the lake. It has a world-class day spa, too. The murals that decorate the ballroom are of castles in Europe, and you can scuba dive, parasail, water-ski, fish, play tennis, or work out in a 24-hour fitness center. There's a Sweet Shoppe and a deli, and even a free movie theater. The Chateau Grille offers fine dining.

Long Creek Herb Farm (417-779-5450; longcreekherbs.com) is nestled deep in the woods on the Long Creek arm of Table Rock Lake. Jim Long calls it an "old-fashioned working herb farm in the heart of the Ozarks," and that describes it pretty well. Guests sip herb tea on the shady porch and listen to the tree frogs. On the 27-acre farm, skullcap, foxglove, and horehound are grown, and goats, chickens, guineas, geese, and steers are raised. Jim grows 400 cultivated and native herbs; many of them, such as sweet goldenrod and horsetail, are unique to the Ozarks. There is a meticulously groomed demonstration garden with winding paths and a bentwood gazebo.

After 20 years as a landscape architect, Jim decided that his love of plants needed a new outlet, and he wanted to share the experience of herbs with people. He also has a gift shop where you can buy about 80 products, including seasonings, teas, and herb blends both medicinal and culinary. You can buy a Dream Pillow to induce dreams that are relaxing, romantic, or action-packed, depending on the herb blend. The farm is open Wed in the summertime (May through Oct) and other days by appointment. You must call first. You will need directions or a map to find the place, because you must cross two state lines and three county lines to get there.

The *Golden Pioneer Museum* in *Golden* (417-271-3300; goldenpioneer-museum.org) can be found between Branson and Eureka Springs on Highway 86. The owner of this museum is Winfred Prier, and the curator is Murry Carmichael. The museum is home to Arlis Coger's collections from the Trail of Tears Museum, which used to be in Huntsville. The 5,200-square-foot museum contains clay pots (800, to be exact), weapons, tools, and clothing made by the Arkansas Osage Indians and found in the War Eagle (Arkansas) mounds. Here is the largest collection of Dalton points (more than 1,000), arrowheads knapped around 8000 BC by Native Americans living along the White River south of Huntsville. On display also is the world's largest collection of Tussinger points. The extensive mineral collection includes the world's largest quartz and crystal cluster—4,200 pounds—found in Hot Springs and displayed in its own glass case, as well as the world's largest turquoise carving, weighing in at 68 pounds. Other displays show rocks that look ordinary until ultraviolet light reveals the vibrant fluorescent color within them. There is also an incredible collection of baseball cards. The guns on display include one of only three or four derringers like the gun that killed President Abraham Lincoln. The museum also has one of the largest collections of carnival glass in the Midwest: more than 72 collections, and still growing. There is a gift shop, too. Call to arrange for a tour. Open Apr through Oct, Tues through Sat 10:30 a.m. to 4:30 p.m.

Dogwood Canyon Nature Park (2038 W. Hwy. 86; 417-779-5983; dogwoodcanyon.org), near *Lampe,* is the dream come true of Johnny Morris, founder of Springfield's Bass Pro Shop. This 10,000-acre property preserves an Ozark wonderland that Morris now shares with the public. Three creeks flow through the canyon—Dogwood Creek, Little Indian Creek, and Hobbs Creek—creating one of the best trout streams in the Midwest. Strategically placed weirs, or dams, and a series of short spillways form terraces in the stream and aerate the water. Each dam creates a pool for the trout. Wet-season, spring-fed water-falls from bluffs above the stream bank were made year-round attractions by the addition of pumps to recirculate water to add oxygen for the trout. Stone walkways and wrought-iron railings built by Bass Pro's staff blacksmiths guide visitors, and 6 miles of paved road pass the most interesting sights in the can-yon. There are 29 stream crossings on the property, and most fords are located at the base of a weir so that passengers in vehicles can view cascading water at eye level. Other crossings include stone bridges built by a local mason and a post-and-beam covered bridge built by Amish craftsmen.

The park is open to the general public year-round and for tram tours from mid-March to Christmas. Horseback trail rides are offered, and bicycle tours are also available. Try a half-day guided trophy fishing excursion on Dogwood Creek (ages 13 and older) or 2 hours of unguided fishing. Tour guides relate the history of the area during the 2-hour tram ride, pointing out caves where work-ers discovered ancient burials. One site high on a bluff contained the remains of a Native American who died more than 1,000 years ago—predating Mis-souri's Osage tribe. Remains (a child and two adults) at another site were dated to 6000 BC by scientists—making them the oldest human remains ever found in the state. The tour crosses into Arkansas and travels among herds of bison, longhorn cattle, and elk. The visitor center has Civil War and Native artifacts. Reservations are required for tram tours, trail rides, and fishing excursions.

Just a mile east of US 65 on Highway 14, the town of ***Ozark*** is a haven for antiques buffs. You will find a couple dozen shops—filled with a gazillion items—in the town of Ozark itself. This town, 15 miles south of Springfield and near enough to Branson to draw its crowds, is a mecca for folks who love old stuff. At ***The Garrison*** at Finley Farms (finleyfarmsmo.com/eat-drink/the-garrison/) in Ozark, you'll go below the Ozark Mill to enter the speakeasy-themed restaurant, a dark and unusual place. While you can dine outdoors, which boasts stunning views of the Finley River, you really must experience this restaurant first. All tables feature a flashlight, so you can easily read the menu. The appetizer menu offers choices like fresh lump crab cake or whipped goat cheese. The main menu isn't huge, but has a selection of yummy entrees, including mini pot roast, sea scallops, and Chilean sea bass. Try the Riverside fried chicken and the porterhouse for everyone at your table.

Best of all is the *Smallin Civil War Cave* at 3575 N. Smallin Rd. (417-551-4545 smallincave.com). You may have stopped at Fantastic Caverns in Springfield, but this is different. It was discovered in 1818 and has a breathtaking 10-story arch. The cave is filled with rich human history, unusual geology, and rare cave life. There are one-hour tours guided by people who really know their Civil War history, and it is open year-round, typically closing at 5 p.m. daily.

Places to Stay in Southwest Missouri

SPRINGFIELD

Holiday Inn
2720 N. Glenstone Ave.
(844) 208–0381
Inexpensive

Lamplighter Inn
2820 N. Glenstone Ave.
(888) 472–5813
Inexpensive

Lamplighter Inn & Suites
1772 S. Glenstone Ave.
(800) 749–7275
Inexpensive

Super 8 Motel
3022 N. Kentwood Ave.

(417) 833–9218
Inexpensive

WEST PLAINS

Holiday Inn Express
1301 Preacher Roe Blvd.
(855) 680–3239
Inexpensive

EMINENCE

Shady Lane Cabins and Motel
19105 Hwy. 19
(573) 226-3893
shadylanecabins.com
Inexpensive

CARTHAGE

Carthage Inn
2244 Grand Ave.
(417) 358-2499
carthageinn.com
Inexpensive

Boots Court Motel
107 S. Garrison Ave.
(Route 66)
(417) 310-2989
Inexpensive

JOPLIN

Holiday Inn
3615 S. Range Line Rd.
(417) 782-1000
Inexpensive

REEDS SPRING

Mountain Country Motor Inn
14930 Business 13
(417) 739-4155
mountaincountrymotorinn.us.com
Inexpensive

FINDING HELPFUL VISITOR INFORMATION

Branson
branson.com
(888) 903-2929 or (417) 334-2360

Kimberling City
kimberling-city.net
(800) 595-0393

Springfield
springfieldmo.org
(800) 678-8767 or (417) 881-5300

Van Buren
seevanburen.com
(573) 323-0800

BRANSON

(Most hotels in the Branson area have specials.)

Econo Lodge
230 S. Wildwood
(417) 336-4849
Inexpensive

Dockers Inn
3100 Green Mountain Dr.
(417) 332-0044
Inexpensive (breakfast included)

Places to Eat in Southwest Missouri

SPRINGFIELD

Nonna's Italian Cafe
306 South Ave.
(417) 831-1222
Inexpensive

WINONA

Flossie's Apple Barrel
Highway 19
(573) 325-8273
Inexpensive

WEST PLAINS

Colton Steak House & Grill
1421 Preacher Roe Blvd.
(417) 255-9090
Moderate

EMINENCE

Ruby's Family Restaurant
408 S. Main St.
(573) 226-3878
Inexpensive

OZARK

Lambert's II
1800 W. Hwy. J
(417) 581-7655
Inexpensive

Central Missouri

Welcome to America's Heartland, where the Mighty Mo marks the end of the glaciated plains, and hill country begins. Remnant prairies tucked between the hills remind us that once these seas of grass covered a third of the state. In this area, there are not one but three big lakes, and from Kansas City to the Lake of the Ozarks lie tiny towns built on gentle ridges, waiting to be discovered. Rough gravel roads wind through dogwood forests, along tentacled lakeshores and into towns that seem to have been protected from the rush like the wild morel hidden under a leaf. The big city here is Kansas City: the birthplace of jazz, the homeland of barbecue, and the Heart of America.

Lake of the Ozarks is not only a tourist area, it is a second home site for people from both Kansas City and St. Louis. The eastern shore, known as the St. Louis side, has million-dollar homes in the Land of the Four Seasons resort area. Six Mile Cove (the 6-mile marker means you are 6 miles from Bagnell Dam) is called Millionaires' Cove by boaters and has some of the most opulent homes in the Midwest. A houseboat business has sprung up on that side, and visitors can now cruise the lake and see both shores without the long drive around the lake. There is also a toll bridge that connects east to west at Osage Beach.

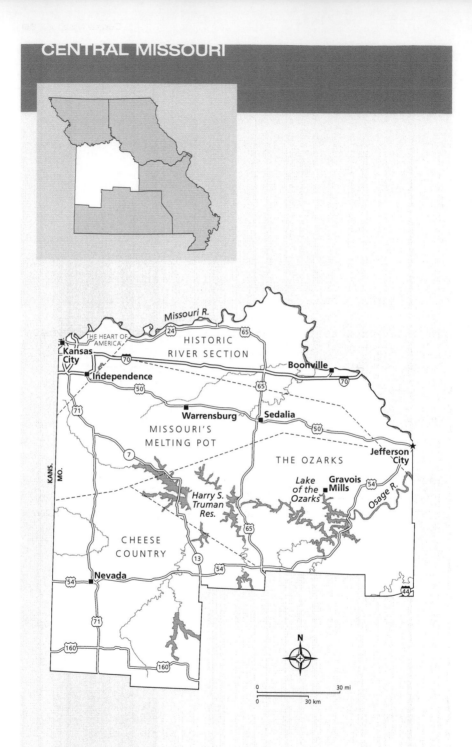

The Heart of America

Describing **Kansas City** as a city with "manure on its feet and wheat in its jeans" was a fair assessment at one time. Its two major industries were meat and wheat—all because a man named Joe McCoy convinced the local powers-that-were in 1871 that the newfangled "bobwire" (barbed wire) made it impossible to herd Texas cattle east. A central shipping point was needed, and the Kansas City stockyard was born. A fine steak house, the **Golden Ox Restaurant** (816-842-2866), is within sniffing distance (if you know the scent of a stockyard, you understand that reference, but the stockyard is no longer in existence so the odor is gone) at 1600 Genessee St. This old vintage steak house has been serving the best steaks in the world since just after World War II. It is the oldest steak house in a city famous for its beef. In fact, the KC Strip steak originated here in 1949. Now the **Stockyards Brewing Company** (816-895-8880) has joined it in the Livestock Exchange Building in the West Bottoms with three of its own beers on tap. The West Bottoms is within walking distance of Kemper Arena, where many sporting events are held. In the fall the American Royal, a longtime cattle and equine event, is held here.

trivia

The blonde bombshell Jean Harlow was born in Kansas City. She was the baddest of bad girls, the first sex symbol in Hollywood, and one of the biggest stars of the 1930s. She died at age 26.

Kansas City is known as the "Heart of America" not because of its location in the center of the country, but because of the people who call it home. Kansas City has a symphony, a lyric opera, the Missouri State Ballet Company, baseball's Royals, and football's Chiefs. Fountains and sculptures grace its wide avenues. Enclosed in the very heart of the city is **Swope Park** and its large zoo. It is the second-largest city park in the nation (after Central Park in New York City), with quiet, tree-shaded picnic areas and a modern zoo now upgraded to world-class. If you haven't been to KC lately, be sure to drive by the futuristic Bartle Hall sculptures at night, beautiful in a strange, space-age way.

The **Nelson-Atkins Museum** owns one of the finest collections of Asian art in the world and has a beautiful outdoor sculpture garden. The museum proves that "everything's up to date in Kansas City" with a new wing and underground parking, and the *Kansas City Star*'s new printing facility is a huge landmark in the downtown loop. The Kansas City studio of artist Thomas Hart Benton is now a state park.

Kansas City has more fountains than any city except Rome, and most of them are on the **Country Club Plaza.** Built in 1922 and modeled after Seville,

Spain, the Plaza's Mediterranean architecture and charming fountains give this suburban shopping center something no other has. Walk around the more than 100 designer shops, cafes, restaurants, and bars lining the wide streets. The Segway store offers guided tours during the day and at night, too. Brush Creek's wide meander through this charming area is broken by a fountain and stone pedestrian bridges right in the middle of the creek. Small boats carry visitors up and down the water. But the Plaza offers more than simply shopping—much more—especially during the winter holiday season after Thanksgiving night, when most of the fountains are turned off but the holiday lights are turned on. After dinner, there is a mass migration to see the famous Plaza lights twinkle on across the entire 15-block area, where each and every building is outlined in sparkling lights. The most popular building looks like Cinderella's enchanted pumpkin. Taking grandchildren through this wonderland has become a holiday tradition in many families. Bundle up and bring along a thermos of hot chocolate. The most romantic way to see this is in a horse-drawn carriage. Dreams are made here on snowy nights as the holiday season begins, with the flip of a switch, in Kansas City. The Country Club Plaza is not off the beaten path—it may be the most famous place in KC—but it is worth spending a day shopping and eating there.

The first question most visitors ask when they get off a plane at Kansas City International Airport is "Where's the best barbecue?" Whether you like it to the sweet side or a bit spicy, that's for you to judge: These places are all good and scattered about town. The oldest contenders are ***Arthur Bryant's Barbecue*** (1727 Brooklyn; 816-231-1123; arthurbryantsbbq.com) and ***Gates and Sons Bar-B-Q*** (1221 Brooklyn; 816-483-3880; gatesbbq.com). Both offer carryout, so you can do comparison tests with their different sauces until you are all "pigged out."

Gates's and Bryant's owe their fame, in part, to the fact that they used to be situated next to the old Kansas City Royals baseball stadium. Not only were they favorite places to eat before and after games, but the announcers would also be happily noshing barbecue and talking about it during the games. Then writer Calvin Trillin, a KC native and New York writer, declared KC the

TOP RECOMMENDATIONS IN CENTRAL MISSOURI

Dutch Bakery and Bulk Food Store	Stroud's Restaurant
Lyceum Repertory Theatre	

barbecue capital of the planet and made Bryant's even more famous. Trillin claims Bryant's is the best restaurant in the world! But no one comes here for the ambience unless you like bright lights and cafeteria-style service. The hunk of meat wrapped between two pieces of white bread is a leader in the best-barbecue-in-town contest. Gates's has the comfy high-back booths and a tangier sauce. The only way to make a decision here is to try both.

<h1>yardbirdatrest</h1>

Charlie "Yardbird" Parker's grave site is in Lincoln Cemetery, at 8604 Truman Rd. The road to the bedraggled cemetery is narrow and unmarked; there is an entrance from Blue Ridge Boulevard. But off the beaten path could be a bit risky here, so if it's really something you want to visit, be careful. Go at high noon and take a bunch of buddies.

But there are between 100 and 150 more barbecue restaurants in the Kansas City area, and most of the best are just joints tucked away somewhere, and "best" is defined by what kind of sauce you favor. ***Danny Edwards Blvd BBQ*** (2900 Southwest Blvd.; 816-283-0880; dannyedwardsblvdbbq.com), for example, has a sign in the window that reads "Eat It and Beat It," which tells you something about its size, popularity, and attitude. Open for lunch only Mon through Sat 11 a.m. to 3 p.m.

B.B.'s Lawnside Bar-B-Que (1205 E. 85th St.; 816-822-7427; bbslawnsidebbq.com) is a fun spot with wooden floors that slope and old blues posters on the walls. There is a definite Louisiana influence in the food there—great gumbo as well as some of the best barbecue in town. B.B.'s is as famous for the blues jam sessions as it is for the food. The owner has a slogan: "B.B.'s restaurant is where barbecue meets the blues." Thursday nights are the best jam sessions, with John Paul's Flying Circus playing live blues music. Wednesday through Sunday nights, local, regional, and national blues acts may be found. They play a two-hour set that may turn into a "jam" session with others joining in. The music is loud, the food fantastic, the crowd enthusiastic, and it is just more darn fun than you can stand. B.B.'s kitchen opens at 11 a.m. and closes at 10 p.m. on Tues, 9 p.m. Wed, 10:30 p.m. Thurs, 11 p.m. Fri and Sat, and 9 p.m. Sun (closed Mon).

Here and there, drowsing on old streets, pocketed in small shopping centers, crouching behind buildings, or even tucked inside buildings, you're likely to find places that definitely qualify as out of the mainstream. After barbecue, Kansas City is famous for jazz.

Eighteenth and Vine in Kansas City was really jumping from the 1920s to the 1950s. There were smoky joints filled with baseball players from the Kansas City Negro League team, the Monarchs, and jazz musicians signing autographs for fans and talking and laughing over drinks. There were restaurants and

TOP ANNUAL EVENTS IN CENTRAL MISSOURI

MARCH
St. Patrick's Day Parade
Lexington
(660) 259-4711

JULY
Fireworks on the Water
Osage Beach
Tan-Tar-A Resort / Four Seasons Resort
(800) 826-8272

AUGUST
Missouri State Fair
Sedalia
(660) 530-5600

Community Fair
Lexington
Old-time fiddlers and skillet-throwing
contest; third week in August

SEPTEMBER
Santa-CaliGon Days Festival
Independence
Celebrates the Santa Fe, California, and
Oregon Trails
(816) 252-4745

Annual Fall Festival of Color
Hot Air Balloon Race
Osage Beach
(573) 365-6663

OCTOBER

American Royal Barbecue
Kansas City
300 teams of BBQers, music, dancing,
and food
(816) 221-9800

Annual Olde Tyme Apple Festival
Versailles
(573) 378-4401

**Annual Lake of the Ozarks Dixieland
Jazz Festival**
Lake Ozarks
Country Club Hotel & Spa
(573) 392-1731

Apples, Arts & Antiques Festival
Lexington
Scarecrow contest with more than
40 unique scarecrows on the lampposts
downtown

NOVEMBER
Plaza Lighting Ceremony
Kansas City
(816) 274-8444

nightclubs there—the Mardi Gras, Blue Room, and Subway Club—and base-ball and jazz are forever linked in Kansas City. An untouched memory of that time can still be found at the *Mutual Musicians'* Foundation (1823 Highland Ave.; 816-471-5212; mutualmusicians.org) in the old Musicians' Union Hall—a hot-pink bungalow in the historic jazz district around 18th and Vine. It is, in fact, the only building inside the city limits that is on the National Register of Historic Places. Tours are available, but the place really jumps on Friday and Saturday nights when musicians from throughout Kansas City gather here to jam after their regular gigs around the city. The traditional jazz jam starts at midnight. There is no cover charge, but donations are always welcome to keep this place open.

trivia

Kansas City has more fountains than any city except Rome, and all of them are turned off in the winter except one, The **Northland Fountain** at the intersection of North Oak Street Trafficway and Vivion Road in Kansas City North becomes a gigantic ongoing ice sculpture, never the same, as the water cascades and melts throughout the winter. Surrounding the fountain are a walking path and park, but the enormous fountain is visible from both Vivion Road and North Oak Street Trafficway.

Now the area is coming alive again, and the link is still strong. At the **American Jazz Museum** (1616 E. 18th St.; 816–474-VINE (8463); americanjazzmuseum. org), visitors can listen to the music of such greats as Louis Armstrong, Julia Lee, Duke Ellington, Ella Fitzgerald, and Charlie "Yardbird" Parker. In fact, the museum is the final resting place of Yardbird's saxophone. The museum has an extensive exhibit honoring Ella Fitzgerald, "The First Lady of Song," with 30 of her most identifiable personal effects, including her famous rhinestone-covered cat-eye glasses and silver pumps.

This is one of the most interactive museums in the country. Music fills the air as the story of jazz is told through sight and sound. Visitors can listen to performances while a giant video wall projects early performances by some of these famous artists. The museum offers something for every level of jazz understanding. You can putter in a mixing station and create your own mix of sounds or enter the Wee-Bob children's activity center. Shop for a CD, T-shirt, or poster in the Swing Shop.

Museum hours are Tues through Sat 10 a.m. to 5 p.m. and Sun noon to 5 p.m. Admission to the museum is $10 for adults, $9 for seniors over 65, and $6 for children.

Kansas City's **Negro Leagues Baseball Museum** (816-221-1920 or 888–221-NLBM (6526); nlbm.com) is at 1616 E. 18th St., too, and it remembers the other half of the jazz and baseball love affair—the league that played in the 1920s and 1930s before the all-white major leagues would accept black players. Black players formed their own league, and some of the best athletes ever to play the game got their start there: Satchel Paige, Ernie Banks, Josh Gibson, "Cool Papa" Bell, and Buck O'Neill. Do these names sound familiar? How about Willie Mays, Hank Aaron, Roy Campanella, or the incredible Jackie Robinson? The Kansas City Monarchs were considered the Yankees of black baseball. The Negro National League drew more than 50,000 spectators from coast to coast. Then in 1947 a guy named Jackie Robinson stepped up to bat for the Brooklyn Dodgers and smashed the color barrier right over the fence. The rest is baseball history.

The museum is more than just a collection of pictures and memorabilia: It re-creates the look, sound, and feel of the game in the heyday of the league. Its centerpiece main gallery has a three-station interactive computer module with video games, historical vignettes, and coaching tips. The museum covers the history of black baseball from its beginning after the Civil War through the end of Negro Leagues play in the 1960s, and it features a custom-designed database to search for the play-by-play of league games. The gift shop features autographed baseballs, Louisville Slugger bats, T-shirts, caps, and jackets. Hours are Tues through Sat 9 a.m. to 6 p.m., Sun noon to 6 p.m. Admission is $10 for adults $9 for seniors and $6 for children.

Right across the street is the historic **Gem Theater Cultural and Performing Arts Center** (1615 E. 18th St.). As early as the 1920s, Kansas City's vibrant theatrical community was known around the world. This reconstructed theater still has the trademark neon marquee hanging outside and once again presents first-class entertainment. The latest in lighting, sound, and acoustical design have been added. The Alvin Ailey Dancers perform here along with renowned jazz groups and theater ensembles. Call the ticket office at (816) 474-8463 for a schedule filled with multimedia events.

At 1722 E. 17th Terrace is the **Black Archives of Mid-America**, where you can find documents, artifacts, paintings, and exhibits that explore the lives of African Americans in Kansas City, including musicians, artists, writers, and leaders in many other fields. The first-floor exhibit features the Tuskegee Airmen of World War II, and the second floor is dedicated to the buffalo soldiers of the Civil War. Hours are Mon through Fri 9 a.m. to 4:30 p.m. Visit blackarchives.org.

trivia

While you are downtown in Kansas City, look for the "cow on a stick." The huge bull used to be atop the American Hereford Association, but the organization has since moved. Now the giant bovine watches over the area from his perch on a pylon above Argus Health Systems. They decided to keep it so folks could find them easily. Another building downtown has a rocket ship on top of it. It used to crest the Trans World Airlines Training Center building back when TWA's home base was KC and it was one of the largest international airlines in the world.

Kansas City has a brand-new mode of transportation that is a great way to see the city without any of the hassle of parking and taxis. KC **Streetcar** is a sleek modern trolley that runs a 2-mile route from Union Station at Pershing and Main Streets in the Crown Center area to the 19th and Main Crossroads District, the 16th and Main Kauffman Center for the Performing Arts, 14th and Main's exciting Power and Light District, 12th and Main downtown KC, the 9th and Main City Library, 7th and Main's North Loop, 5th and Walnut for the fabulous City Market, and 4th and Delaware's River Market District. There are plenty of stops along the way with things to see and do and places to eat and drink. The streetcar runs just about all the time—every 10 minutes or so—and makes 16 stops so you can get off about every 2 blocks to explore. And it's *free*. This is so great. Let's see what we can see by streetcar. Go to kcstreetcar.org for route maps and the latest Ride & Dine list. Hours of operation are Mon through Thurs 6 a.m. to midnight, Fri till 1 a.m., Sat 7 a.m. to 1 a.m., and Sun 7 a.m. to midnight.

Hallmark Crown Center (2450 Grand Ave.; crowncenter.com) is a little city of its own with luxury residences and hotels and several levels of shopping. It even has an outdoor ice-skating rink. This is not off the beaten path, though; it is one of the city's most popular areas. Across the street—or over the skywalk if the weather is bad—is Union Station. You *can* buy the **Best of Kansas City** (816-303-7330; thebestofkc.com) at the shop of the same name at Crown Center. Everything from art to Zarda barbecue sauce is sold here. Order gift baskets at (800) 366-8780. Hours are Mon through Sat 10 a.m. to 9 p.m. and Sun till 5 p.m.

Afterward Tavern & Shelves is at 1834 Grand Blvd. (816-299-8360). Owners Christian Overgaard and Luke Pitz believe that books share beer, wine, spirits, and food's quality of bringing out the best in strangers, opening discussions, encouraging thinking, and making friends. A small but mighty collection of in-store books is available for purchase as well as the food and drinks to mellow disagreements and keep people talking. They call it "pedaling discovery, a tranquil escape from the chaotic." It is a unique place in downtown KC. Hours are Tues through Fri 4 p.m. to 11 p.m., Sat 4 p.m. to 1 a.m., and Sun noon to 1 a.m.

There is a little-known museum under a well-known tower standing sentry on a hill across from Crown Center. *The National World War I Museum at Liberty Memorial* (2 Memorial Dr.; 816-888-8100; theworldwar.org) is in a new complex and uses interactive technology to bring alive the history of this "war to end all wars." Then ride the elevator to the top of the tower for a breathtaking view of Kansas City. Open Tues through Sun 10 a.m. to 5 p.m.; the Over the Hill Cafe is open until 3 p.m.

Christopher Elbow Chocolates (1819 McGee St.; 816-842-1300; elbowchocolates.com) is where every piece of chocolate is a work of art. Christopher's signature Stiletto vodka chocolates compete with the strawberry balsamic caramel (from Modena), rosemary caramel (locally grown rosemary), caramel with fleur de sel (a soft ganache infused with French sea salt), or a personal fave, the Bourbon pecan (with dark chocolate making it very healthy). This famous chocolatier is open Mon through Fri 8 a.m. to 5 p.m.

One of the most interesting shops to visit is **Webster House** (1644 Wyandotte; 816-800-8820; websterhousekc.com), a circa 1885 schoolhouse restored and filled with European antiques, gifts, clothing, jewelry, and home goodies. It is a unique destination for lunch and right next door to the Kauffman Center for the Performing Arts. It has a spectacular view of the Liberty Memorial and downtown KC.

The **Crossroads Art District** began in the 1980s when a professor from the Kansas City Art Institute bought an old building in the warehouse district and turned it into lofts where young artists could afford to live. Their rent subsidized the gallery downstairs, where their work was displayed. Today that building is the **Leedy-Voulkos Art** Center (2012 Baltimore Ave.; 816-474-1919; leedy-voulkos.com), and many other galleries and lofts have made this a popular urban art community. This area is the up-and-coming art district of KC. It is situated between Crown Center and downtown, just behind Union Station. A 100-year-old railroad trestle bridge was moved from the river, through downtown KC, and placed at Union Station, and now is used as a walkway from the station to the nearby art district. The amazing move was filmed and shown on the History Channel. For a really fun evening, join the 6,000 other people who flock to First Fridays, the city's monthly art walk, from 7 to 9 p.m. Shops and galleries stay open late and the restaurants tease you with scents of wonderful food to nibble as you walk. You will find not just art and food, but retail shops, entertainment (comedy shows), and enough to keep you busy all day.

The Crossroads area is worth a trip for the different kinds of food. **Grinders Pizza** is at 417 E. 18th St. (816-472-5454; grinderspizza.com). It's in a large outdoor area where some really good live music happens. Inventive and authentic Mexican street food is at the **Mission Taco Joint,** next door at 409 E. 18th St.

KC is so eclectic. Next is **Affäre,** a German restaurant also in the Crossroads at 1911 Main St. (816-298-6182. affarekc.com). It boasts one of the more eclectic wine lists in the city, with rare and hard-to-find offerings from around the world, and of course an ample selection of German wines. The owners, executive chef Martin Heuser and Katrin Heuser, put a German twist to farm-fresh and seasonal dishes and handmade brats. There is an outdoor dining spot that is one of the more beautiful in Kansas City.

Another must-see but not exactly off-the-path is the **Kauffman Center for the Performing Arts** (1601 Broadway; 816-994-7200; kauffmancenter. org). Tours of the center are $5 per person and reservations are required (816-994-7222, ext. 3), but the best way to see it is to enjoy a performance in this remarkable theater.

KC Power and Light District downtown offers nightlife and more (800-767-7700; visitkc.com). People from Kansas City remember when downtown was the go-to place. There was jazz, there were parties, it was alive with rhythm and blues, and one of the places remembered fondly is still tucked away in the historic Hilton President Kansas City hotel, within walking distance of the Power and Light District.

If you want to sit a spell, the downtown library is a streetcar stop you can take advantage of. It is a beautiful piece of architecture. There's a little cafe and a children's area your kids will love. The parking next door looks like a giant bookshelf, so you can't miss this attraction while touring downtown.

If you are looking a bit disheveled and want a quick fix-up, stop by **Posh KC Blow Dry Bar** at 1211 Main St. (816-974-7674; poshkc.com), where they can give you a quick turnaround between work and play with a change of makeup (complete makeover $60) or hairstyle. Ask for the $30 quickie, no wash but perhaps a fast fishtail braid, up-do, or blowout. Men can have a $20 wash and style. And such fun, SuperDad! Take your little girl (under 12) in for The Princess: wash (optional), style, glitter spray, and lip gloss for just $35.

Oh, dear, just look at those nails. Quick, **Polished** at 1221 Main St. (polishedkc.com) can come to the rescue. This classy shop offers a quick pedi in a shiatsu massage chair for $30, and you get your legs rubbed down and wrapped in a hot steam towel. You will be ready to jump back on the streetcar and take off for more of the small side streets of KC. Call (816) 221-2888 for an appointment.

Downtown (way downtown near the Missouri River) is the **City Market,** where you can shop outdoors with a big wicker basket for just-picked produce in the wonderful atmosphere of a European marketplace. You can buy everything from morel mushrooms in early May to late-harvest turnips in October. There are always fresh eggs and fresh or even live chickens, and on Saturday mornings local farmers and buyers meet over the freshest produce this side of the garden. The area by the Missouri River has undergone restoration, complete with a riverboat museum.

The year was 1856 when the steamboat *Arabia* set out for the West, loaded with trade goods and passengers. As the folks at the **Steamboat Arabia Museum** (400 Grand; 816-471-1856; 1856.com) say, you'll find everything from axes, awls, and augers to zillions of other treasures restored to near-mint condition. How did they manage to amass all this in one place? Well, the *Arabia* hit a cottonwood snag in the Missouri River and sank like a stone. There it rested from 1856 to 1988, a time capsule waiting to spill its treasures, both everyday and exotic, into the present. But, of course, even the everyday from more than 150 years ago is exotic now. You'll find spurs, tinware, perfume (that retained its scent after its sojourn under 45 feet of mud and water), wine, whiskey, champagne (still bubbly), canned goods, hairpins, inkwells, and clothing.

The Hawley family excavated the boat and spent untold hours painstakingly restoring the artifacts they found. To our good fortune, rather than selling

Wearin' o' the Green—Italian Style

The North End is where I grew up. We lived with my grandmother, "Nana" Randazzo, until I was about 12 years old. I went to the Catholic school a couple of blocks from our home—Holy Rosary School—and rarely left the neighborhood. My grandma spoke Sicilian, my parents were bilingual, and I grew up knowing just enough Sicilian to stay out of trouble with my Nana. Everyone in the neighborhood was Italian. There was a pennycandy store on one corner, an Italian bakery on the other, and a park with a bocce court and a swimming pool a half block away. A good restaurant served the area, and we could open fire hydrants on hot summer days and play kick-the-can in the streets. Yelling "first light!" when the streetlights came on was a nightly contest. We even had lightning bugs. Why would anyone want to leave a neighborhood so wonderful? It was safe. It was home.

But one of my earliest childhood memories, in kindergarten or first grade, was of walking to school on March 17—a day that meant absolutely nothing to my family—and finding everyone else dressed in green. Now remember, this was an Italian neighborhood. There was not a drop of Irish blood anywhere for miles. Suddenly everyone was Irish, and I was the one who got pinched dozens of times—for not wearing green—before the bell rang to begin classes. I was terrified, and when the lunch bell rang, I took off for home with my lunch tucked under my arm like a football. (We wrapped our lunch in newspaper; sacks didn't exist for us.) When I arrived home unexpectedly, crying, my Nana couldn't understand what the problem was. I refused to go back to school until she found me something green to wear. When she saw that I was adamant, she began to rummage in the closets, muttering "*manacia l'America!*" under her breath. (That is phonetically spelled and is some sort of Sicilian-American *slanguage*. It means "blame it on America" and was used whenever American things got to be too much for her.) I returned to school wearing green but not understanding why. I noticed that nobody pinched Sister Mary Margaret. Although she was wearing black, she had a green shamrock pinned to her habit.

off the bounty, they opened a museum, and this treasure trove now tells casual visitors, schoolkids, scholars, living-history reenactors, and just plain history buffs volumes about what life was like on the frontier; civilization was built with the bits and pieces of trade goods carried by packets like the *Arabia*. A short film introduces you to the museum and to the excavation and restoration process. Admission is $14.50 for adults, $13.50 for seniors, $5.50 for children ages 4 to 14, and free for younger kids. Hours are Mon through Sat 10 a.m. to 5 p.m. and Sun noon to 5 p.m. (last tour begins at 3:30 p.m.). In winter, Jan through Mar, closing is at 4:30 p.m. and the last tour begins at 3 p.m.

Catty-corner from the City Market, across the street at 513 Walnut, is **Planters' Seed and Spice Co.** (816-842-3651; plantersseed.com). Step inside this old building and inhale the wonderful odors of fresh bulk herbs and spices, the scent of old wood, the aroma of exotic teas and coffees, and the clean smell of seeds. Need a watering can? They've got 'em. Want to buy a pound of dried bay leaves? Look no further. It's a delightful place. Hours are Mon through Fri 8 a.m. to 5:30 p.m., Sat. till 5 p.m.

Nowhere in KC will you find a more diverse dining experience than the City Market area—Italian, of course, as well as Chinese, Ethiopian, Mexican, French, American, and everything in between. If you love to cook, Asian, African, Italian, and Mediterranean markets are scattered all over the area along with shops for meat, coffee, and tea. Enjoy a night out at one of several hot spots for some late-night libations. There are more than 25 merchants, markets, grocers, and shops, so stroll the neighborhood to see what's going on.

Just down the street from the City Market is a French bistro—admittedly a most unlikely spot to find such a place—but it is as authentic as it can be, with an outdoor cafe in the alley just as they are in Paris. **Le Fou Frog** (400 E. 5th St.; 816-474-6060; lefoufrog.com) isn't really faux at all (it means "the crazy frog"), as owner and chef Mano Rafael will tell you. He is from Marseilles and made his reputation as head chef in some New York hot spots (Petrossian and Casanis). He met and married Barbara Bayer from Kansas City, and the rest is history.

The real test of a French bistro is the *soupe a l'oignon gratinée* with a bubbly top of Gruyère cheese. This one passes with gold stars. Of course, it is impossible to taste everything on the menu, but give it a good try. The *poulet aux olives et herbes de Provence* (whole baby chicken roasted in a fragrant sauce of olives and fresh herbs and served with garlic mashed potatoes) is a personal favorite. Seasonal menu changes daily. Entrees range from $29 to $62—and are worth every franc. Le Frog is open for dinner Tues through Sun 5 to 9 p.m. There is an excellent wine list with some very good and inexpensive wines available, just as there should be in a bistro.

Keep going east on 5th Street to Harrison, and on the corner is a restaurant that has changed hands a few times but has always been Italian, because this is a neighborhood simply known as "the North End." It is the Little Italy that many big cities have. Here Mass was said in Italian at nearby Holy Rosary Catholic Church in the old days. Now the neighborhood has blended into a more Vietnamese/Italian mix, but it still has the feel of the streets we played on as children—where opening a fire hydrant was the coolest thing that happened on a hot summer day—and that ambience is still there. **Garozzo's Ristorante** (526 Harrison; 816-221-2455; garozzos.com) has soft music by Frank Sinatra, a lively bar, and really, really huge servings of pasta. Do not, repeat, do not order spaghetti and meatballs unless you want to eat it for a week or can share it with several other people. The other dishes are more moderately proportioned but also excellent. If you like, no, love, garlic, order some olive oil to dip your Italian bread into and you will get a bowl of oil smothered in garlic and Parmesan cheese.

The neighborhood was entirely and completely Italian when I was growing up here. There was the Italian bakery on the corner with hot loaves of bread behind the counter every day, and the Italian candy store where we bought penny candy (remember penny candy?). Holy Rosary Church and school dominated the corner at 911 Missouri Ave., and the nuns who taught there dominated the local Italian children. Mass was in Italian at 8 o'clock on Sunday morning, and the only restaurant in the neighborhood was Italian. Period. Then things changed when thousands of Vietnamese refugees fled their country after the war ended and were placed in American cities. The North End of Kansas City became home to many of them because it had a good Catholic school, and most of those fleeing their homelands were Catholics. So the area changed, and now Kansas City locals would agree that the **Vietnam Cafe** (522 Campbell St.; 816-472-4888; vietnamcafe.us) is one of the best Asian restaurants in town. Located in a quaint corner of a building just up the street from Garozzo's, the Vietnam Cafe is known for its amazing pho noodle soup, but also try the spring rolls with peanut sauce. There are lines of customers on the street at lunchtime. Great food, friendly service—you will love it. Hours are Mon through Sat (but closed on Wed) 9 a.m. to 8 p.m. and Sun till 6 p.m.

St. Mary's Episcopal Church (1307 Holmes; 816-842-0975) is a grand old church in downtown Kansas City. The redbrick church has been there forever (since 1888), and as with many old churches, it has some interesting history and a good ghost story. Amazingly, the building was spared when the neighborhood around it was razed during urban renewal in the 1960s. It is a

The Ghost of St. Mary's

The **ghost of St. Mary's** is believed to be that of Father Henry Jardine, who was rector of St. Mary's in 1879. A crypt was built under the altar for Father Jardine's body before his death. Because he suffered from a painful facial nerve disorder, he took laudanum (tincture of opium) and used chloroform to help him sleep. One night he died from the combination. The bishop declared it a suicide, and therefore Father Jardine's body was buried in unconsecrated ground rather than in his beloved church. There have been several ghostly incidents. When one acolyte arrived at the church, he saw a priest, in vestments, who stood facing the altar. He hurried to the sacristy thinking he must be late, only to find the rector waiting for him there. When they went back to the sanctuary, no one was there. Several people have sensed a presence in the gallery where his restless ghost hovers. A former rector at St Mary's attempted to have Father Jardine's remains moved from the cemetery to the church's columbarium, perhaps allowing his spirit to rest in peace at last.

wonderful Sunday morning experience to follow the sound of the carillon and to hear the organist make the huge pipe organ sing for the Solemn High Mass celebrated at 10 a.m., complete with incense and bells. The congregation is an interesting and varied collection of people from the urban area as well as suburban people who make the drive into the city every Sunday. Call for the times of other services.

Along Southwest Boulevard the scent of chili peppers fills the air. This is Kansas City's Hispanic neighborhood, and the restaurants here are very popular, especially at lunchtime.

There is always some discussion about which, exactly, is the best Mexican restaurant in the Southwest Boulevard area. It just depends on whom you ask. One favorite of people who work downtown and eat there often is *Manny's* (207 Southwest Blvd.; 816-474-7696; mannyskc.com). The Lopez family has been here for years and years—about 30, actually. They bottle their salsa to take home because there is such a demand for it. If you have never tasted real Mexican pork chili, it should go to the top of the list. Manny's is open for lunch and dinner Tues through Sat 11 a.m. to 10 p.m. and makes a mean margarita.

Another favorite is *Ponak's Mexican Kitchen* (2856 Southwest Blvd.; 816-753-0775; ponaksmexicankitchen.com). This place has great margaritas on tap and a covered outdoor dining patio. There is a special every night, and a personal favorite is the spinach enchilada on Wednesday—no, wait, maybe it's the Mexican pork tips stew cooked slow in a tomato-jalapeño-garlic sauce on Thursday. Maybe everything at Ponak's is good. You decide. Open Sun through Thurs 11 a.m. to 9 p.m. and Fri and Sat till 10 p.m.

Union Station in KC, built in 1914 in grand Beaux-Arts style—with vaulted ceilings and giant chandeliers—is historic not just for its architecture but also for June 17, 1933, when four unarmed FBI agents were gunned down by gang members attempting to free captured fugitive Frank Nash. The "Kansas City Massacre" resulted in the arming of all FBI agents. You can still see chips in the marble from the bullets.

Although not off the beaten path by any means, there's something old and something new in Kansas City at 30 W. Pershing Rd. It has been restored to its glorious original beauty and is now an urban plaza and entertainment center. There are several restaurants, evening entertainment at *City Nights* with live performance theater, motion pictures, and laser and magic shows as well as music and theater performances. There are also shopping areas and, best of all, especially for the kids, Science City, featuring more than 50 hands-on environments for all ages to explore.

Science City is a city-within-a-city on multiple levels with streets and alleyways. Each exhibit is a realistic environment that offers interactive experiences with costumed citizens who live and work in the "city's" Festival Plaza, Uptown, Downtown, Southside, and Old Town. You can even explore an excavation dig site in prehistoric Kansas City or assist a surgical team in the operating room. Want a chance to be on TV? You can broadcast news from the television station. You can bake a cake in the test kitchen, try your hand at being an astronaut in the space center, or board a real locomotive located just outside the station. Science City is open daily. Call (816) 460-2020 or visit unionstation.org com for times. Do not miss the ***Arvin Gottlieb Planetarium***. It is the best thing ever.

The ***Freight House,*** across the tracks from historic Union Station at 101 W. 22nd St. in the Crossroads Art District, is worth looking for. It has several really good restaurants tucked inside and is connected via a pedestrian bridge to Union Station.

Fiorell's Jack Stack Barbeque is the first stop. The menu is extensive, and fresh seafood is flown in every day. Although the barbecue is what many come here for, the signature dish is a "crown prime rib" that is obscenely good. The Hickory Pit Beans are as good as they get. It's usually pretty packed but booths are big and comfortable. Hours are Mon through Thurs 11 a.m. to 9 p.m., Fri and Sat till 10 p.m., and Sun till 8:30 p.m.

Lidia's (816-221-3722; lidias-kc.com) is also in the Freight House. Lidia Bastianich is a renowned chef with other restaurants. Fine Italian food, a beautiful setting, what's not to love? This isn't just the usual spaghetti and meatballs kinda place. There's a good wine list, of course. Try the osso buco, a pork shank slow-braised in red wine with garlic mashed potatoes, and you will come back again and again. Hours are Mon through Thurs 11 a.m. to 2 p.m. for lunch and 5 to 9:30 p.m. for dinner. Fri and Sat dinner hours are 5 to 10 p.m. and Sun 4 to 8 p.m.

Grünauer, still at 101 W. 22nd St. (816-283-3234), is where Austrian cuisine is offered in Kansas City. Brother and sister Nicholas and Elisabeth Grünauer opened in the historic Freight House. The restaurant is named for the restaurant of the same name the family owns in Vienna's artsy Neubau neighborhood. They bring the same Austrian cooking, hospitality, and atmosphere to Kansas City's art and dining area. Open Mon and Tues 4 to 9 p.m., Wed and Thurs 11:30 a.m. to 9 p.m., Fri 11:30 a.m. to 10 p.m., Sat 11 a.m. to 10 p.m., and Sun 11 a.m. to 8 p.m.

The buildings at the ***Kansas City Museum*** (3218 Gladstone Blvd.; 816-702-7700; kansascitymuseum.org) are in the process of renovation. Corinthian Hall (originally the carriage house) has been restored and is open to the public. Visitors are welcome daily. The museum visitor center can provide an introduction to the Long family, who owned the home, and the history of Kansas City. History-themed films, such as the pre–Civil War epic *Bad Blood,* are shown frequently in the StoryTarium. A new exhibition, *The Long Family and Corinthian Hall,* has opened on colorful informational panels around the perimeter of the estate.

The 39th Street area of Kansas City is a wonderful old area in which to stroll. There are antiques shops, crystal shops, and just a lot of interesting places. At 1800 W. 39th St. is **Prospero's Books & Media,** a three-story bookstore for the book nerd in you. Plan for plenty of time to rummage, and if you are a local, there are book readings and discussions as well as live music at different times. It is open Mon through Sat 10:30 a.m. to 10 p.m. and Sun 11 a.m. to 7 p.m.

The area is also home to some of the city's best restaurants. Now, before we get all fancy-schmancy with the new bistros, let's talk about—what else?—barbecue.

Q39 (1000 W. 39th St.; 816-255-3753; q39kc.com) is a new contender to the barbecue scene in KC and has the lunch crowds "queuing up for their 'cue," including slow-smoked barbecue with sweet, tangy pepper sauce, wood-fired grilled steaks, and sides like apple slaw. If you are looking for something more brunch-like, try the Oink & Cluck, made with house-made chipotle sausage, cheddar cheese, and an egg over easy topped with the barbecue sauce. That will start your day right. Hours are Sun through Thurs 11 a.m. to 9 p.m. and Fri and Sat till 10 p.m.

About a half-mile away is another, but different barbecue, the **Genghis Khan Mongolian Barbecue** (3906 Bell St.; 816-753-3600; gkbbq.com), an eat all you can meat, seafood, and vegetable grill that is well worth its modest prices. Don't be misled by the name. It is not a barbecue in the KC sense of smoked ribs. This is fresh raw meat cooked before your eyes on a huge griddle-type cooking area. You choose your shrimp, calamari, meat, veggies, whatever, and they throw it on the grill and stir-fry it while you watch. Hours are Tues through Fri 11 a.m. to 9 p.m. and Sat noon to 9 p.m.

There is more good jazz and blues in Kansas City than anywhere in the country. Pick up a copy of *Jam (Jazz Ambassador Magazine),* with listings of all the jazz clubs in town and who is playing where. Watch for Karin Allison, a very talented jazz singer who calls KC home. Then you can search out nightlife at such places as the **Levee** (16 W. 43rd St.; 816-561-5565; thelevee. net), with wonderfully loud rock 'n' roll to dance to on Saturday afternoons until 8 p.m.

In case you are cruisin' on your Harley (or even if you're not) and want to experience an upscale "biker-bar atmosphere," check out Frank Hick's **F.O.G. Cycles & Knucklehead's Saloon** (816-483-1456; knuckleheadskc. com). It's a honky-tonk blues bar next to F.O.G. bike shop at 2715 Rochester in the East Bottoms just off I-435 and Front Street. Live bands play that cool Kansas City blues music. It's an entertainment venue smack dab between two railroad tracks, in an old neighborhood surrounded by industrial buildings. (If you get caught waiting for a train to pass, you can always enjoy the tagging on many of the cars . . . I like to think of it as a traveling art gallery.) Wear your leathers if you want to fit right in. Knucklehead's is open Wed and Thurs 7 to 11 p.m., Fri 7 p.m. to midnight, Sat noon to 5 p.m. and 7 p.m. to midnight, and Sun noon to 6 p.m. It is an over-21 club, so minors must be with their parents. The saloon took some top honors for blues clubs and is the premier club for that venue in KC. It has been awarded Best of KC by *Pitch,* a Kansas City newspaper, and won the "Keepin' the Blues Alive" award. Want more encouragement to visit? *Kansas City Magazine's* 2022 Reader's Choice #1 Best Bar with Live Music, #1 Best Rock Music Club, #1 Best Country Music Venue, and #1 Best Jam. Still not sure? What more can you ask for? Check out the mural of past performers outside on the Garage.

At Knucklehead's, you can have the usual hamburgers, tacos, or sausage, of course, but you gotta try the Knuckle Sandwich. Don't ask what's in it, just order it. (Okay, if you must know, it's fried bologna.)

J. Rieger & Co. (2700 Guionotte; 816-702-7800; jriegerco.com) is more than just a distillery. It's in an elegant brick former industrial building in the old Electric Park Neighborhood. It's a great place to tour and enjoy whiskey tastings or a full meal with pairings, along with a surprising variety of other offerings. The Monogram Lounge overlooks the distillery and offers small plates, cocktails, and Heim beer on draft. The Electric Park is a seasonal outdoor patio named after the amusement park that was there from 1899 to 1908. It features swing-set tables and boozy snow cones, frozen cocktails, and good food. The tasting room is open seven days a week and the Tasting Room Atrium with covered open-air seating is open year-round. The history here is interesting because in 2021 this distillery released the first Bottled in Bond Straight Rye Whiskey bottled in KC since Prohibition. Now they have partnered with the KC Chiefs for the official 2022 World Champion Premium Wheat Vodka (*Go Chiefs!*). A must-have souvenir of KC. Be sure to get your **Missouri Spirits Expedition** log stamped before the evening ends.

At the corner of the block at 1700 Summit, the ***Bluebird Bistro*** (816-221-7559; bluebirdbistro.com) serves lunch daily—great homemade soups and interesting sandwiches on crunchy sunflower-seed bread. This corner cafe is much larger than it looks from the outside, but it fills up quickly at lunchtime. The tin ceilings and antique cabinets make the high-ceilinged rooms cozy. A long bar along one wall is a fine spot to wait for a table. Hours are Mon through Sat 7 a.m. to 9 p.m. and Sun 9 a.m. to 1 p.m.

Historic Westport, some 40 blocks south of downtown, was the whole city at one time. Some of us think it still is. The **Broadway Cafe** (301 Westport Rd; 816-531-2431) and the **Broadway Roasting Co.** (4012 Washington St.; 816-931-9955; broadwayroasting.com) are just two neighborhood coffeehouses in Westport. There is a blackboard where colorful chalk lists the day's beverages and baked-today scones, biscotti, and cakes (its famous apple cake, for example). Sara Honan and Jon Cates invite you to taste samples of that day's baked goods and have a cup of one of the more than 20 types of coffee they roast every day (Ethiopian Harrar, for example). The coffee is roasted at the roastery on Westport Road, but "when the wind's right" you can still smell the coffee roasting at the other address, too. Why two cafes so close together? They like the Westport area. And so will you. The cafe is open daily 7 a.m. to 8 p.m. and the Roasting Co. is open Mon through Fri 8 a.m. to 3 p.m.

hasanyoneseen dan'snephew?

Kelly's in historic Westport (500 Westport Rd.; 816-561-0635; kellyswestportinn.com) is a good place to sip a brew. This has been a very popular Kansas City nightspot for more than 30 years. In fact, Daniel Boone's nephew used to hang out here. Well, he once ran a trading post in the building, which is the oldest in Kansas City. He hasn't come in lately. The hard-core regulars are called "squirrels" and have a designated table for Thursdays.

Looking for a way to express your individual style, and sick of the same old/same old available in most clothing stores? Don't wait, get yourself to **Wonderland** at 307–309 Westport Rd. (816-674-9645). It truly is a wonderland of glorious, quirky vintage clothing, curated by brilliant fashion maven Andy Chambers. It has recently expanded to nearly double its original size, and you're sure to find something perfect there—if you don't, you're either not trying or it doesn't exist. This isn't a Goodwill wannabe thrift store, but a great place to find the highest-quality vintage clothing for men and women. The window displays alone are worth the trip to Kansas City's original arts area.

Visit the **Classic Cup Cafe** at 301 W. 47th St. (816-753-1840; theclassiccupcafe. com). The all-time favorite entree here is the raspberry Dijon mustard sauce on grilled pork tenderloin (sometimes it's blueberry, blackberry, or tart cherry Dijon sauce). Hours are Mon through Fri 7 a.m. to 2 p.m. and Sat and Sun 9 a.m. to 3 p.m.

In the Brookside neighborhood, you can get really small. If you love tiny things (or if you haven't quite grown up), don't miss Kansas City's **Toy and Miniature Museum** (5235 Oak St.; 816-235-8000; toyandminiaturemuseum. org). Childhood friends Mary Harris Francis and Barbara Marshall started the museum in a Mediterranean-style mansion built in 1906. It has been expanded to 21,500 square feet. The mansion and the surrounding property are owned by the University of Missouri–Kansas City, but the toys and miniatures belong to a private nonprofit foundation. Miniatures are not toys; scale is important in a miniature—everything in a miniature room must look exactly like a full-size room. Toys are a separate collection.

Tucked upstairs is a Victorian nursery with a brass cradle made in Paris in 1850. It had been in Mary's family for several generations. Barbara's father, Hallmark Cards founder Joyce C. Hall, had a dollhouse built for his daughter at a local high school. When it was time to pick it up for Christmas, it was too big to take out of the school, so she did not get her dollhouse. Now it's part of a museum recognized as one of the largest museums of miniatures in the world. There are more than 85 antique furnished dollhouses at least 100 years old, scale-model miniature rooms, and toys. The museum is open Mon through Wed 10 a.m. to 4 p.m. Admission is $10 for adults.

The Crestwood Shops around 55th and Oak Streets lure antiquers. **Charlecote** (337 E. 55th St.; 816-444-4622; charlecoteantiques.com) specializes in 18th-century English furniture from Queen Anne to George Hepplewhite, when craftsmanship was at its height. **Pear Tree** (303 E. 55th St.; 816-333-2100; peartreedesignantiques.com) is open Mon through Sat 10 a.m. to 5 p.m. and is full of really cool stuff—really nice, albeit not inexpensive, antiques from the world over, plus accessories, lighting, mirrors, and decorative arts for both home and garden. If you want it, it's probably here and fun to search for, too. Look at the website to see some examples of what you will find.

If you have children along, you might want to swing by **Brookside Toy & Science** (330 W. 63rd St.; 816-523-4501; brooksidetoyandscience.com), where a fine display of bugs under glass and an array of toys not to be believed will keep the kids busy for a while.

For the grown-ups, a well-named place called **Stuff** (316 W. 63rd St.; 816-361-8222; astorenamedstuff.com) is packed with the same: stuff such as antiques, collectibles, fine art, and gifts. No, it's more than that—it is a shopping experience designed for shoppers looking for stuff. Real shoppers who like stuff. The "lookie here!" shoppers who always find things they weren't looking for and stock them away as "gifts." The "where in the world did you find that" kinda gifts. You know who you are. Do not miss this place.

Cross one of the many bridges spanning the Missouri River and head into the northland area. This is still greater KC. We will explore North Kansas City and other towns north of the river later. **Stroud's Restaurant** is located north of the Missouri River, just off I-35 and Brighton (5410 NE Oak Ridge Rd.; 816-454-9600; stroudsnorth.com). The motto stated on the waiter's T-shirts is

"We choke our own chickens." Be prepared for a wait, but it is worth it. This picturesque farmstead is a walk back in time. You can stroll the garden, take a walk down to the lake to see the swans, or have a seat in an old buggy and contemplate the big family-style chicken dinner you are about to enjoy. Meals come complete with green beans, mashed potatoes and gravy, and homemade cinnamon rolls that melt in your mouth. There are plenty of things on the menu, but the fried chicken is what keeps people coming back for more. Open Mon through Thurs 4 to 9 p.m., Fri 11 a.m. to 9 p.m., Sat 2 to 9 p.m., and Sun 11 a.m. to 9 p.m.

As long as you are north of the Missouri River, take I-35 north to I-29 North to the Barry Road exit. Go left (west) and take a right into *Zona Rosa* (8640 N. Dixon for the GPS), a neighborhood of shops, restaurants, and condos. There are plenty of well-known names along with some homegrown ones. Go to the Zona Rosa website to see what else is in store for you: zonarosa.com. Hint: There is a winter wonderland with an ice rink for skating.

Want to have a real Kansas City steak? This is a personal favorite for steak, I promise you, a steak you will remember. The *Hereford House* (8661 N. Stoddard Ave.; 816-584-9000; herefordhouse.com) has been a local tradition for more than 50 years. Probably the first restaurant KC natives remember (from prom night, say) and still one of the best places to have a KC steak cooked just right. It used to be downtown but has moved to the 'burbs, with a location in Zona Rosa, but the quality has not changed a bit. Whether you like it "black and blue" or "done all through," you will get the perfect steak here. Hours are Mon through Thurs 11 a.m. to 9 p.m., Fri till 10 p.m., Sat 3 to 10 p.m., and Sun 3 to 8 p.m. In fact, Zona Rosa is a pleasant way to spend an evening strolling after eating a steak.

strangeas itseems

Want to see the mantel that Jackie Kennedy started a feud over? When Harry Truman moved this mantel to the Truman Library in Independence, the former first lady had a fit and wanted it returned to the White House.

The city of *Independence,* just east of downtown Kansas City on I-70, could be a day trip in itself: There's Harry S Truman's home, now a national park, and the *Truman Presidential Library* at 500 W. Hwy. 24 (816-268-82005; trumanlibrary.gov). The library is open Mon through Sat 9 a.m. to 5 p.m. and Sun noon to 5 p.m. (closed Thanksgiving, Christmas, and New Year's Day). There's a special program night on Thursday, when the museum is open until 9 p.m. Admission is $8 for adults, $7 for seniors, $3 for children ages 6 to 18, and free for children younger than age 6. Self-guided tours.

In Independence you'll also find the world center for the Reorganized Church of Latter-day Saints and the RLDS Auditorium. There are also Civil War battlefields, as well as the beginnings of the Santa Fe Trail, still visible in the worn earth. (Sometimes it seems as if half the towns on this side of the state claim the trail, but in Independence they still celebrate the Santa-Cali-Gon, where the Santa Fe, California, and Oregon Trails jumped off into the wilderness.) The **National Frontier Trails Center** is a fine place to learn more about the hardships and adventures of those who dared to leave civilization behind and strike out across the wilderness to a new life. It's in the historic Waggoner-Gates Milling Company building. Call (816) 325-7575 or (800) 810-3900, or go to visitindependence.com for further information about the city.

Stop in at **Vivilore** at 10815 E. Winner Rd. in the Englewood Art District (816-836-2222; vivilore.com). Owners Cindy Foster and her brother, master chef Whit Ross, invite you to the ivy-covered brick building and the restaurant serving lunch and dinner, and to peruse the art gallery, antiques, and home decor from estate sales and European travel. Find the magical garden where you can eat (weather-permitting) and wander, or have something to drink while you enjoy the art gallery and antiques shop before your meal. Vivilore is described as upscale and sophisticated, which is true because it has a fine wine list. It could also be called quietly romantic. Open Wed through Sat 11 a.m. to 8 p.m.

There are antiques stores, bed-and-breakfasts, and dandy places to eat in Independence—in short, there's entirely too much to include in a single volume. We've narrowed it down to these few, which are off the beaten path by virtue of location, arcane historical significance, or ambience. Of course, the best tenderloin in town is at the **Courthouse Exchange** (113 W. Lexington; 816-252-0344; courthouseexchange.com). The portion is huge. The pie list will make you weep. Along with the ordinary kinds of pies hide pies from your youth: sweet potato, pecan, old-fashioned raisin, gooseberry, Dutch triple berry, and the list goes on—27 kinds of pie at last count—and you can order a whole pie to go. Sweet. Hours are Mon through Thurs 11 a.m. to 9 p.m. and Fri and Sat till 10 p.m.

Don't miss **Clinton's** (816-833-2046; clintonssodafountain.com), on Independence Square at 100 W. Maple Ave. When he was on the campaign train in Independence, President Bill Clinton visited here; the owners have photos and a thank-you letter to prove it! (He's wearing a Clinton's sweatshirt.) Just how long has it been since you've had a real chocolate soda or cherry phosphate? While you're there, ask them to make a chocolate-cherry cola; it's like a liquid, chocolate-covered cherry with a twist. This is a real old-time soda fountain, complete with uniformed soda jerks and a marble counter with a mirrored back; the malts still whir in those tall, frosty metal containers as they did when we were kids. Clinton's is open Tues through Sat noon to 5 p.m.

And if all this hedonistic revelry doesn't get you, maybe the historical angle will: Truman's very first job was at Clinton's. You don't have to be a soda jerk first to be president, but maybe it helps. Harry was one of our most popular commanders in chief. Here at Clinton's you can buy a bottle of Polly's Pop, once again in production at *Polly's Soda Pop Factory* at 306 W. Maple (816-859-5666; pollyssodapop.com). The factory is the love child of Ken and Cindy McClain, who started it up again after it had been closed since 1967. The original bottling plant opened in 1923, and the local soda was—and is again—sold in most of the eateries on the square. Good old-fashioned favorites like cream soda, root beer, and, of course, orange join grape, pineapple, and strawberry for the six original flavors made with pure, natural cane sugar. The glass bottles move along the original 66-year-old bottling machine just like in the old days. The plan is to have a glass wall so that folks can come in and watch the bottling live and in color.

Visitors to the historic Independence Square can now experience the excitement and charm of Scandinavia. Just a few steps from the Harry S Truman Home ticket office, *Scandinavia Place* (209 N. Main; 816-461-6633) in downtown Independence features a smorgasbord of traditional Scandinavian gifts complemented by a splash of the unique and the unexpected. In addition to the wide selection of items from Denmark, Sweden, Norway, Finland, and Iceland, a shopper can also find an assortment of gifts from other European countries, especially packaged gourmet foods. Gift wrapping and shipping are available. Come and browse the many fine foods and gifts and visit with Nina, the Icelandic owner. Hours are Mon through Sat 10 a.m. to 6 p.m. and Sun noon to 4 p.m.

Ophelia's Restaurant and Inn (201 N. Main; 844-208-9439) is in the heart of Independence near the Truman National Historic Site, Kauffman Stadium, and Arrowhead Stadium (*Go Chiefs!*). Very convenient. The rooms are comfy, and the food is good.

Scandinavian, German, sophisticated, and a diner: What kind of food hasn't been mentioned for a couple of pages? Oh yes, barbecue. Independence is a part of the Greater Kansas City area so it has *A Little BBQ Joint,* too, and that's the name you see out front at 1101 W. Hwy. 24 (816-252-2275; alittlebarbqjoint.com). It's fun. The decor is all old auto—booths are backseats of Chryslers, Caddies, and Chevys (might make you want to do a little canoodling), and old car parts hang on the walls. An outside deck has live music when the weather is good. Just to remind yourself that you are not in KC, order the Harry S—a grilled hot dog with pulled pork and pepper jack cheese. Hours are Tues through Thurs 11 a.m. to 7 p.m., Fri till 8 p.m., Sat noon to 8 p.m., and Sun noon to 7 p.m.

You think celebrity prisoners in our jails are pampered now. When Frank James, Jesse's brother, was held at the jail in Independence, his cell sported an Oriental carpet; he had guests in for dinner and served them fine wines. For that matter, so did William Quantrill when he was incarcerated here. Remember, Missouri had a star on the Confederate flag and one on the Union flag as well.

Although the dank cells with their monolithic stone walls were decorated when company called, they were still jail. More than 145 years after the fact, the cells are still dark, forbidding holes that look impossible to escape. The 1869 jail and ***Marshal's Home and Museum*** (816-252-1892) are at 217 N. Main in Independence. The two-story, brick, Federal-style Marshal's Home continues to front North Main. What you don't see (until you surrender a small admittance) is the Jackson County Jail, huge limestone jail cells that are situated at the back of the Marshal's Home. The home and the lockdown were both constructed beginning in 1859. As the 12 new limestone jail cells were opened, hostilities between free-state and proslavery forces were reaching a boiling point in this area. By 1854 Congress had passed the Kansas-Nebraska Act, which opened the Kansas Territory to settlement. The result of this act was violent guerrilla fighting that terrorized local populations on both sides of the Missouri-Kansas line as abolitionists poured into the Kansas Territory. The state of Missouri was held in the Union by martial law even though the elected governor and legislators had voted to secede from the Union, so the history is very interesting here. The museum is open Apr through Oct, Mon through Sat 10 a.m. to 5 p.m. and Sun 1 to 4 p.m.; Nov, Dec, and Mar, Tues through Sat 10 a.m. to 4 p.m. and Sun 1 to 4 p.m.; closed Jan and Feb. Admission is $6 for adults, $3 for ages 6 to 17, and free for children age 5 and younger.

Perhaps you remember the 19th-century painting of two trappers in a long wooden canoe. A big black animal—perhaps a bear—sits in the bow gazing enigmatically at the viewer. Or maybe *The Jolly Flatboatmen* is more your style, with the rivermen dancing at the dock, playing instruments, and generally raising a ruckus. Artist George Caleb Bingham painted both, along with many others depicting life along the western frontier.

Bingham made his home in Independence for a time at the elegant ***Bingham-Waggoner Estate*** (313 W. Pacific; 816-461-3491; bwestate.org), where he watched two Civil War battles rage across his front lawn (not conducive to painting a decent picture—think what that would do to your concentration!). Visit from Apr through Oct, Mon through Sat 10 a.m. to 4 p.m. to find out how "the other half" lived in the 19th century—or rent the mansion for a festive event and make the past your own. The mansion is also open late Nov through

Dec for the Christmas season; staff decorates all 26 rooms. Admission is $10 for adults and $5 for children ages 6 to 12, with slightly higher winter fees to defray the cost of all those decorations. Local rumor is that the estate is haunted by a ghost bride who appears on the staircase on occasion.

The **Mound Grove Cemetery** is known for its white apparition, too: Apparently a woman in a nightgown or perhaps a wedding gown has been seen following visitors. She disappears at the cemetery gate, as if she is unable—or perhaps unwilling—to go past it. Could it be the same woman from the Bingham-Waggoner Estate?

Another beautiful visit in Independence is to the **Vaile Mansion** (1500 N. Liberty; 816-325-7430; vailemansion.org). Built in 1881, the Vaile stands as one of our nation's premier examples of Second Empire Victorian architecture. This 31-room mansion includes painted ceilings, flushing toilets, nine marble fireplaces, and a wine cellar. But that is just the beginning of the story of over a century of history that has unfolded in this house. It is open Apr through Oct, Mon through Sat 10 a.m. to 4 p.m. and Sun 1 to 4 p.m. Admission is $6 for adults and $3 for children ages 6 to 16.

There is great antiques shopping in this region. Independence was the jumping-off point for pioneers heading west, so this is as far as a lot of their furniture got. Schlepping across the country with a wagon full of sideboards and armoires didn't seem practical, so Independence is where many pioneers began jettisoning large pieces of furniture. (Rocking chairs often made it as far as the Platte River.)

More of this kind of fascinating information can be found at the **National Frontier Trails Center** (318 W. Pacific St.; 816-325-7575), where exhibits commemorate the Santa Fe, California, and Oregon Trails, all of which passed through or began in Independence. The center doesn't feel like a museum, because it presents the trails through the words of the pioneers who traveled them. The layout of the center is patterned after the trails. At one point, a fork in the path forces visitors to choose between taking the Santa Fe or the Oregon-California routes. One route dead-ends, so if you choose that route, you have to go back and try again. Voice-activated boxes tell stories of how the West was settled, and the murals by Charles Goslin show how it was accomplished. There are thousands of original diary accounts of emigrants who traveled the trails. You can discover your pioneer ancestors at the Merrill J. Mattes Research Library (by appointment during regular hours at the museum). The pioneers' journals make fascinating reading, and there is a theater with a trails film. Hours are Thurs through Sat 10 a.m. to 4 p.m.

The **Woodstock Inn Bed & Breakfast** (1212 W. Lexington; 816-886-5656; woodstockinnmo.com) was originally a doll and quilt factory. It features

11 uniquely and beautifully appointed guest rooms, all with private baths. Inn-keepers Todd and Patricia Justice have completely refurbished the place, which now features a fenced-in courtyard and garden area, thermo-massage spa tubs, fireplaces, and a wealth of fine collectibles, rare antiques, and priceless artwork from around the world.

Silver Heart Inn & Cottages at 1114 S. Noland Rd. is a beautiful old home with private terraces and patios near town and can be booked online with booking.com.

Every town tries to have the weirdest little museum, and *Leila's Hair Museum* (1333 S. Noland Rd.; 816-833-2955; leilashairmuseum.net) gives Independence a lock on that title. (Ow! Sorry!) It is the only hair museum in the country, and probably the only place you can see a 14-inch-high tree made of human hair. The museum is inside Leila Cohoon's Independence School of Cosmetology. Her collection of more than 2,000 wreaths, brooches, watch fobs, bracelets, and buttons (all made from human hair) began in 1956 when she found a little square frame made of hair. She was a hairdresser then and it piqued her interest. Hair art was a reminder of a loved one before cameras were invented. You must see the wreaths (she has more than 300 now), which were created by carefully weaving hair over fine wires to make tiny flowers. Her oldest piece is a finely detailed brooch from 1680, brought to this country from Sweden. *And* this is the only hair museum in the country, so get it checked off your bucket list now. The museum is open Tues through Sat 9 a.m. to 4 p.m.

Community of Christ's International Headquarters is located at the center of Independence. The 1,600-seat temple at 201 S. River, featuring a spiral ceiling rising 195 feet and a 102-rank, 5,685-pipe organ built by Casavant Frères Limitée in Quebec, Canada; and the auditorium across the street with more than 5,000 seats and an Aeolian-Skinner organ with 113 ranks and 6,334 pipes are certainly something to behold. That is only the beginning. The rest you should see for yourself. These two structures are truly magnificent. The temple offers self-guided or guided tours by appointment. Visit the website at cofchrist.org/independence-temple-and-auditorium/ for hours of operation and to fill out a Temple Tour Request Form. Organ recitals, a daily prayer for peace, concerts, special services, and other events are also offered free to the public. Check the website for more information.

At the old RLDS auditorium, the one with the green dome at 1001 W. Walnut, you can take your children to the nondenominational *Children's Peace Pavilion.* There they will have a good time playing in the "Do Touch" museum. Inside are games that help them build self-esteem and learn cooperation and communication. The Peace Pavilion is on the fourth floor.

Harry Truman was not the only famous person from Independence. It is also the birthplace of Academy Award–winning actress Ginger Rogers, dancer, singer, and movie star of the Golden Age of Hollywood.

whatgoes aroundcomes around

William Clark returned from the historic expedition with Meriwether Lewis to become administrator of the Missouri Territory. Respectful and frail, Clark was accorded similar courtesies by the tribal chiefs, sparing the state some of the woes brought upon other areas by mismanaged dealings with the Native Americans.

Just outside Independence is the town of **Sugar Creek,** where you can have dinner at **Salvatore's** (12801 E. Hwy. 40; 816-737-2400; salvatores.us). Try some of the excellent *spiedini* and a glass of Chianti. Remember Garozzo's in Kansas City's North End? Well, this is the same family: owner Mike Garozzo's cousin and godson, Sam Garozzo. It's open for lunch and dinner.

Historic River Section

How about a day trip back in time? It's 1803, the year of the Louisiana Purchase: Imagine Missouri nearly empty of "civilization," as it was when it became part of the US. Early fur trappers traded necessities such as tobacco, tomahawks, blankets, fabrics, and cookware. The Osage people were the most common Native tribe in this area, and they did business amicably with both French and American trading posts.

East of Independence you'll explore **Fort Osage** (816-650-5737; fortosagenhl.com), a National Historic Landmark and the westernmost US outpost in the Louisiana Purchase. Its site was chosen by Lewis and Clark; construction was originally supervised by William Clark himself. Strategically overlooking the Missouri River, the fort was reconstructed from detailed plans preserved by the US War Department. The factory building stands today on its original foundation. Artifacts unearthed during the excavation are on display in the visitor center.

You may find a living-history reenactment in progress, complete with trappers and military men, Native Americans, explorers, storytellers, and musicians. Clothing displayed is authenticated down to the last bit of trim, and guides learn their alter egos' life and times so thoroughly that you forget you are only visiting the past. Sit inside the blockhouse looking out at the river, watch arrowheads being made from local flint, or visit the gift shop to purchase unique items with a sense of history (such as real bone buttons). Rustle up a group to enjoy one of the after-hours programs offered by the Jackson County Heritage Program. You can reserve a place at a hearthside supper in the factory's dining rooms, for example. Enjoy an authentic 19th-century meal by candlelight, then cozy up to the fireplace and savor the entertainment.

Several weekends a year, special events such as the Sheep Shearing (May) or the Militia Muster and Candlelight Tour (October) are offered, or spend the Fourth of July as our forebears did—the fort's a great place for it. To find Fort Osage, take US 24 from Kansas City east to Buckner; turn north at Sibley Street (Highway BB) and follow the gray signs through the tiny town of Sibley. The fort is open year-round on weekends from 9 a.m. to 4:30 p.m. You can explore on your own Tues through Sun. Admission is $8 for adults, $4 for senior citizens, and $4 for children.

A more historic (and scenic) route between Fort Osage and Lexington will take you down the Highway 224 spur through Napoleon, Waterloo, and Wellington. This is Lafayette County (must have been history buffs around this area). The road runs along the Missouri River, sometimes almost at water level, other times from a spectacular river-bluff view. Don't miss the turnoff to tiny downtown Napoleon. A bit farther on is Waterloo, just between Napoleon and Wellington— the obvious place, don't you think? There's not much here but a sign and a few houses, but it would be perfect even if it were only the sign! A great photo-op.

On the way into **_Lexington,_** watch for colorful sights guaranteed to make you smile, and that glorious old river. Once you enter historic Lexington, soak up the antebellum ambience. The homes along US 24 and on South Street are wonderful examples of Victorian charm—and remember, we're not just talking 1890s gingerbread here. The Victorian era began in the 1840s. You'll itch to get inside some of these beauties; check with the chamber of commerce for dates and times of historic homes tours. Lexington has four national historic districts and 110 antebellum and Victorian homes and shops. There are several good B&Bs, too.

rideonby

The Pony Express house at 1704 South St. is not open to the public, but it is interesting that one of the founders of the Pony Express, William Bradford Waddell, built it, and family members have lived there since 1840. The person who now occupies the house—Katherine Bradford Van Amburg—is his great-great-granddaughter.

There are a couple of nice shops for the ladies in town. **_Gigi's Boutique_** (922 Main St.; 660-259-4050) is in the historic 1880s Eagle Building. Hours are Mon through Sat 10 a.m. to 5 p.m. and Sun noon to 4 p.m.

There are about 20 shops in the downtown area, so it can be more than a day trip from Kansas City to enjoy the over 100 antebellum homes and historic structures. The **_Inn on Main,_** circa 1840, at 920 1/2 Main St. (660-259-8000), is right downtown and has four huge rooms decorated in period decor. Rooms are $100 a night, and rollaway beds are available.

The Battle of Lexington was fought in September 1861 when General Sterling Price moved his Confederate troops north after the Battle of Wilson's Creek and the fall of Springfield. After 52 hours of fighting, Union troops surrendered to the invaders. General Price took 3,000 prisoners and broke the chain of Union-held posts along the Missouri River. Remnants of the battle endure; a cannonball remains lodged in a pillar of the courthouse. You can still find earthworks out behind the ***Battle of Lexington State Historic Site*** (660-259-4654; mostateparks.com) overlooking the Missouri River. This redbrick house served as headquarters and hospital for both sides and is now a Civil War museum.

Creighton is a little town with no stoplights. But, are you needing another stamp on your **Missouri Spirits Expedition?** ***Rockin A Distillery*** (44307 E. Hwy. B; 847-863-4929; rockingadistillery.com) is nearby. It is open weekend evenings with different hours for summer or winter, so best to check it out online ahead of time. This small craft distillery is located on a farm in the middle of the corn belt. There is no traffic, and everything is sourced from local farmers, from the wheat and corn to the grapes used in the brandy and grappa. You must try the Rockin A Moonshine, made from the local corn. It's a mash whiskey handmade in all-copper pot stills. Everything ages in white oak barrels—also local—and milling, mashing, fermenting, distilling, barreling, and bottling is all done here. The MO Shine mash whiskey is bottled in mason jars and looks a lot like moonshine, but it is much, much better.

Buckner is home to the ***Bone Hill View Distillery*** (321 S. Hudson St.; 816-650-0655), another chance to get a stamp on your **Missouri Spirits Expedition.** You can also enjoy live music in the wine and cocktail garden when the weather is right. You gotta try the Strawberry Sweet Sorghum Shine; you won't find it anywhere else, for sure. Or perhaps the Peanut Butter and Jelly Sweet Sorghum Shine. You are going to have fun here. I guar-un-teee it.

andthestate mottois

The state motto is a quotation from Cicero: *"Salus popali suprema lex esto."* (Let the welfare of the people be the supreme law.)

Along US 24 toward ***Waverly,*** the land undergoes a change from fenced, row-cropped fields to orchards. The peach crop is always at risk in Missouri's unpredictable weather. Blossoms are often teased out early by a mild February only to be punished by an April freeze. It is a dangerous business, but the area around Waverly perseveres. The best peaches from this area are huge and sweet and dripping with juice. A bad year for the peach business is when the fruit is too big, too juicy, and not nearly plentiful enough to make shipping profitable. This is bad for orchard owners but wonderful for anyone lucky enough to be driving through.

US 24 is the old Lewis and Clark Trail along the river. Now it is filled with markets where orchard owners sell their bounty to travelers. Pick up peaches and apples or honey, homemade sausages, cheese, and cider along this scenic drive.

The Santa Fe Trail ran through here at one time, and it is still a trail of sorts for people living here in Missouri's apple and peach country. The Santa Fe Trail Growers Association is made up of 17 members in the area. On a drive along US 24 you will see a bountiful expanse of apples, peaches, nectarines, strawberries, raspberries, and blackberries—and all for sale if the season is right. Schreiman and Burkhart are just two of the orchards you will pass along the road. Greenhouses along the way are filled with vegetables, sweet corn, cider, and honey. In July and August, follow the scenic bluffs along the Missouri River to **Peters Market** (32615 Hwy. 65 S.; 660-493-2368; petersmkt.com), the largest apple grower in the state. The family has operated these 500 acres of apples and 20 acres of peaches for over 110 years, five generations since the original founder, Hermann Peters, began. Beginning with the earliest apple, the Ginger Gold—which is often sold out—to the Pink Lady, the last apple to ripen, these apples take you back to your childhood lunchbox. Every apple is special in some way—sweet, tart, long lasting—but the Jonathon is the undisputed best for pies. Peaches begin to ripen in the middle of July. Most popular are freestone and semi-cling peaches. Hours are Sat 9 a.m. to 5 p.m. and Sun noon to 5 p.m.

Pioneers stopped at historic **Arrow Rock** on their way west; it was a Santa Fe Trail town, a river port, and a meeting place for those who shaped history. More than 40 original buildings remain. Arrow Rock is still a real town, with permanent residents, a grocery store, a gas station, and a post office, but it is also a state park and historic site. The population numbers only 70 (and the historic district is so tightly controlled that someone has to die before someone new can move in, they say), but the place is packed in the summertime when the Lyceum Theatre is active. Arrow Rock looks like a normal town, but normal for a long time ago. It became a town in 1829 but for generations before that it was known as *pierre a fleche,* literally translated as "rock of arrows." In the 1820s the Santa Fe Trail crossed the river and travelers filled their water barrels at Arrow Rock. In 1829 the town was founded and named Philadelphia, but, thank goodness, the name was changed in 1833 to match the landmark for which the town was known. Streets and gutters are made from huge blocks of limestone; board sidewalks clatter with footsteps. The old bank acts as ticket office for the Lyceum, and the tiny stone jail still waits for an inmate. You may camp at Arrow Rock State Park; sites are available for groups or individuals. Visit the website at arrowrock.org.

Today the **Lyceum Repertory Theatre** (114 High St.; 660-837-3311) offers performances throughout the summer in an old church building; it's Missouri's oldest repertory company. Call ahead for a list of plays and their rotating dates, or visit lyceumtheatre.org.

Flint Creek Inn at 507 7th St. (660-837-3352) is surrounded by history. Ardee and Penny opened the inn in September 2017, and named it Flint Creek after the creek running along the property. It has a relaxed prairie style with authentic art and artifacts collected from states along the Sante Fe Trail. There is a bakery on the main level of the house, and the walkout lower level has the bed-and-breakfast area. A boardwalk leads to a covered patio and the inn entrance from the parking area. It is perfect for those who don't want to climb stairs. The common area is full of windows along one side for bird-watching and a view of the wooded area along the creek.

Artist George Caleb Bingham's home is here (remember him from Independence?), as is the home of Dr. John Sappington, one of the first to use quinine to treat malaria. The historic **J. Huston Tavern** (305 Main; 660-837-3200) dates from 1834, when Arrow Rock was a thriving river port. The most-ordered item on the menu is the specialty of the tavern, fried chicken. And why not? This recipe, like many others here, has been handed down for generations. Ole-time hominy salad, bread pudding, and fudge pie are included in those hand-me-downs. Blueberry cobbler and wonderful bread pudding make people come back again and again. There is more, too. The 190-year-old tavern (that word was synonymous with "hotel" then) was home to travelers on the Santa Fe Trail or people bound for Independence and the Oregon Trail. Some died here of the cholera and typhus that stopped the westward trek of many. And so, the place is haunted. Beds used in exhibits on the second floor have been found mussed, quiet voices have been heard as well as the cries of a child whose mother died here, photos show strange images that are not really there, and once, a mysterious cloud of smoke appeared in the manager's upstairs bedroom. They seem to be friendly spirits, though. The museum is upstairs. The restaurant opens Easter and serves Sunday lunch only through May 12, when the regular season begins: lunch Tues through Sun 11 a.m. to 2 p.m., dinner Sat 5 to 8 p.m., plus Wed and Fri 5 to 8 p.m. if there is Lyceum performance.

cupid's arrow

Legend has it that the town of Arrow Rock was named after a bow and arrow competition between Native warriors vying for the hand of a chief's daughter. One arrow—the winner's, no doubt—shot from a sandbar in the river flew so far that it lodged in a distant bluff above the river.

At **Boonville** (mile 191.8 on the KATY Trail), following the river east, the western prairie meets the Ozarks. The town was settled in 1810 by the widow Hannah Cole, who with her nine children built cabins on the bluffs overlooking the Missouri River. During the War of 1812 the settlement was palisaded and named Cole's Fort. It became the main river port for all southwestern Missouri.

The older residential section of Boonville has an unusually well-preserved collection of antebellum brick residences with wide halls and large rooms. Modest neoclassical homes are mixed with more flamboyant Victorian ones; many are on the National Register of Historic Places. The MKT depot is now the visitor center and features Missouri artists, but the real jewel is the ***Hotel Frederick*** and ***The Fred Restaurant*** (501 High St.; 660-882-2828; hotelfrederick. com). The hotel is wonderful. It's been restored and made into a European-style boutique hotel but has lost none of the charm, retaining its beautiful worn marble tile floor, original woodwork, stained glass, and antiques throughout The glass bathrooms in the rooms are a hoot—not for someone with privacy issues (there are shower curtains for the more modest among you). There's a bar in the lobby and the Fred Restaurant is in the back of the hotel. (Try the butternut squash ravioli sautéed with a brown butter sage sauce for a unique vegetarian dish.) The views out over the old river bottom on one side and old town Boonville on the other are gorgeous.

Thespian Hall (522 Main St.; friendsofhistoricboonville.org/thespianhall. html) is the oldest theater still in use west of the Alleghenies. Originally built in 1857, it has been used as an army barracks, Civil War hospital, and skating rink, among other things. It featured gymnastics, opera, and movies in its day and is now home to Boonville Community Theatre.

If you have come to town for one of Boonville's many bluegrass festivals—where musicians play everything from harmonicas to paper bags—Thespian Hall is the center of the activity. The folk-music tradition lives on here through the efforts of the Friends of Historic Boonville. If you can, try to coordinate your visit with one of these festivals. The Big Muddy Folk Festival is in April, and the Missouri River Festival of the Arts is in August.

If you are out walking around, search out ***Harley Park,*** where Lookout Point sits atop a bluff over the Missouri River, and get a feel for what early townsfolk saw along the long bend of the river. A Native burial mound surmounts this high point; imagine the prospect of immortality with such a view.

The mid-Missouri area was the site of many of the key battles of the Civil War. The first land battle of the war was fought 4 miles below Boonville on June 17, 1861. State troops under the command of Confederate Colonel John S. Marmaduke were defeated by federal forces led by Captain Nathaniel Lyon. Military historians consider this victory important in preserving the Union.

One more must-see place near Boonville is the ***Warm Springs Ranch*** (25270 Hwy. 98), home and breeding farm of the Budweiser Clydesdales. It has a foaling barn, veterinary lab, and 10 pastures and is home to more than 70 Clydesdales ranging from foals to stallions. These gentle giants will steal your heart. There is a guided walking tour or, if you have the time, the Clydesdale Behind-the-Scenes Tour for groups of up to 16. Call (888) 972-5933 to arrange tours.

Jefferson City, Missouri's capital (mile 143.2 on the KATY Trail), is smack in the center of the state on US 50, handy to legislators and lobbyists. Built on the steep southern bluffs of the Missouri River, the city and the surrounding rural landscape offer considerable scenic variety. Large streams are bordered with steeply sloping and heavily forested hills. Bottomland here is rich with alluvial and yellow loess soils that don't look the way you expect fertile topsoil to look but support more wheat and corn than any other section of the Ozarks.

Here also is Jefferson Landing, one of the busiest centers of the 19th century. It's still busy; the Amtrak station is at the landing, as are the Lohman Building, the Union Hotel, and the Maus House.

The state capitol is certainly on the beaten path; however, once inside the House Lounge, you will find a mural painted in 1935 by Thomas Hart Benton. This mural stirred controversy in 1936 because some of the legislators said it lacked refinement. Always quick with an answer, Benton retorted that he portrayed "people involved in their natural, daily activities that did not require being polite."

Central Dairy (610 Madison St.; 573-635-6148; centraldairy.biz) still has old-fashioned ice cream and old-fashioned ice-cream prices. This is a must-stop place for people on the KATY Trail on a hot summer's day—and for everyone else, for that matter. Hours are Mon through Sat 8 a.m. to 6 p.m. and Sun 10 a.m. to 6 p.m. One of the specialties is called the Rock and Roll. It's like a banana split but with four, count 'em, four flavors of ice cream and toppings. Betcha can't eat one!

Arri's Pizza (117 W. High St.; 573-635-9225; arrispizzaplace.com) is a local favorite with the members of congress in the capital city. Hours are Mon through Sat 11 a.m. to 9 p.m.

Also near Jeff City is the **Missouri Wildflower Nursery** (9814 Pleasant Hill Rd.; 573-496-3492; mowildflowers.net), where plants and seeds of the state's native flora are available. The nursery also has a good color catalog to help identify plants you are curious about. Or take Highway 50 east approximately 23 miles through *Linn.* You will see a big barn sitting high on the hill on the right-hand side of the road (do not use your GPS for this or you will end up in Nowheresville) and find America's only pig museum, **Where Pigs Fly Farm and Pigs Aloft Museum** (2810 Hwy. 50 E.), which has one of the largest pig collections and, in fact, is the only pig museum in the world. If you have a pig collection yourself that needs a new home, give them a call at (314) 241-3488—they are happy to take in homeless pigs, ceramic or otherwise. This is also one of the largest petting zoos in the state. If you like pigs, you are going to love this place. Admission is only $5 for adults and $3 for kids under 12. Shop in the Farm & Resale Shop Fri through Sun 10 a.m. to 6 p.m.

Nearby is the little town of **Lohoman,** where you can visit the **Blacksmith Distillery** (11517 Branch Rd.; 573-469-8580; blacksmithartisanalspirits. com) for handcrafted, small-batch spirits. Family recipes handed down for generations range from an award-winning corn whiskey, bourbon, and apple pie whiskey to more modern inspirations such as the limestone-filtered vodka and unique botanical gin to the Iron Forge Corn Whiskey that started it all. Quench Tank Gin has a unique selection of botanicals: Sugar snap peas, cucumber, mint, cilantro, and a rare Japanese mountain pepper give this gin a green, refreshing taste with a subtle hit of heat. Smashed Apple is a refreshing, crisp, apple wine–flavored whiskey with sweet apple flavor (but not too sweet) and a lovely, warm whiskey finish. Get your **Missouri Spirits Expedition** stamp, but also go to the website and read about the team who runs this place—it is one funny read.

Missouri's Melting Pot

Head west to California (that's Missouri, of course) on US 50 to the town of **Tipton.** Follow the signs to the **Dutch Bakery and Bulk Food Store** (709 US 50; 660-433-2865), located on Highway 5 and US 50 at the west end of Tipton. Here the pies are baked from homegrown berries and fruit; fresh vegetables from the garden are available in season. Homemade breads (a favorite is a wonderful oatmeal bread) and rolls fill the shelves along with bulk foods. But the primary reason for stopping here is the "Dutch letters"—crisp, thick pastry rolled and filled with almond paste and shaped into letters. They are cheaper if you buy five, and you might as well so you won't have to turn around and come back in an hour. Open Mon through Thurs 7 a.m. to 6 p.m., Fri till 7 p.m., and Sat till 5:30 p.m.

While in Tipton try to visit the circa 1858 **Maclay House** at 209 W. Howard St. and Highway B (660-433-2068; tiptonmo.com), which is open on the second or fourth Sunday of each month for a modest fee of $10 for adults and $5 for kids under 12. This beautiful old three-story house has been restored and contains the original furniture. It is the site of the annual Fourth of July ice-cream social and features dinner and entertainment in September. The first Saturday in July is called Super Saturday around here and draws a thousand visitors for the barbecue contest, volleyball, and three-on-three basketball contests. Call the Tipton Chamber of Commerce (660-433-2068) for more information about the Maclay House and Super Saturday. Be sure to notice the "eight-ball" water tower; there's a Fischer's Pool Table manufacturing plant in town.

Slip into the **Downtown Café** at 116 W. Moniteau St. for lunch before you hit the road again. This is one of those places where the locals eat, and it's only open for breakfast and brunch Mon through Fri 5:30 a.m. (you read that right) to 11 a.m., Sat till 11:30 a.m., and Sun till 4:30 p.m.

If you're in the mood for some really good barbecue, turn south on US 65 where it intersects with US 50 and drive to 1915 S. Limit (mile 229 on the KATY Trail) to **Kehde's Barbeque** (660-826-2267) in **Sedalia,** where John and Chelsea Kehde (pronounced K.D.) serve the best barbecue in the area. But that's not all. Kehde's also has jalapeño fries (french fries dipped in some kind of spicy coating) and a grilled tenderloin sandwich that is as good as the fried kind but without all the fat. It is a regular stop for folks headed to or from the Lake of the Ozarks and Kansas City. Kehde's added a railroad dining car to the building to handle the extra crowds from the state fair and the summertime Lake of the Ozarks crowd. It's fun to sit up in the old dining car and watch the traffic go by while enjoying the best barbecued ribs in the area. Take home a bottle of the sauce. In fact, take a couple or you will have to send for more when you get home. Hours are Wed through Sat 11 a.m. to 8 p.m. and Sun till 3 p.m.

If you drive into Sedalia on US 65, you will probably pass (off to your left and way up) a beautiful stone mansion overlooking the highway. This is Stonyridge Farm in **Bothwell State Park** (19350 Bothwell State Park Rd.). Bothwell chose limestone as his primary building material for the lodge and cliff house. There are more angles to this place than a Chinese puzzle—it must have driven the roofers crazy. The original carriage road rises almost 100 feet but in a gentle ascent, with the lay of the land; hand-laid stone culverts allow water to pass under the road. Take the first left after you pass the house on US 65 going toward Sedalia (or, driving north, watch very carefully for the small sign marking the turn or you will have to turn around and go back when you finally see it). It is worth the trouble to find; there are spectacular views and wonderful walking trails near the house.

There are several antiques malls in Sedalia, but remember that in August this is the home of the **Missouri State Fair,** which attracts more than 300,000 people. The path gets beaten smooth, but it leads to midway rides, big-name entertainment, livestock shows, and car races—good, clean, all-American fun.

There's a B&B in the little community of **Georgetown,** just 3 miles north of Sedalia. **Georgetown Country View Estate** (22378 Hwy. H) is on 80 acres of Missouri farmland and has an outdoor porch and swing just like a farm-house built in 1869 should. Private baths and two-person jetted tubs make it much more modern than the old-fashioned farmstead, but the antique furniture keeps the mood right. It went from being a country home for a banker to the county poor farm in 1894 when the banker died. It's a beautiful outdoor set-ting (great for weddings) and has a swimming pool as well. Visit the website at georgetowncountryviewestate.com for prices and more information, or call (660) 826-4046.

The **KATY Trail** snakes along the river from Clinton to Machens for 237.7 miles, burrowing through tunnels and also treating you to the only Missouri River railroad bridge near Franklin before passing glittering Burlington limestone bluffs containing millions of fossils from the sea. The Mighty Mo has been out of its banks twice since the trail was begun, once in the Great Flood of 1993 and again in the almost-great flood of 1995, but work is progressing to connect the trail here with its other end in St. Charles. When the river is behaving, you can look "across the wide Missouri" and have a magnificent view of the river traffic of barges and boats. The trail is open to hikers and horseback riders.

thekatytrail

The **KATY Trail** is named for the MKT (Missouri-Kansas-Texas) Railroad tracks laid down more than a century ago. The MKT came out of Fort Riley, Kansas, in the mid-1890s and shot into Indian Territory. It was the heart of the area, rumbling in and bringing the lifeblood of freight, newspa-pers, and passengers needed to make the Midwest part of the Industrial Revolution. By 1892 the KATY had a direct route to St. Louis and connec-tions to the eastern seaboard. Many of the small towns along the trail were born—and died—with the railroad.

Western Missouri waited a long time for a botanical garden; St. Louis, in the east, has one of the finest in the country. Finally, after much hemming and hawing among folks in the greater Kansas City area and those just over the Kansas border, the people of **Powell Gardens** (1609 NW US 50; 816-566-2600; powellgardens.org), just south of US 50 in **Kingsville,** couldn't wait any longer and began their own. Hurrah for private initiative! This almost 25-year-old garden is a beautiful 915 acres of blooms and a natural resource center where you can wander among the flowers and indig-enous plants; learn about "S-s-s-snakes!"; make an all-natural wreath; or learn how to plant, prune, and harvest your own back-yard botanical garden—you get the idea. The size sounds a bit overwhelming, but this oasis has free trolleys to help you cover the ground. Notice the hen and chicks and the sedum and other plants peeking out from the crevices of a 600-foot-long stone wall in the Island Garden. Take time to visit the secret sunken garden where floating lotus blossoms glisten in the dappled sunlight. The Humming-bird Garden calls these little creatures in droves, and although pockets of blooms pop up around every corner, be sure to find the Perennial Garden, which has 1,200 kinds of flowers covering 3.5 acres. The stunning redwood and glass Marjorie Powell Allen Chapel at the gardens was designed by E. Fay Jones, a nationally honored and recognized architect who built Thorncrown Chapel in Arkansas.

The gardens are food for the soul as well as the tummy. You can see a Missouri Star quilt pattern planted in vegetables, a demonstration kitchen, and a kitchen garden. Powell Gardens has opened the 12-acre Heartland Harvest Garden, where everything is edible and visitors can learn about the path of food from seed to plate. Hours are 9 a.m. to 6 p.m. daily May through Sept, until 5 p.m. Oct through Apr. Workshops and seminars are scheduled year-round. There are also a cafe and a gift shop, which opens at 10 a.m.

Watch for signs from I-70 (or Highway 291) for **Fleming Park** and **Lake Jacomo.** You'll find the usual sailing, swimming, and fishing as well as the **Burroughs Audubon Society Library** in **Blue Springs** (7300 SW West Park Rd.; 816-795-8177; burroughs.org). Learn about the birds, take a hike, browse through the books, and discover how to turn your backyard into a wildlife sanctuary. The library offers not just viewing but free Wi-Fi access, nature photography, birdseed and feeders, and gifts and cards. Check the website for seasonal hours.

Stop in your tracks. The world is moving altogether too quickly, but there's an antidote: **Missouri Town 1855** in **Lee's Summit.** Managed by the Jackson County Parks Department, one of the two largest county parks departments in the US, it is a collection of original mid-19th-century buildings that were moved on-site and now make up a brand-new old town founded in 1960.

what'sinaname

In 1868 when 51 pioneer families settled in the area, they applied for a post office and name for their town. Excelsior was suggested, but it was already taken. More names were sent, and more had already been assigned. Finally the frustrated citizens of this settlement on the east branch of the Grand River sent one last request: "We don't care what name you give us, so long as it is sort of 'peculiar.'" Well, that's exactly what they got: *Peculiar,* Missouri.

A wide variety of architectural styles add to the historical significance of the town. It's just that sort of progression from rugged log cabins to fine homes that would have taken place in the 19th century as settlers arrived and commerce thrived. You'll find antebellum homes, a tavern, a schoolhouse, a church, a lawyer's tiny office (apparently the law was not quite so lucrative then), and the mercantile, where settlers would have bought outright or bartered for their goods. It has even been the setting for several movies, including the television version of *Friendly Persuasion* and the more recent movie *Across Five Aprils,* a story of a family split by the Civil War.

If the buildings alone aren't enough to pique your interest, this is a living-history experience. You're liable to see the blacksmith at work, watch oxen tilling the soil, or be followed by the resident flock of geese. You can wander around a real herb garden and discover how many herbs were used as medicine in the 19th century—hospitals were rare in those days, and medical insurance was unheard of.

Missouri Town 1855 is at 8010 E. Park Rd. in Lee's Summit, on the east side of Fleming Park. Take Colbern Road east to Cyclone School Road. Turn north (left) and follow the signs 2 miles to the entrance. Admission is $8 for adults and $7 for youths; children younger than age 4 get in for free. The town is open Apr 1 through Nov 15, Tues through Sun 9 a.m. to 4:30 p.m.; and Nov 16 through Mar, weekends only 9 a.m. to 4:30 p.m.

Ray Julo's place is always full of ice-cream connoisseurs, people who know how special frozen custard is. ***Custard's Last Stand*** (308 SE Hwy. 291) has been in town since 1989, and business is fine even with the competition. Frozen custard is a super-premium ice cream with one-third less air than regular ice cream and is served at 28 degrees Fahrenheit instead of 10 degrees like regular ice cream. It doesn't freeze your taste buds. And, Ray points out, it has eggs in it, which makes it creamier and very thick—so thick it is handed to you upside down.

Custard's Last Stand was voted best ice cream in the Kansas City area two years in a row by a local magazine. There are 45 flavors to choose from, including peanut butter, bubble gum, and the ever-popular Berry, Berry, Berry (a combination of strawberry, blueberry, and raspberry). Visit the website at custardslaststand.com or call a member of the Julo family (there are three generations working there) at (816) 347-9922. Open Mon through Thurs 11:30 a.m. to 9:30 p.m., Fri and Sat till 10:30 p.m., and Sun noon to 9:30 p.m.

Lee's Summit is also the home of the ***Midwest Genealogy Center*** at 3440 S. Lee's Summit Rd. (816-252-7228; mymcpl.org). It is the largest public genealogy facility in the country and has more than 750,000 free resources and librarians on duty to help you begin research into your family's history. Hours are Mon through Sat 10 a.m. to 8 p.m. and Sun 1 to 5 p.m.

Once upon a time there was a little village named Cockrell on Old US 50, and in that little village was an old mercantile general store. But that was more than 115 years ago. Today the vintage village is known as ***Cockrell Mercantile Company*** (30003 E. Old US 50; 816-697-1923; cockrellmercantile.com) and is located between Lee's Summit and Lone Jack. Proprietors Chris and Becky Glaze have made the five cottages and barns home to five unique shops. The Mercantile carries gadgets galore—aprons, tea towels, glassware, pots and pans—and treats you to a free cup of coffee or tea while you shop. The Fiesta Cottage has the largest selection of Fiestaware in this part of the country. The Morton House features bakeware and most anything a baker could need, including King Arthur Flour products. Cockrell Cottage is filled with home decor items, barbecue supplies, gift books, candles, and the line of Aromatique products. There are butcher blocks, pot racks, and gourmet foods throughout the village, and gift wrapping is complimentary. Last—but certainly not least if you are a gardener—is the Cockrell Annex, an outdoorsy shop full of surprising garden accessories. To find the village, travel east on US 50 through Lee's Summit and go 0.75 mile past the Highway 7 exit. Turn right at the Cockrell sign and follow the road for 0.5 mile. The store is on the right. Hours are Mon through Sat 10 a.m. to 6 p.m. and Sun noon to 5 p.m.

Lake Lotawana is a fine place to be on a warm summer night. If you are out in a boat, it's even better. Float up to the docks at **Marina Grog and Galley** (22 A St.) and enjoy great food and a view to match. The circa 1934 building has been renovated. There are four dining options, and all are elegant. The main dining room overlooks the lake on one side and a 1,500-gallon saltwater aquarium on the other. The upper deck features two fireplaces and provides a cozy atmosphere for dining. On a warm summer night, you can sit on the outer deck, right at water's edge. The newest addition is the luxurious Marina Bay Club, a private dining area available by reservation Sun through Fri. The cozy dining room with fireplace overlooks the lake and seats only 12 to 16 guests at one hardwood table. A sunken bar and more than 200-bottle wine list make this a fine-dining experience. Guests are invited into the kitchen to watch the chef and sous chef prepare the courses. Only USDA prime dry-aged steaks are offered, as well as Alaskan king crab legs. The house specialty is deep-fried lobster. This is a very nice restaurant and there is a dress code, so please don't jump out of a boat in a bathing suit. Call (816) 578-5511 to get directions by car or check the Web at marina27.com.

Take Highway 7 from the Lake Lotawana area to East Colbern Road and then south to 9512 S. Buckner Tarsney Rd. in **Grain Valley,** and pig out, so to speak, at **Porky's Blazin' BBQ** (816-566-0203; porkysblazinbbq.com). This barbecue comes highly recommended by weekend bikers—businesspeople, lawyers, doctors, etc., disguised in leathers—who really know how to find good food on straight roads. Hours are Fri and Sat 11 a.m. to 8 p.m., Sun till 3 p.m.

Unity Village, on US 50 just west of Lee's Summit, is an incorporated town with its own post office and government. It's a peaceful setting with an old-world feel; spacious grounds contain a natural rock bridge, Spanish Mediterranean–style buildings, and a formal rose garden with reflecting pools and fountains. A 9-hole golf course and hiking trails will keep you moving. People of all faiths use the resources at Unity for holistic healing. The restaurant, bookstore, and chapel are open to the public, and you can arrange an overnight stay at the "spiritual life center" by calling (816) 524-3550 or going to unityvillage.org.

Little *Greenwood* is just south of Lee's Summit on Highway 291, then east on Highway 150. This was once a bustling place with not one but two train stations. It was a major shipping center for cattle and lumber. It still has two explosives factories and a rock quarry nearby, accounting for the heavy trucks rumbling through this sleepy town.

An old wooden bridge marks the end of downtown proper; watch for signs to find any number of little antiques stores and factory outlets. *Greenwood Antiques and Country Tea Room* (502 Main St.; 816-537-8434; greenwood-countrytearoom.com) is a mall-type operation by the railroad bridge and just full of small booths. More than 70 shops occupy 15,000 square feet of space. The food is excellent; add your name to the waiting list when you go in the door, and they'll find you. Hours are Wed through Sat 11 a.m. to 2 p.m.

Lone Jack is another unlikely spot for a winery. *Bynum Winery* (13520 S. Sam Moore Rd.; 816-566-2240) is 3 miles east of Lone Jack at the intersection of US 50 and Sam Moore Road. The Bynum family was among the earliest settlers here in 1836. Mr. Bynum's great-great-uncle George Shawhan was a well-known whiskey maker before Prohibition. Carrying on the family tradition, Floyd Bynum opened the winery in 1989. Bynum Winery is a 6-acre vineyard tucked in Missouri's rolling hills, with plans to develop over 30 acres in time. Both red and white wines, along with fruit wines, are made here. The winery is open seven days a week. Hours are Mon and Wed noon to 4 p.m. and Tues and Thurs through Sun noon to 5:30 p.m. Visit missouriwinecountry. com/wineries, which is a good resource if you want to visit wineries along any route in the state.

Warrensburg is the home of the *University of Central Missouri.* It is a fair-to-middlin'-size city now as it grows with the university. The oldest dorm on campus is Yeater Hall, built in 1940. It is said to be haunted. The redbrick walls surround a single window in the attic that overlooks the campus. Here students have seen the image of a woman standing in the window even though the attic is not accessible at all. Mysterious footsteps and strange lights reinforce the legend. It was the first dormitory for women, built by Laura J. Yeater, who was head of the Latin and Greek department from 1901 to 1917—certainly a woman ahead of her time—and a strong advocate for women's housing on campus.

Perhaps she is still there, and proud of what she sees women doing today. It so happens this is where this writer lived while attending what was then Central Missouri State College. The website for Warrensburg is warrensburg.org.

There's plenty to do in Warrensburg since it is a college town, but find the **Dutch Valley** (760 Hwy. 13; 660-553-3496), an Amish shop where you can have a really good cup of coffee and something from their bakery while you shop for CBD products, herbs, groceries (really fresh brown eggs), bulk foods, candy, or Amish-made furniture.

Look up while driving through Knob Noster, because there are interesting things in the air above **Whiteman Air Force Base.** The previously very, very top-secret Stealth Bomber calls this base home, and its eerie Batman-like silhouette can be seen low in the sky on approach to the base's runway. If you see it, you might as well pull off to the side of the road—as everyone else is doing—to watch it land.

North of Knob Noster on Highway 23 is the town of **Concordia,** where residents take their German heritage very, very seriously. It is home to St. Paul's College and the state's only Lutheran boarding school, a school that has been in operation for 130 years. Check out the **Concordia Area Museum and Historical Society.** It is interesting, especially if you have German heritage, that in 1864 the German settlers (who were against slavery and fought with the Union Army) were massacred in an attack by Confederate sympathizers—bushwhackers, they were called—and some say it was Jesse and Frank James, who were known to be in the area. The **Plattdutsch Hadn Tohopa** (Low German Club) of Concordia has an annual Low German Theater at the Concordia Community Center at 802 Gordon St. This lavish fall production is compiled and written by people of the town. Saturday night offers a dinner theater serving German delights such as peppered beef and bratwurst. Sunday is usually a matinee theater only. Call (660) 463-2212.

Concordia's rich German heritage draws thousands of visitors each year for the annual **Concordia Fall Festival** (concordiafallfestival.com) in September. There are exhibits, carnival rides, and German food and beer at the "Heidelberg Gardens" in one of the two beautiful parks in town. Visit the website or send an e-mail to concordiafallfestival@gmail.com for more information.

The Ozarks

Cole Camp is a tiny town that would be easy to miss, but don't. The first place to stop, if you have planned this right and it is lunchtime, is **Handel Haus Tea Room** (101 S. Maple; 660-668-9952) at the four-way stop in the heart of town— you can't miss it; the town is small. This European bistro cafe has a fireplace to keep you warm in the fall and winter and a trickling fountain to keep you cool in the spring and summer. Everything is made from scratch—quiche with blends of cheese and homemade crust, salads, soups, and croissants. The tearoom serves Mon through Sat 11 a.m. to 2 p.m. The building that houses the tearoom was built in 1920 as the Cole Camp Mercantile and now is filled with antiques, art, pottery, linens, and quilts. You can rummage through the treasures. *The German Table* at 107 E. Main St. (660-668-0019) is full of German comfort food made from scratch. Open Fri and Sat; call for reservations.

At *Triple Creek Golf Course* (660-668-4653; triplecreekgolf.com), located on Highway B 0.5 mile south of Cole Camp at 333 Triple Creek Dr., you can play one of the most unique golf course layouts you have ever experienced. It has 18 tee boxes and wide, zoysia fairways hitting to nine large, bentgrass greens.

trivia

Cole Camp was at the hub of four major roads at the time of the Civil War. It became the site of one of the first battles of the war on June 19, 1861. A force of around 700 Union Home Guards was mobilized on June 13 and had its "baptism by fire" that same week. The pro-Confederate Missouri governor, Claiborne Jackson, was retreating from his defeat at Boonville, but the Home Guards were blocking his escape route, which would have brought him through Cole Camp. A force of Confederate sympathizers was organized at Warsaw and on June 19 launched an early morning attack on the Home Guard encampment. The Home Guard was routed and the way cleared for Governor Jackson to escape, adding another bloody footnote to Missouri's Civil War history.

If you decide to stay near Cole Camp, check out the *Silos at Prairie Vale* (29300 Hwy. 127; 573-280-3947) in nearby *Green Ridge.* It is a unique farm stay complete with animals. The kids will love it. Guests stay in their own silo apartment and can enjoy farm life, and it is convenient to the KATY Trail.

Highway 52 runs into Highway 5 at the city of *Versailles* (pronounced just as it looks, Ver-sales, not the French way). Versailles is the gateway to the Lake of the Ozarks area. Here you make the decision to go east on Highway 52 to the St. Louis side of the lake or southwest on Highway 5 to the Kansas City side. Versailles has a lot going on. Nearby is Jacob's Cave, and there is the annual Olde Tyme Apple Festival the second week of October, but the biggest draw is the giant flea market also held in October (as well as April and June). This is a 40-acre event (you need a golf cart to see everything) that draws about 11,000 people. The October flea market also coincides with the apple festival.

Just half a block southeast of the square in Versailles, a brick walkway leads to a two-story white Victorian home that has become the **Hawthorne Inn.** Built in 1877, it sits, still in its former magnificence, at 206 E. Jasper St. Host Melanie Littlefiels will make sure you are comfy. There is a sitting room if you are just looking for a peaceful afternoon and a quiet library filled with good books if you just want to veg, or you can wander around Versailles, play on the water at Lake of the Ozarks, or look for Amish horse and buggies. All the rooms have private baths, and some can be combined into a suite for families. Call (573) 378-2020 for reservations.

World Craft and Thrift Shop (123 E. Newton St.; 573-378-5900) is owned by the Mennonite Church. Crafts are imported from throughout the world, and you can browse in the thrift shop in the back room for great used stuff as well. Profits from this shop support Mennonite missions all over the world. Summer hours are Mon through Fri 9 a.m. to 5 p.m. and Sat 9 a.m. to 2 p.m. Winter hours are Tues through Fri 10 a.m. to 4 p.m. and Sat 10 a.m. to 1 p.m.

In recent years, Versailles has become home to a number of gift and coffee shops, a group of rug weavers, and other arts-oriented businesses.

Emme's Attic (113 W. Jasper; 573-378-5999; emmesboutique.com) has become a destination shopping experience, with free wine tastings every day so you can browse around the shop and look at bags and jewelry, candles, antiques, and wines. This is a great way to spend a rainy day at the lake, or a day when the guys are going fishing, just relaxing in the pleasant atmosphere of this friendly shop. Hours are Mon through Fri 10 a.m. to 5 p.m., Sat till 3 p.m.

The **Lake of the Ozarks** area is called the "Land of the Magic Dragon." If you look at the lake on a map and go snake-eyed, it has a dragon shape; hence the name. The Ozark heritage stems from the first immigrants here, who were from Tennessee, Kentucky, and nearby parts of the southern Appalachians. The Upper South hill-country folks were descended from Scotch-Irish stock. For many years the Ozark Mountains sheltered these folks, and few outsiders entered the area; you may have heard of the "Irish Wilderness." Because of the rough topography, the railroads avoided the area, and this extreme isolation until a little more than 50 years ago created the "Ozark Hillbilly." The values, lifestyle, and beliefs of those first settlers are still much in evidence.

The building of Bagnell Dam to form the Lake of the Ozarks eroded that isolation and turned the area into the Midwest's summer playground. Because it is not a US Army Corps of Engineers lake, homes can be built right on the water's edge; the 1,300 miles of serpentine shore has more shoreline than the state of California!

Miles of lake coves, wooded hills, and steep, dusty roads are still unsettled. Most undeveloped areas have no roads at all leading to them. The east side of

Winter Solace

The Missouri Ozarks are a quiet labyrinth of rugged hills and deep valleys, as famous for the folk culture as the beauty. Our home was perched high above a lake looking down at the very tops of the old oak trees with dozens of dogwoods sprinkled among them. The glass front let us watch the summer people on the lake; the screened porch was a perfect spot for breakfast. A telescope allowed us a view of the other side of the lake, a toll call away by road.

The chimney of the stone fireplace rose to the second-story ceiling; a loft above the one-room living area held our bed. The change of the seasons moved like a kaleidoscope across the north window glass; the spring dogwoods and wild pear trees splashed white and pink across the barely budded trees. Bright daffodils popped up in the woods where earlier settlers must have planted them. Summers were intensely green, with ivy taking over the woods around the house. Deer and almost-tame raccoons and foxes shared the woods around the cottage with us. The roar of the boats and shouts of the skiers began early and continued until after sunset.

When the leaves changed in the fall, the quiet made the woods a private place. The color, not so garishly bright as New Hampshire's maples, but a rustic red and gold of Missouri oak, gave the hills a new texture, a different feel. The leaves fell—some years slowly, one by one; other years, it seemed, all at once—leaving the view unobstructed and breathtaking when the cool, early-morning lake fog hung over the still-warm water.

The most beautiful spectacle I remember took place deep in winter. One special day the sun was warm, the air crisp and cold. We built a huge fire in the fireplace and grilled steaks and baked potatoes there that evening. In the morning the whisper of snowflakes woke us. The sleeping loft was bathed in the reflected light of a deep snow. The quiet was almost tangible; I could feel it, taste it, touch it. We threw more logs on the smoldering fire and curled up on the couch with the down comforter and a cup of hot coffee. We were treated to the sight of a bald eagle perched on a tree limb outside the window. We watched it dive for fish twice and carry them off to a nearby nest.

Putting the for-sale sign by the roadside of our little wooded acreage was a sad day. But like the seasons, the times of our lives change, and with those changes come new colors and new sights. Our lives move in new directions, just as the winds change from south to north and back again. The memories, though, will be mine forever.

the lake, which houses the dam, has become the drop-in tourist side. The track is beaten slick over here. There are restaurants, shopping malls, and waterslides galore.

Some of the unique places on the east side deserve a mention before you head to the west side of the lake, where the more fascinating spots hide. If you go to Bagnell Dam from Eldon, watch for wintering eagles—here and at most of the lake crossings. They retreat from the Arctic chill up north, following flocks of migrating geese.

You may not have thought of Missouri as a state for bald eagle watching—and spring through early fall, it's not, though a captive breeding program by the Missouri Department of Conservation has been in effect since 1981 to reestablish a wild breeding population. But come winter, these big birds take up residence wherever they can find open water and plentiful feeding. One recent year, more than 1,400 bald eagles were counted, making this state second only to Washington in the Lower 48 for eagle sightings. At most Missouri lakes, their main diet consists of fish—they have far better luck with fishing than most humans.

Charley's Buffet is a unique spot on this side of the lake, and well worth the drive if you can find it. People come from all around to eat there (and get lost in the process), and because it's only open on Friday and Saturday evenings, folks line up for the delicious Mennonite-cooked and -served food. This restaurant has taken third place in the *Rural Missourian*'s "Best of Missouri" polls in the "Places Worth the Drive" category. They don't advertise and apparently don't need to, based on the size of the crowds there on weekends. If you have a GPS, you can cheat and enter 23785 Hwy. B, Lincoln, but that would take away the challenge. In the day, you were lucky to have a number to call, because many Mennonite businesses had neither. Call (660) 668-3806 if you accept the challenge and get lost. When you find it, bon appétit! Hours are Fri and Sat 4:30 to 8:30 p.m.

Taking the back way around the lake along Highway 52 to Eldon and then US 54 to Bagnell Dam is more interesting than the much-traveled and very crowded Highway 5/US 54 route. A left turn (north) on Highway 5 puts you in the middle of the Mennonite community. On the roads around Versailles, horse-drawn buggies carry Mennonite citizens on their daily tasks. They are less strict than the Jamesport Amish—the somber black attire is uncommon—and most of the homes have telephones and electricity, though many don't. Old Order Mennonite women wear prayer bonnets but dress in printed fabrics. Some families have cars, but many of the cars are painted black—chrome and all. To get a good tour of the area, begin where Highway 5 splits into Highway 52 and follow 52 to Highway C on the left.

Follow Highway C about 6 miles to ***Pleasant Valley Quilts*** (17019 Meadowbrook Rd; 573-378-5782; zquilts.webs.com) in ***Barnett.*** There is a sign by the road where you can turn and drive about three-quarters of a mile on gravel. Lydia Zimmerman makes each of her unique quilts by hand, all hand-stitched and no two the same. Not only are they detailed and beautiful, but they are also durable and usable fine art. You can call and order the size and colors you want.

Follow the sign off Highway C down a gravel road to the **Dutch Country Store** (18268 Kelsay Rd., Barnett; 573-378-4395), which carries bulk foods as well as a huge selection of freight-damaged groceries and toiletries. There are usually buggies parked out front along with the automobiles. The store always has a good selection of name-brand cereals and canned goods, shampoo, and dog food—just about anything. The selection is different every week.

Turn north on Highway E, then follow E to Highway K (this sounds harder than it really is), but watch closely for horse-drawn buggies and bicycles on these hilly back roads. Highway K leads east to the tiny, tiny town of **Excelsior** and **Weavers' Market** (113920 Market Rd., Versailles; 573-378-4672; weaverscountry-market.com), serving this community of about 250 Mennonite families. Weavers' carries fresh-frozen farm produce, frozen homemade pies ready to pop into your oven, an enormous assortment of teas and spices, and other bulk foods, including homemade noodles. Hours are Mon through Sat 8:30 a.m. to 5 p.m.

Nearby (follow the signs) is **Excelsior Fabric** (13142 Hopewell Rd.; 573-378-7448), where Anna and Sam Shirk and their family carry an extensive collection of quilting fabrics.

Driving along Hopewell Road is an adventure all by itself. You will find the **Excelsior Book Store** (13142 Hopewell Rd.; 573-378-1925) and the **Excelsior Harness Shop** (13142 Hopewell Rd.; 573-378-7218) along there, too, although even though you are off the beaten path, you probably won't need harness repair if you are just a visitor to the area.

If you decide to turn left back at Highway E on some pretty Sunday morning about 10 a.m., you will come to the Clearview Mennonite Church and see dozens of horse-drawn buggies tied up in stables and at hitching posts around the church. It's quite a sight.

The difference between the east and west sides of the lake has been described as like "flipping channels between *Hee Haw* and *Lifestyles of the Rich and Famous*." Welcome to the St. Louis side, a road more traveled but still lots of fun. The Ozark website has plenty of information about the area: ozarkmissouri.com. The new-ish Community Bridge linking Lake Ozark and Sunrise Beach (the St. Louis side and the Kansas City side) has joined the two and made everything accessible to everyone. It was a "you can't get there from here" Ozark experience before the bridge was built.

US 54 through **Osage Beach** is, in a word, touristy. The path here is not only beaten, but also six lanes wide and heavy with traffic in the summer—the bumper-to-bumper gridlock type you came here to get away from. The road is filled to overflowing with craft shops, flea markets, bumper cars, and waterslides. A new expressway that bypasses Highway 54 is about 12 miles long and helps speed up the trip. There are plenty of good eating places, from fast-food chains to little places tucked in corners. You are on your own here.

If you have taken the route along the west side of the lake, you will begin to see the real Ozarks now. Missouri has surprisingly diverse wildlife, from the blind cave fish to the black bear, which still forages in the heavy woods. The pileated woodpecker (the size of a chicken, no kidding!) will certainly wake you up in the morning if it decides to peck on your shake shingles. The west side of the lake is still undiscovered except by Kansas City people, who have tried to keep it quiet. Here, great eating places abound and small shops hide off the beaten path.

The newest place in town is a favorite with the locals and still somewhat unknown by tourists. **Wok N Roll** (1359B Bagnell Dam Blvd.; 573-365-2090; woknroll1359.com) has Thai and Chinese food by Nok Knernschield (she's called Kok Noi, Thai for "Little Bird"), who was born in rural Thailand where she learned traditional Thai cooking in her family's restaurant. She went on to cook in some of the best dining establishments in Bangkok. Kok Noi has lived in this country for more than 30 years and understands American tastes, as well. She serves dishes that range from Chinese family food to more intense and complex Thai dishes. Of course, all the sauces are made by Kok Noi, and I can almost guarantee it will be the best Thai food you have ever had. Open Tues through Sat 11 a.m. to 7 p.m.

Highway 5 cuts like a razor slash through the hills between **Gravois Mills** and Laurie. There are some quiet, low-key places not to be missed. Locals recommend a couple in Gravois Mills. **Taboo Ice Cream & Grill**, for one, at 200 N. Main St. (573-207-5202). Then there are the spots for the party animals around the lake. One with a serious party reputation is **Big Dick's Halfway Inn** (halfway between Truman and Bagnell Dams), at 1038 Cup Tree Rd. It is not just drinking and partying here; there is a local sport called "minnow shooting" that involves swallowing live minnows while you're cheered on by fans of all ages. You can be the next shooter and even the kids can participate.

Just outside **Laurie** on Highway 5 is **St. Patrick's Catholic Church.** This unique church sits on acres of outdoor gardens that feature waterfalls, fountains, and a shrine dedicated to mothers, the **Shrine of Mary Mother of the Church.** You may add your mother's name to the list to be remembered in ongoing prayers. On summer Sundays, Mass is at 8:30 a.m. at the shrine, and casual dress is in the spirit of a Lake of the Ozarks vacation. The outdoor candlelight procession and Mass on Saturday at 8:30 p.m. at the shrine are beautiful and open to anyone. Times change in winter, so call (573) 374-MARY (6279) for a current schedule.

Slip into **Chances 'R'** (310 S. Main St.; 573-374-8770) for a quick bite at a little mom-and-pop place with great fried chicken. It is a local favorite hangout, and you may be the only one there that the waitress doesn't call by name. Chances R you will be back. It is open 7 a.m. to 9 p.m. every day but Tues, till 10 and 11 p.m. on Fri and Sat; a breakfast buffet is offered on Sun.

From the town of Laurie you can turn right onto Highway 135, which wanders back to **Stover** and Highway 52, over some genuine roller-coaster dips and beautiful, unpopulated Ozark country.

In the rolling Missouri foothills between Osage Beach and Camdenton lie 160 acres of vineyard. **Seven Springs Winery** (846 Winery Hills Estates, Linn Creek; 573-317-0100; sevenspringswinery.com) is less than a 10-minute drive from either town. Missouri wines and microbrews are served on the covered porch and patio area. There is a light menu of soups and sandwiches, cheese trays, and dipping oils for bread. The winery is open 11 a.m. to 7 p.m. daily.

Either way you circle the lake, east or west, you will end up in **Camdenton** at the intersection of Highway 5 and US 54. Continue west on US 54 and turn onto Highway D to **Ha Ha Tonka State Park.** High on a bluff overlooking an arm of the Lake of the Ozarks, poised over a cold, aqua-blue spring that bubbles out from under a limestone bluff, are the ruins of a stone "castle" with a story to tell. There is a European feel to the ruins; it's as if you have stumbled onto a Scottish stronghold here in the Missouri woods. The place was conceived in 1900 as a 60-room retreat for prominent Kansas City businessman Robert Snyder. But tragedy struck; Snyder was killed in an automobile accident in 1906 and construction halted. Later, the castle-like mansion was completed by Snyder's son, but in 1942 a fire set by a spark from one of the many stone fireplaces gutted the buildings. All that was left were the stone walls thrust up against the sky. Ha Ha Tonka is now a state park, although the mansion is still a ghostly ruins half hidden in the trees.

strangeas itseems

Native Americans valued caves for their shelter and storage capabilities. They would mark the location of caves by creating thong trees—forcing a sapling white oak to a horizontal position using green, forked limbs thrust into the earth. Throughout the Ozarks, these thong trees can still be seen.

The park is a classic example of karst topography, with caves and sinkholes, springs, natural bridges, and underground streams. (This typical southern Missouri geology is responsible for the many caves in the state.) There are nine nature trails here; explore on your own or check in with the park office (573-346-2986) for a naturalist-guided tour; programs are available year-round.

Missouri places second nationwide for the largest number of caves, but the state beats number-one Tennessee in the number of "show caves" that are developed for touring. The state records more than 5,000 caves. The southern half of Missouri—in the Ozarks region—is where most of the caves are because of the limestone deposits there. The complex of caves, underground streams, large springs, sinkholes, and natural bridges at Ha Ha Tonka State Park makes it one of the country's most important geologic sites.

Casa de Loco Winery (442 Riverbird Ln.; 573-693-1441; casadelocowinery.com) in Camdenton is more than a winery, it is also a beautiful inn about 5 miles out of town. It's a favorite place for weddings and reunions around here. The deck hangs over the bluff overlooking the Big Niangua River. You can enjoy float trips, wine, and a great view. Or you can just pop in for lunch or to taste some wine. The winery is open all year seven days a week: Sun through Fri 10 a.m. to 5 p.m., Sat till 6 p.m.

About halfway between Warsaw and Clinton on Highway 7 is the town of **Tightwad** (population 56). There's a UMB Bank in Tightwad, and the branch manager says that people from as far away as Florida have accounts there just to get the checks with "Tightwad" on them.

The city of **Clinton** (mile 264.6 on the KATY Trail) is every chamber of commerce's dream come true. It has one of the most active squares in the country, filled with more than 150 shops and services, and there is lots of parking. You can't miss the wonderful old courthouse and outdoor pavilion in the center of the square. The town has changed little since 1836, when it began as an outpost in the heart of the Golden Valley.

History buffs will find plenty of research material at the **Henry County Museum** (203 W. Franklin St.; 660-885-8414; henrycountymomuseum.org), just off the northwest corner of the square in Clinton. The building itself was owned by Anheuser-Busch from 1886 until Prohibition. Huge blocks of ice (often cut from the nearby lake) were used to chill the kegs in the cooling room. The second room contains a skylight and double doors leading to the old loading dock and courtyard. Quick dashes in horse-drawn wagons were necessary to transport the beer while still cool to the depot, where there was access to three railroads. The building houses the Courtenay Thomas room, commemorating the Clinton native who became an international operatic soprano.

Another don't-miss town is **Pleasant Hill,** at the intersection of Highway 7 and US 58. Way back in 1828 David Creek settled a piece of land and became the first recorded non-native settler in Cass County. A town grew here until the Civil War. The "border war" between Kansas and Missouri, which was waged long after the Civil War officially ended, decimated the population. The next big event was the coming of the railroad, when the town began to resurrect itself. Each year the town celebrates Pleasant Hill Railroad Days in September. The town has a cupola-design caboose on display here that was part of the Missouri Pacific Railroad. This captivating little town has much to offer. Let's start on First Street: At 113 First St. is the **5 and 10 Antiques** (816-987-0214), filled with boutique gifts and antiques as well as creations by local artisans. At 117 First is **Brown's Vintage & Variety** where Julie and Alice Brown have vintage toys to take you back in time.

One of the more unusual places in town is **The Knot Hole Woodcarving** at 118 First St. The gallery is filled with carvings for sale by many different carvers from around the Midwest. There are also seminars led by well-known carvers Joyce and Andy Anderson for people who want to sharpen (no pun intended) their skills at woodcarving. Call ahead for times at (816) 987-2214 or check out the website theknothole.net. Drop the guys off at 118 S. First St. for a quick game of pool at the **Pleasant Hill Pool Hall** (816-540-2004). It is said to be the oldest functioning pool hall west of the Mississippi. Owner Jeff Johnson calls it a hole-in-the-wall bar, but it isn't. It is almost always open and serves the best beer in town, he says. At 120 First St. is **R & S Mercantile,** where Rich and Sara Kitchel have a unique gift shop full of unusual and handmade things, and at 121 S. First St. is **American Dwelling,** where Eric and Sara Tangblade have a selection of locally made apparel and gifts. At 138 First St., Debbie Aiman operates **A Sweet Expression,** with custom candies and cookies, a good place to find a candy bouquet to send to a friend who is having a birthday. She has a website for that at asweetexpression.net, or call (816) 405-7704.

Now move on to Wyoming Street and look for 113 Wyoming and the **Big Creek Café** (816-987-0524) for some home cooking (and breakfast all day), then 115 Wyoming for the **Wyoming Street Wine Shop** (816-987-0228). Rob and Julia McBride have not only wines, but pizzas, paninis, and desserts to feed your soul and your belly. At 129 Wyoming is **Willow Boutique** (816-651-9286), with clothes, accessories, and gifts.

Pleasant Hill Thrift Store at 100 Veterans Pkwy. is always fun to poke around in. **Resto 101** is a full-service restoration shop at 101 N. Boardman St. where you bring in something really old and Jeff makes it look really new again. Call (816) 540-3443.

There is also the Pleasant Hill Golf Course and a year-round pool in town. You might also want to take advantage of the **Big Creek Country Music Show** (110 S. Lake; 816-524-6856 or 816-987-3919 on Sat; bigcreekcountry. com). The show has entertained thousands of people every Saturday night since 1982. Showtime is 7:30 p.m.

Cheese Country

Large dairy barns and silos built around the turn of the 20th century are still in use, and dairy cattle—Holsteins and Guernseys—graze alongside beef cattle. This is not the kind of background you would imagine for someone who made his living writing the very best sci-fi ever. Robert Heinlein was born in Butler, right up the road from Nevada. He was an aeronautical engineer and naval officer who wrote science-based fiction, not just sci-fi. Perhaps that is why his first book was named *Stranger in a Stange Land.*

The **Bushwhacker Museum** (212 W. Walnut; 417-667-9602; bushwhacker .org) is in the public library facility in **Nevada** (pronounced neh-VAY-duh) and is open May 5 to Oct 31, Tues through Sat 10 a.m. to 4 p.m. (closed July 4). Groups may call the museum to schedule special tours: $5 for adults, $2 for ages 12–17, and $1 for kids under 12.

This next place will be a talking point of your trip. **W. F. Norman** (214 N. Cedar; 417-667-5552; wfnorman.com) makes pressed-tin ceilings just like they have always been made. Tours of the factory allow you to watch the tin hauled up and dropped. You need earplugs, which are provided, to protect your ears from the crashing sounds. Other metal items are created here, but this is the most fascinating to watch. Call to make an appointment to visit.

Go east on US 54 to **El Dorado Springs** (da-RAY-do, this being a very non–Spanish speaking part of the country) as a shortcut to the Osceola area. This is a pretty little town complete with a nostalgic bandstand in the tree-shaded park at the center of town. It looks like something straight out of *The Music Man.* There's a band here every Friday and Saturday night and Sunday afternoon; a local band has played in the park for more than 100 years. The old spa town was once crowded with bathhouses and hotels, but the spa business ended long ago for most towns like this one. El Dorado Springs has done a great job of preserving itself anyway.

Hammons Black Walnut Emporium (2 Public Square; 800-872-6879; black-walnuts.com) in **Stockton** is the world's largest processor of black walnuts, and its retail store has been moved, enlarged, and improved ("like Starbucks, only better"). Not only can you get walnut brittle or chocolate-covered walnuts for your sweet tooth, or a nutty breakfast with black walnut pancake and waffle mix and a bottle of walnut syrup, but you can have gourmet ice cream, pastries, espresso, or a latte, or buy coffee beans (maybe a walnut-flavored coffee?) as well. Visit the website for recipes using black walnuts in not only cookies, fudge, and muffins, but everything from fish to, well, nuts.

This quaint little lake town only has 1,800 residents, and the peaceful lake is popular for sailing. Stockton is also home to **The Squeez Inn,** (404 RB Rd.; 417-276-6302), where you can get deliciously cheesy burgers and fries.

If you don't take the shortcut, you will continue down I-71 to **Lamar,** where history fans will find **Harry S Truman's Birthplace.** (No, remember, there is no period after the S, because the president didn't have a middle name—his folks just put an S in there.) It's a long way from this little house at

1009 Truman St. in Lamar to the big white one on Pennsylvania Avenue in our nation's capital. Hours are Mon through Sat 10 a.m. to 4 p.m. and Sun noon to 4 p.m. Call (417) 682-2279 or visit mostateparks.com/trumansite.htm.

trivia

Ground black walnut shell is a hard, chemically inert, nontoxic, and biodegradable abrasive. It makes up a large percentage of the nut and is a very useful product with a wide range of applications. Hammons began marketing this product more than 50 years ago and is now the world's leading supplier of black-walnut soft-grit abrasives.

In **Golden City** bicyclists know a place called **Cooky's** (529 Main; 417-537-4741), at the junction of Highways 126 and 37 south and east of Lamar. Out of season it's a small-town cafe on the south side of the main drag. During bike-riding season, though, Cooky's is the place to dream about when you are 300 miles out on the trail. Bikecentennial Inc., of Missoula, Montana, put Cooky's on the map—the TransAmerica Trail map, that is—and riders have flocked here ever since for some serious carbohydrate loading. It's not uncommon to watch a rider from Australia chow down on three or four pieces of Willie and Holly Stefan's terrific pies; you can be more moderate, if you like. You can get an affordable steak dinner here, too; the home-raised beef will keep you going down the trail whether you come by car or bike. Cooky's opens at 6 a.m. every day and closes at 2 p.m. on Mon, 8 p.m. Tues through Thurs, 9 p.m. Fri and Sat, and 8 p.m. Sun.

Jerry Overton, president of the Missouri Prairie Foundation, puts in a good word for **Golden Prairie,** designated a National Natural Landmark by the US Department of the Interior. It's not reclaimed prairie or replanted prairie—this is a virgin remnant of the thousands of acres of grassland that once covered the Midwest, important not only for the historic plants it contains, but also for the varieties of wildlife that inhabit it. Here you can still hear the sound of the prairie chicken. Listen for them exactly 3 miles west of Golden City on Highway 126 and exactly 2 miles south of Highway 26 on the first gravel road.

A roadside park just outside **Osceola** on Highway 82 West will show you what attracted both Native people and settlers to the area: the breathtaking view of the white bluffs where the Sac and Osage Rivers meet. Highway 82 also has a Sac River access point and boat ramp if you are hauling a boat to the Truman Reservoir.

The **Historic Commercial Hotel** (610 2nd St.; 319-939-8288) was built in 1868. It has been a hotel and a nursing home, but now it is the lap of luxury with themed rooms named after famous people who have slept there. Suites are named for Jesse and Frank James, the Younger Gang, Tom Mix, Sally Rand, and

President Truman. That's a pretty rowdy bunch—well, except for Harry S—if only walls could talk.

Highway 13 bypasses the town square but is home to **Osceola Cheese Shop** and **Ewe's in the Country** (3700 NE Hwy. 13; 417-646-2396; osceolacheese.com). Mike and Marcia Bloom own both shops, which share the building. The Blooms buy the cheese in bulk and smoke and flavor it in the former cheese factory; they have been at this same location for more than 50 years. They now offer more than 275 varieties of cheese, mostly from Missouri, with each type cut for sampling. Try the jalapeño (extra hot), instant pizza, or chocolate (yes!) cheese. Pick up a catalog; they ship cheese anywhere in the world—except from Apr to Sept, when it might arrive as hot cheese sauce. Hours are variable depending on the season: Mon through Thurs 8 a.m. to 7 p.m. and Fri through Sun 8 a.m. to 8 p.m.

Places to Stay in Central Missouri

KANSAS CITY

Hotel Phillips
(downtown KC)
106 W. 12th St.
(844) 208-5523
hotelphillips.com
Moderate

InterContinental Hotel
(on the Country Club Plaza)
401 Ward Pkwy.
(816) 756-1500
kansascityic.com
Expensive

Raphael Hotel and Restaurant Country Club
Plaza 325 Ward Pkwy.
(816) 756-3800
Moderate

INDEPENDENCE

Truman Inn (Best Western)
4048 S. Lynn Ct. Dr.
(816) 254-0100
Inexpensive

BOONVILLE

Days Inn
2401 Pioneer
(660) 672-4310
daysinn.com
Inexpensive

Holiday Inn
2419 Mid America
Industrial Dr.
(660) 882-6882
Inexpensive

JEFFERSON CITY

Capitol Plaza Hotel
415 W. McCarty St.

capitolplazajeffersoncity.com
Inexpensive

Holiday Inn Express
1716 Jefferson St.
(573) 634-4040
Inexpensive

SEDALIA

Best Western State Fair Motor Inn
3120 S. Limit 65 Hwy.
(660) 826-6100
Inexpensive

Bothwell Kensington
103 E. 4th St.
(660) 826-5588
Inexpensive

WARRENSBURG

Days Inn
204 E. Cleveland St.
(660) 429-2400
Inexpensive

OSAGE BEACH

Tan-Tar-A Resort and Golf Course
494 Tantara Dr.
(573) 348-8594

tan-tar-a.com
Moderate

LAKE OZARK

Lodge of the Four Seasons
(spa and golf course)
(573) 365-3000
fourseasons.com
Moderate

WHEATLAND LAKE POMME DE TERRE

Sunflower Resort
(RV sites available)
22792 Sunflower Dr. (call, do not rely on GPS)
(417) 282-6235
pommedeterreresort.com
Inexpensive

Places to Eat in Central Missouri

KANSAS CITY

Corvino Supper Club & Tasting Room

1830 Walnut
(816) 832-4564
Moderate

RAYTOWN

Harp BBQ
6633 Raytown Rd.
(816) 886-6208
Inexpensive

SUNRISE BEACH

Sunrise Cantina
264 Sunset Hills
(573) 374-8185
Moderate

Shrimp Daddy's
16218 Sunset Blvd.
(573) 374-7800
Moderate

JEFFERSON CITY

Das Stein Haus
1436 S. Ridge Dr.
(behind the Ramada Inn)
(573) 634-3869
dassteinhaus.com
Inexpensive

Madison's Cafe
216 Madison St.

(across from parking garage)
(573) 634-2988
madisonscafe.com
Inexpensive

BELTON

Oden's Family Barbecue
1302 N. Scott
(816) 322-3072
Inexpensive

GRAVOIS MILLS

Vinny's Cafe and Lounge
751 N. Main (Highway 5)
(573) 374-9982
vinnyscafe.net
Inexpensive

Laurie Val's
610 N. Main (Highway 5)
(573) 374-0922
Inexpensive

LAMAR

Lamarti's Truck Stop
54 SE 1 Ln.
(junction Highways 71 and 160)
(417) 682–6034
Inexpensive

FINDING HELPFUL VISITOR INFORMATION

Arrow Rock
arrowrock.org
(660) 837–3231

Independence
visitindependence.com
(800) 748–7328

Jefferson City
visitjeffersoncity.com
(800) 769-4183 or (573) 632–2820

Kansas City
visitkc.com
(800) 767-7700 or (816) 691–3800

Lake of the Ozarks
funlake.com
(573) 348-1599 or (800) 386-5253

Northwest Missouri

It does get cold in northwest Missouri—make no mistake—especially near the northernmost border, where the plains are chilled by every stiff wind howling down from the frigid north. Alberta Clipper, Siberian Express—whatever you call it, Missouri catches hell in the winter, bringing to mind that old joke: "There's nothing between here and the North Pole but two bobwire fences, and one o' them's down." In 1989 all records were broken—along with that fence—when the nighttime temperature bottomed out at −23 degrees Fahrenheit (windchill made that −60 degrees). It also gets hot in Missouri; August days can soar over the 100-degree mark.

But at its temperate best, Jesse James country is a great place to visit that's filled with great hideouts. (James knew them all. It seems that, like George Washington, Jesse James slept almost everywhere—in northwest Missouri, anyway.)

Not that that's all there is to this section of the state; we'd hate to say we're living in the past on the rather unsavory reputation of our own "Robbing" Hood. There is a national wildlife refuge on the Central Flyway that is absolutely essential to migrating waterfowl. There is Excelsior Springs, where folks

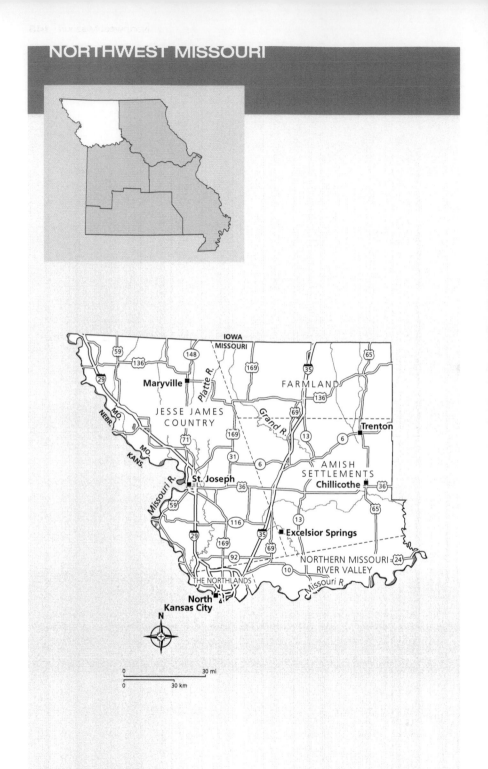

once came to take the waters and where Harry S Truman read that he had lost the presidential election to Thomas Dewey—at least according to the *Chicago Daily Tribune.*

The Northlands

Just across the Missouri River from the town with a similar name is **North Kansas City.** This is a separate city, with a healthy industrial tax base and a coordinated downtown shopping area complete with plazas, fountains, and wide streets. "Northtown" has its own mayor, its own police department, and its own quirky charm. There are cafes and delis and bakeries; North Kansas Citians know how to eat. Northtown has a website at nkc.org, and the North Kansas City High School Hornets (*Go Hornets!*) still attract crowds to football games.

As long as you are in Northtown, visit **_Furniture Solutions!_** (7311 N. Oak Trafficway, Gladstone; 816-471-0092). Jeff Porter focuses on furniture restoration, a nearly lost art, but he also makes some incredible modern art, which you can see in his small showroom. Open Tues through Sat.

Restless Spirits (109 E. 18th Ave.; 816-492-6868; restlessspiritsdistilling. com) calls itself an Irish American distillery because the Shannon family came from Ireland in 1867 during the great famine and settled in the Kansas City area. The Irish pride shows in the Sons of Erin whiskey and Pádraig's Rebellion Poitin, but a personal fave is the Irish Cream Bottled Cocktail. And fair play to ya when you be getting' the **Missouri Spirits Expedition** stamp. Hours are Tues through Thurs 2 to 7 p.m. and Fri and Sat till 9 p.m.

Since you are north of the Missouri River, swing by the **_TWA Museum_** at the Downtown Airport at 10 NW Richards Rd. (816-234-1011 twamuseum.org). If you flew when flying was glamorous and fun, then this will be a nostalgic visit. See the planes that flew when the Connie, a four-engine prop, was the queen of the fleet. Enter the Boeing 707, when uniforms became sexy and flight attendants were called "hostesses" and it was the see-the-world job of a lifetime I was lucky enough to have done so for 10 years. I flew on Air Force II—a TWA 707—when Hubert Humphrey was VP. MATS (Military Air Transport Service) to Vietnam was also part of the airline's history and mine as well, and celebs galore—before they all had private jets.

Hayes Hamburgers (2502 NE Vivion Rd. at Antioch Rd.) in suburban Kansas City North serves the kind of hamburgers that you could order before "fast food" was invented. This is the place to go for a burger after a North Kansas City High School Hornets football game (*Go Hornets!*—Are you sensing an alum in here?) or late at night on a date you don't want to end. The hamburgers are small (like sliders) and made of fresh chopped meat rolled into a ball and mashed onto the grill with a handful of onions. The aroma of onions and hamburger grilling together sparks an appetite. People buy them by the bag and have been known to eat a dozen. The chili is all-American good, too. The diner is open 6 a.m. to 10 p.m. every day. Thank goodness! Because you never know when you will need a hamburger.

Take the I-435 exit north off I-35 and keep an eye out for Highway 152. A right turn will take you to **Hodge Park** (9598 NE Reinking Rd., north off Hwy. 152), a fine place to get away from the "two Ps": progress and people. Those big, hairy critters you spot as you enter the park are American bison; the Kansas City Zoo maintains a small herd here, where once there were thousands. Elk and deer share the enclosure; you may be able to get "up close and personal" with some of the Midwest's largest indigenous animals. If human history is more your thing, park your car in the lot and keep walking. **Shoal Creek** is a restored frontier town at Hodge Park, full of historic buildings moved here by the Kansas City Parks and Recreation Department. The tiny, two-story jail built of monolithic limestone blocks (how did they lift those things?) came from nearby Missouri City. What a place for a lockup! Local ne'er-do-wells slept off Saturday-night festivities here some 100-plus years ago. Other buildings include square-hewn log cabins, a one-room schoolhouse, a barn, a replica of an old mill complete with mill wheel and race, and some pretty fine houses for the gentry. Stop by during one of the living-history weekends for a re-creation of frontier life; you'll feel as if you've stepped back to the 19th century. Fine nature trails lead into the woods from Shoal Creek. The park is open 5 a.m. to midnight every day.

Do you want to have some real fun now? Well, there is a most unusual place in Kansas City North to do just that if you are up to trying something different. **Jaegers Subsurface Paintball,** deep in the caves at 9300 NE Underground Dr. (816-452-6600; jaegers.com), is the place to find. For $35, manager

TOP RECOMMENDATIONS IN NORTHWEST MISSOURI

Church of St. Luke, the Beloved Physician	Inn on Crescent Lake
	Jamesport
Elms Hotel	
	Martha Lafite Thompson Nature Sanctuary
Hall of Waters	
Hayes Hamburgers	

TOP ANNUAL EVENTS IN
NORTHWEST MISSOURI

MAY
The Gatsby Festival
Excelsior Springs
(816) 630-0750
epsi.net/gatsby/welcome.htm

Morel Mushroom Festival
Richmond
Parade, food and craft booths, model
train show, carnival
(816) 776-5304 or (816) 776-5306
cofcommerce.home.mchsi.com/festival.
html

SEPTEMBER
Waterfest
Excelsior Springs
Second Sat in Sept; arts, crafts, and
food booths, plus games, music, and
rides
(816) 630-6161

DECEMBER
Christmas Festival
Jamesport
jamesportmissouri.org

J. J. Johnson will give you a safety briefing, helmet and goggles, and a semiautomatic weapon with 130 rounds of ammunition—i.e., paintballs.

The caves are spooky—dark stone walls and dirt floors—and littered with washing machines, wire spools, and a beat-up delivery van to hide behind or trip over. Old paintball pellets and shards of exploded ones are debris on the floor. Fluorescent lights illuminate parts of the cave; other parts are dark. The color of your helmet designates the team you belong to. You are the hunter—and the hunted—on a field that consists of the cave's labyrinthine stone passages and lots of sand.

"Paintball . . . may be an inherently dangerous activity that can result in loss of life, eyesight, or hearing," says the waiver you sign before entering the field, and although harmless, those little pellets *hurt* when you are hit. So it is easy to follow the next rule: When hit, you raise your gun above your head and yell "I'm hit!" and run off the field while the referee counts to 10. Aficionados of the game find the rapid-fire shooting under pressure and the thrill of catching the enemy unaware exciting and exhilarating (along with the satisfaction of hitting a moving target). Jaegers is just off I-435 near Worlds of Fun. Take I-435 to the Highway 210 exit. Turn right at Randolph Road and go south to Underground Drive.

Northern Missouri River Valley

Head east back on Highway 152 and you'll come to historic **Liberty.** The downtown square has been restored to Civil War–era glory, with authentic paint colors and fancy trim—most of it original. There are several great eating spots, recommended by the locals, here on the square or close by.

Huey's Café (816-415-4727) has a deli menu, a salad menu, a lunch menu, and some killer desserts. Don't see what you want there? Hard to believe, but right on the menu it says "Request? Just ask." Hours are Mon through Sat 7 a.m. to 2:30 p.m. At 9 W. Franklin St. is *Anna Marie's Teas* (816-792-8777; annateashop.com), specializing in loose-leaf herbal and organic teas, as well as the classics and tea ware. Open Tues through Sat 10 a.m. to 5 p.m. Try *Ginger Sue's* at 12 W. Kansas (816-407-7707) for a hearty brunch. This is a popular place with locals. Open 6:30 a.m. to 2:30 p.m. daily.

Two things that go together and are magnets to some is coffee and books. *Holy Grounds Coffee & Book Shoppe* is a new spot for both in the St. James Cathedral building at 342 N. Water St.

Belvoir Winery & Inn is in the old Odd Fellows Home at 1325 Odd Fellows Rd. Let's begin with the old building, reputed to be haunted by deceased Odd Fellows. Actual paranormal investigators will give you the gear you need to detect ghostly activity in the rooms and hallways. Or you can attend a Murder Mystery Dinner; for $52 you will enjoy dinner, two drinks (and an open bar), and the show. Order tickets at belvoirwinery.com. On to the real reason for finding the winery—wine—which is good and plentiful. These wines are all made with Missouri grapes, bred to withstand the temperatures of the state. The Norton is the state grape, but there is also the Concord, St. Vincent, Chambourcin, and Catawba red wine grapes, while the Seyval, Traminelle, and Vignole grapes are grown for the white wines. Check out the tiny museum and browse the original art in other parts of the big brick mansion. The place is also a B&B/inn, with sweeping views . . . and perhaps a resident ghost. Call (816) 200-1811 for reservations or information.

There are three museums in downtown Liberty, either on the square or within easy walking distance, among them the *Jesse James Bank Museum Historic Site* (103 N. Water St.; 816-781-4458) and the *Historic Liberty Jail* (216 N. Main St.; 816-781-3188). The jail provides exhibits, audiovisual presentations, and art to help visitors understand the significant events that took place there. It is sponsored by the Church of Jesus Christ of Latter-day Saints. Hours are daily from 9 a.m. to 9 p.m. The Jesse James Bank Museum Historic Site was where the first successful daylight peacetime bank robbery in the nation took place in 1866. Although the robbers were never caught, the James gang took the blame. The bank is still the same as it was then. For more information or to schedule a tour, call (816) 736-8510. Hours are Mon through Sat 10 a.m. to 4 p.m.

The town is chock-full of antiques and craft shops, so plan on browsing. You can check out the website at ci.liberty.mo.us.

A block east of the square at 7 N. Missouri St., you'll find **Sorella's Deli** (816-781-1200), which has paninis, soups and salads, spreads, sauces, meatballs, and take-and-bake lasagna. Share a huge oatmeal-raisin cookie.

Taylor Family Orchard is tucked into the northern edge of the downtown area, an unexpected delight at 1 Crawford Ln. (816-262-8613), on a dead-end street off Gallatin. Owner Brandon Taylor is rightly proud of the family's accomplishment, and you'll be sure to enjoy your visit, as well as some mouth-watering fresh fruit in season. It's just below one of the city water towers and surrounded by neighborhoods, but unexpectedly secluded and country-feeling. There's a big red barnlike building overlooking the ranks of trees, where sales and events take place. It's a great spot for a photo shoot, as well. Open by appointment on Thurs, Sat, and Sun 10 a.m. to 5 p.m.

William Jewell College is the alma mater of internationally known writer Patti DeLano (brother in California, cousins in New York, and friends in most states and Canada defines "internationally known" for a writer from Missouri). But seriously, the college often hosts celebrity events open to the public. Luciano Pavarotti made his international recital debut at William Jewell College. New York City Ballet's Patricia McBride danced here, and violinist Itzhak Perlman played here. **Jewell's Stocksdale Art Gallery** space is located on the second floor of Brown Hall. The college campus is also the location of one of the most interesting little cemeteries around. The college was founded before the Civil War and used as a military hospital during the war. The cemetery has tombstones dating from the 1800s. Walking around there, you can see the dates of flu epidemics and wars and discover husbands with several wives, and those wives buried with their newborns. It is a lesson in history for a sunny afternoon.

The **Martha Lafite Thompson Nature Sanctuary** (816-781-8598; naturesanctuary.com) offers a wonderful place to watch wildlife, take a naturalist-guided walk, or enjoy special programs—from making your own bird feeder to learning about the constellations on a night hike. More than 600 species of plants and many fish, reptiles, amphibians, and mammals make their homes here, and more than 160 species of birds have been sighted. Worn out? Take in the lovely new sanctuary building with its displays of indigenous plants, watch snapping turtles and catfish in the creek-habitat aquarium, or enjoy one of the sanctuary's many programs. Relax on the spacious deck in redwood Adirondack chairs, or buy a book, a bird feeder, or birdcall to take home. Watch for the sanctuary sign at 407 N. La Frenz Rd.

North Water Street is in the Lightburne Historic District and contains a diverse collection of structures built during the late 19th century, such as Lightburne Hall, an elaborate 1852 mansion, and the 1898 Simmons house. These are all private homes.

Leave Liberty via Highway H, and you'll find *The Red Apron* at 1090 E. CR H. It has fun collectibles and home decor, a few vintage books, toys, and even a bit of original art. The shop is only open on the third Fri and Sat of the month, so mark your calendars. Hours are 9 a.m. to 5 p.m. both days.

I-35 South from Liberty will take you to the little town of *Claycomo,* known mostly for the giant Ford Motor Plant that resides there. Of course, if there is a Ford plant in town, then there must be somewhere that serves home cookin' to the people going to or coming off the 24/7 shifts there. That place would be *Nelle Belle's Diner* (150 NE Hwy 69; 816-452-9786). Owner Dixie Edwards knows what to cook for hungry people. Her specials are on the wall, and you can get an early start there because the hours are 6 a.m. to 2 p.m. Mon through Fri, until 1 p.m. on Sat.

howmanytons ofsiltayear?

As the Missouri River cut through mountains and prairie, it gathered huge quantities of silt and sand. It earned its nicknames—the "Muddy Mo" and the "Big Muddy"—because it used to dump about 200 million tons of silt a year into the Mississippi River.

Heading North from Kansas City? There's a new BBQ restaurant near MCI Airport called *Scott's Kitchen BBQ,* at Hangar 29 (11920 N. Ambassador Dr.; 816-270-0505; scottskitchenandcatering.com). It's a hole in the wall, hidden away in the hangar, but oh so worth the search if you love smoky meat and all the fixins—the food has won numerous awards and competitions. Hours are Mon through Fri 7 a.m. to 6:30 p.m.

Highway 210 east from downtown NKC runs through the tiny river towns of Missouri City, Orrick, and Camden, dotted along the Missouri River. But hang on there, back up . . . take Highway 291 toward Liberty to find the turnoff for Old Highway 210, almost abandoned after the new highway was built. A vast automotive junkyard is to your right just after turning off Highway 291, but look to the left to find the *Fish Market in Liberty,* a huge favorite of locals. It really was a fish market before it closed, but like the Phoenix it rose again as a popular seafood venue. The shrimp chowder and crayfish are both seasonal, but you can get fish-and-chips, smoked or fried catfish fillets, or even alligator, and some of the best coleslaw ever. Try a Cajun remoulade. Find the Fish Market—and its photo-op shark—at 1120 Old Hwy. 210, (816-781-8705). Hours are Sun and Tues through Thurs 11 a.m. to 8 p.m. and Fri and Sat till 9 p.m.

Watch for the turnoff going east on Old Hwy 210; a left turn will take you back to the new highway and the rest of the small towns along the river road, but take it slow. The views are spectacular along the Missouri River, especially from the observation stop just this side of Missouri City. At your back is **Nebo Hill,** an important site for pre-contact Natives and the perfect place for ceremonies and camps; the site was in use for hundreds of years. After a rain, artifact aficionados are out in force on weekends.

Continuing east on Highway 210 will take you to **Cooley Lake** and **Cooley Lake River Access** (mdc.mo.gov/discover-nature/places/cooley-lake-conservation-area), where you may see thousands of resident and migrating birds, including pelicans and trumpeter swans, once almost extinct in this country, and bald eagles that follow the crowds, the eagles also making a comeback from near-extinction. Keep an eye open and you may see a flatboat pushing its heavy load against the current just as Mark Twain did. Wave and the captain may toot the horn at you. The lake was part of the nearby Missouri River until it changed course and abandoned the oxbow. Since it is no longer fed by the river, water levels fluctuate in dry or rainy years. Lots of fish, turtles, and muskrats make their homes here.

The tall loess bluffs you see to the north are also part of the conservation area. Hop onto Highway N and turn on the second gravel road to wind up the bluffs between oak/hickory forests. Keep going and you'll find an observation tower with truly spectacular views. It's a great place to star-watch as well, maybe even catch a meteor shower on a clear night.

heatherlywar

The *"Heatherly War"* of *1836* made it into the history books. Some sources list this as an Indian war; in fact, it was a family of white outlaws who killed their neighbors and laid the blame at the feet of the Iowa Natives. Several companies from Clay and Ray Counties were dispatched to investigate and/or quell a supposed uprising. Ma Heatherly instigated the murders that were carried out by her brood of mixed-blood offspring.

Farther on Highway 210 is the town of **Orrick,** hard by the Missouri River, and there you can find Missouri's greatest tenderloin sandwich. This is delta land from the Big Muddy Mo. The place to find that tenderloin is **Jayder's** in beautiful downtown Orrick (109 Front St.; 816-770-3878). You will have a memorable meal in this old storefront. They feature a terrific walleye dinner as well as catfish on Friday—or hold off until Saturday for prime rib—whatever you choose, top off your meal with homemade blackberry or peach cobbler. The breakfast menu features the Farmer's Special—enough food to keep any farmer going all day for the reasonable price of $5.45. Open Tues through Sat 11 a.m. to 8 p.m.

Adrian's Pioneer Kitchen (14711 Hwy. 13; 816-853-6066) is where you can buy high-quality baked goods—the chocolate cake is killer. It has home-made cookies, pies, and wonderful cinnamon rolls. It is only open on Fri and Sat, so be sure to time your visit accordingly.

About 35 miles east of Kansas City, the small town of *Camden* has a little surprise for you. *Elements* (7851 Southport Dr.; 816-496-0165; elementsdining. com) is a destination restaurant—the kind of place you take a secret love for a quiet dinner far from the city. It has the feel of an exclusive urban restaurant, but without the crowds and hustle and waiting in line. Take a special friend there for an unexpected surprise that will keep them guessing the whole drive. Entrees begin at $18, but the four-course meals that make this restaurant special are $30 to $46 and worth every romantic penny. Reservations are required.

Amish Settlements

For a visit to a very special small town, spend some time in *Chillicothe.* Don't pass it by. (It has a website at chillicothemo.com.) Chillicothe is also known as the *Home of Sliced Bread.* A plaque notes the spot where bread was first sliced by machine on July 7, 1928. In two weeks, the bakery's bread sales increased by 2,000 percent. There's also a *Home of Sliced Bread* mural at Webster and Washington Streets.

The Parlor Bakery & Café, tucked away inside a plain white storefront at 1007 Bryan St. (660-646-3333), is the place to go if you are looking for some warm, fresh-from-the-oven treats. The just-like-mama-made apple and cherry pies are the favorites, but how about a Cow Pattie for breakfast? It's a delightful Danish sweet roll, albeit with a yucky name. Hours are Tues through Fri 6:30 a.m. to 1:30 p.m.

There are actually plenty of places to eat in Chillicothe—you don't have to settle for fast food. Check out *Cool Beans Coffee House* (701 Webster St.; 660-973-9525); *Corporal Blue 's Smoothie Shack* (315 Washington St.); *The Sip,* a wine bar with dine in and take-out at 304 Park Ln.; or *Murray's Family Buffet* (719 S. Washington St.). There, that ought to keep you busy and well fed.

North on US 65 is the town of *Trenton.* Don't mistake *Trenton Cemetery Prairie* for a neglected eyesore, with its rough grasses obscuring some of the old tombstones. Established in 1830, its protected status as a cemetery happily resulted in one of the few precious parcels of native prairie remaining in the state. Today it is maintained by the Missouri Conservation Department. Preservation is especially crucial; prairie north of the Missouri River is scarce.

"Real World" Experience

It was a warm and wet November day, the color gray and dismal. Yellow leaves had begun to stick to the raindrops and fall with them, cluttering the streets with mats of browning vegetation. We were looking for a day trip from Kansas City and chose Jamesport. Saturday is a busy day in this Amish community. Local residents were hurrying by in their horse-drawn carriages—wooden boxes with tiny windows in the back—headed for the nearby bulk food stores.

Books give only the minimum information about the Amish, the strictest branch of the Mennonite Church. The founder, Jacob Amman, was a Swiss religious reformer who laid the foundation for the difficult lives the Amish lead. It is strange to see the farmhouses sitting unattached to the life-giving power poles we are so accustomed to seeing in neat rows down the roadway. Forbidden modern conveniences, the Amish live in a sunrise-to-sunset world. The absence of television antennae or satellite dishes transports the little farms' appearances back to simpler times. The people shun vanity. Their clothes are black and fastened with straight pins—they are forbidden the vainglory of buttons—and their hair is hidden under bonnets and hats. They will not allow themselves to be photographed.

We bought handmade quilts and hand-loomed rugs. We drove away in our fast car, back to our modern lives, stocked with every possible convenience, from zippers to microwave ovens. So why do the women of the Amish community have the time to quilt by the light of a kerosene lamp while we are so busy we barely have time to sew on a lost button? Ah, vanity. It is such a time-consuming sin.

These patchwork remnants produce the seeds adapted to the northern Missouri climate that are essential to reestablishing prairie ecosystems.

This is an area of oddities; what you see may not be what you get. ***Riverside Country Club*** (660-359-6004), Trenton's golf course, has tree stumps carved into life-size animals around the fairways. (If you hit a birdie or an eagle around here, it may be a wooden one.) Former greenskeeper Don McNabb was an artist with a chainsaw and salted the 9-hole course with bears and other critters. The club is open for golf to anyone for the cost of a greens fee (and cart rental, if you wish), but nongolfers are welcome to check out the carvings.

Jamesport is a different world. It is the largest Mennonite settlement in Missouri and home to the most orthodox "horse-and-buggy" Mennonites. Here the Amish wear black, fasten clothes with pins, and allow no electricity in their homes. Don't ask the Amish to pose for pictures, though; it's against their beliefs.

There are lots of shops in the area, so you can, and should, pick up a map of Jamesport. Now, with map in hand, let's tour the town. Remember, just about everything in town is closed on Thursday and Sunday. You can begin and end where Highway 6 meets Highway F and leads into the western part of downtown. ***Anna's Bake Shop*** (660-684-6810) off Highway F in Jamesport would be a good place to start, with fresh-baked doughnuts, pies, breads, and cinnamon rolls. It opens at 8 a.m., so you can get an early start, and stays open until 6 p.m. (closed Christmas until February).

Still in the city square just past the four-way stop at 115 E. Aulbury Grove is ***Downhome Collectibles*** (660-684-6526; jamesportmo.com), specializing in oak furniture and woodcraft. It's open Mon through Sat 9 a.m. until 5 p.m. The Mennonite-owned ***Gingerich Dutch Pantry and Bakery*** (660-684-6212; gingerichdutchpantry.com) is right at the four-way in Jamesport and has real Amish-style meals with lots of wonderful homemade food and baked goods. It is open Mon through Sat 6 a.m. to 9 p.m.

Now let's get out of town a bit. The roads here are described as "gravel roads," but gravel would be a big improvement. You won't need an all-terrain vehicle to negotiate them, but driving slowly is definitely in order unless you want to disappear into a pothole, never to be seen again. The horse and buggies pack down a couple of very strong little paths in the center of the road, but the rest of the road is pretty much shot. It makes passing another car going the other way a bit of an adventure, and the buggies, understandably, won't leave the path under any circumstances. But aside from a bit of horse poop on your tires, you will emerge undamaged if you go slowly. Remember, most of these shops are closed on Thursday and Sunday and have no telephones or electric lights.

Kerosene lamps light the ***H & M Country Store*** (660-684-6108), just south of Jamesport. It's a good place to stock your kitchen. You'll find bulk groceries at great prices (wonderful high-gluten flour for your bread machine), dried fruit, beans, homemade mixes for just about anything you want (biscuits, pancakes, muffins), and spices and herbs by the wall-full. You want noodles? Every kind you can imagine is here. You can buy fresh produce and brown eggs, too.

To find a nice selection of hand-quilted pieces, venture out of town east on Highway F and 1 mile south on Highway U for ***Shearwood Quilts and Fabrics*** (204 S. Broadway; 660-684-6121; quiltsnfabricstore.com), which has a large selection of handmade quilts, rugs, and baskets. It has a bed piled high with beautiful quilts; dig through until you find the one you can't live without. The shop offers embroidery supplies and classes, as well. It is open Mon through Sat 10 a.m. to 5 p.m.

South of town on Highway 190 is the ***Rolling Hills Store,*** offering sturdy dry goods at excellent prices and lots of natural-fiber fabrics, plus boots and shoes.

You can stay at the **Country Colonial Bed and Breakfast** (106 E. Main; 660-684-6711 or 800-579-9248) and allow hosts Myrick and Nina den Hartog to tell you a little bit about the area. After shopping, you can return to this early 20th-century home and enjoy playing the baby grand piano, and when night falls again snuggle back into the featherbed. You will awaken to the aroma of a large country breakfast being prepared, and if the weather is fine, it will be served in the flower garden. Ladies, you can have a free facial, sigh, and you can even take a sunset or moonlight carriage ride for $25 and see Jamesport Amish-style. There are murder mystery weekends, too, if you want to play.

So many places to see, so little time! If you leave town the way you came in, you can stop at the **Country Cupboard Restaurant** (1011 Old Hwy. 6; 660-684-6597), in downtown Jamesport. There's always a daily special and homemade pies and breads—well, actually, everything is homemade, hometown cooking. Open Tues through Sun 6:30 a.m. to 9 p.m.

The territory was initially inhabited by Sacs, Foxes, Pottawatomies, and Musquakies. The Treaty of 1837 removed the Sac and Fox Nation of Missouri into Kansas. Check out the **Rotary Jail** (rotaryjail.com), a brick hexagonal building. Cells are pie-shaped around a central core with a sanitary plumbing system, which was considered a luxury at that time. The cell block could be rotated by a single man hand-turning a crank that connected to gears beneath the structure, which rotated the entire cell block. The structure was supported by a ball bearing surface to allow for smooth rotation. Now a museum, you can see this architectural marvel at 310 W. Jackson St.

Morrel Ranch (22782 Hwy. DD; 660-334-0507; morrellranch.com) is a gorgeous luxury lodge in the country with beautiful views. There are cozy fire pits, and horses as well as baby llamas to feed. Located 70 miles northeast of Kansas City, Morrell Ranch is a hidden retreat. Stay in the lodge or rent individual cabins that peer out over two lakes. Morrell Ranch also offers campgrounds so travelers can enjoy the 600 acres of trails and lakes from their RV or tent.

The Mormons settled in western Daviess County in the 1830s. Just north and west of Gallatin (take Highway 13 north and turn west onto Highway P) is the historic **Adam-Ondi-Ahman Shrine,** believed by Mormons to be the place where Christ will return. Northwest Missouri is important historically to the Mormon people; there were once thousands of them here. The majority were forced out during the Mormon Wars, when the state militia was ordered to drive them out of Missouri. The town of **Far West,** now no more than a historical marker, comprised 5,000 souls, all exterminated or driven from their homes. Many died during a forced march in this land of religious freedom. The marker is off Highway 13, west on Highway HH and north on Highway D, near Shoal Creek (just northwest of Kingston).

Ever wonder where retail giant J. C. Penney got his start? No, not New York, or even Chicago. It was right here in **Hamilton** in 1895 that he got his first job at Hale's Department Store. By the time he returned to Hamilton to buy his old employer's place of business in 1924, it was number 500 in his chain of stores. His company motto was "Honor, confidence, service, and cooperation"—no wonder he did so well.

The **J.C. Penney Memorial Library and Museum** (816-583-2168), uptown on Davis Street in Hamilton, is open Tues through Sat 10 a.m. to 5 p.m. You'll love the displays of early merchandise—makes you wonder who wore the stuff. The Penney farm cottage has also been restored.

Even cattlemen like this area's history. J. C. Penney once raised great herds of Angus, and at the Penney farm there is a monument—a big monument—to Penney's prize bull.

Jesse James Country

Take the Business 69 exit to **Excelsior Springs.** Once a magnet for people who wished to "take the waters," this old spa town has enough moxie to try for a comeback. The health-spa ship was scuttled in the 1950s when an article in the *Saturday Evening Post* declared mineral waters an ineffective form of treatment; the demise was clinched when Missouri passed a bill prohibiting advertising by doctors. So now we enjoy the waters—and the baths and massages—for the lovely, hedonistic fun of it. The town was founded in 1880 for the waters. Even the Native Americans living here valued the healing properties.

Visit the **Hall of Waters** (201 E. Broadway; 816-630-0750; cityofesmo.com), the world's longest mineral-water bar, and sample some of the waters that attracted thousands near the turn of the 20th century. There are more naturally occurring types of mineral waters here than anyplace else on earth except the German city of Baden-Baden, which ties Excelsior Springs. The lovely art deco–style building, built in 1937 as "the finest and most complete health resort structure in the US," is a fine example of a WPA project begun during the Great Depression.

trivia

Frank and Jesse James's dad was a preacher at the Pisgah Baptist Church in Excelsior Springs. They moved to the farm in 1843.

Slightly Off Broadway at 114 Marietta St. (slightly off Broadway, look at the street signs), in the old Methodist church, is the home of the community theater here. For ticket information call 816–637-ESCT (3728). Who would have thought a smallish town like this would have two theater groups? The other theater? You'll love the

Paradise Playhouse, too, for dinner, theater, live music, dining, and events. Find it at 101 Spring St.

If you miss old-fashioned diners with 10 stools and 3 booths, and like old-fashioned burgers, don't miss **Ray's Diner** (231 E. Broadway; 816-637-3432). The hash browns are killer good, and the secret chili recipe (passed down from previous owners and still top secret) is a favorite with locals. It's the kind of small-town diner where men hang out for coffee every morning at 6 a.m. to straighten out the world situation. Ray's is open until 2 p.m. every day but Sunday.

The **Old Bank Museum** (101 E. Broadway; 816-630-3712), in a former bank building, circa 1906, and itself an interesting architectural achievement, preserves spa-town history. Check out the dentist's office, and thank your lucky stars you live in the present. Look up to find a pair of murals; they're wonderful copies of Jean-François Millet's *The Gleaners* and *The Angelus,* which hang in museums in France. The amazing copies were painted by a Hungarian count, Edmond de Szaak. The museum's murals were painted more than 100 years ago and are local treasures. The museum also has two of de Szaak's own landscapes. He returned in 1937 and did some touch-ups on them. You can buy postcards, homemade lye soap, or a museum membership; you may find the Women's Auxiliary of the museum quilting or weaving rag rugs when you visit on a Wednesday. The chamber of commerce is here, too.

Ventana Gourmet Grill (117 W. Broadway; 816-630-8600) offers casual upscale dining. In fact, the chef was recently named greater KC's Chef of the Year. Grilled mahimahi; chicken smothered in mushrooms, bacon, and yellow onions served over mashed potatoes; and salmon with rosemary mashed potatoes and zucchini are all on the menu. Friday and Saturday features the juiciest, most delicious prime rib ever. Hours are Mon, Wed, and Thurs 4 p.m. to 8:30 p.m., Tues till 9 p.m., Fri 11 a.m. to 9:30 p.m., and Sat till 10 p.m.

What do Harry S Truman, Al Capone, and Franklin D. Roosevelt have in common? They all stayed at the **Elms Hotel** at Elms Boulevard and Regent Street in Excelsior Springs (800-843-3567; elmsresort.com). The elegant old hotel, built in 1888, has been a resting place for the famous and the infamous, from Presidents Roosevelt and Truman to gangster Capone, who hosted all-night drinking and gambling parties here during Prohibition. The look celebrates the time of that bygone era. In fact, the workers in the renovation process claimed to have seen the ghost of someone who looked a lot like Al Capone drifting down the hall of the fourth floor. Look up when you're in the Three Owls Restaurant just off the lobby—the murals above the bar are a delight, capturing that period of the hotel's long history—then settle in for a gourmet meal. Or visit The Tavern for cocktails, on the upper level overlooking wooded grounds, the outdoor

Hometown Notes

From a childhood in Kansas City's North End, an inner-city Italian neighborhood (maiden name Randazzo), to my years at North Kansas City High School (*Go Hornets!*), I am a Missouri girl born and reared. I call Excelsior Springs my hometown because of the many years I lived there. I have always been very active in the community, beginning with a few years as PTA president when my children were young. To say I was active in the community is probably an understatement, but I loved it. I was on the Planning and Zoning Commission, the Road and Bridge Commission, and the Beautification Committee. I was on the board of directors of the Good Samaritan Society, a local charitable organization that ran a food pantry, among other things. Then I ran for and was elected to the city council. I ultimately became the mayor. While on the council, I was elected to the board of directors of the Missouri Municipal League and so traveled around the state and met people from other small cities who were working through the same problems our city was facing.

For three years I wrote a weekly humor column for the *Daily Standard,* the local newspaper. I then went back to school at William Jewell College in Liberty and earned my BA in communication. I worked for the college as a recruiter for the reentry program, to encourage older people to go back to school, and wrote a weekly humor column called "A Different View" (looking at college life from the perspective of a 42-year-old wife and mother) for the school paper. I was even a DJ at the radio station with my own late-night jazz program. I am proud to say that I was the oldest graduating senior, and on the dean's list. I gave those college-age kids a run for their money and had great fun doing it. My home became the home-away-from-home for all the Japanese exchange students at the college who had nowhere to go over the holidays when the dorms closed. We even had a full-time exchange student from Japan from our own high school living with us. Excelsior Springs will always be my hometown; though I now live far away, my family still lives there.

pool, and a huge gazebo. The Café Soterian, in the lobby, offers the perfect cup of espresso, and pastries are fresh from the oven.

Look for the 1948 Chevrolet Stylemaster in front of the hotel. President Truman arrived in just such a car on election night in 1948. He came to avoid the press on a night when everyone thought he would be defeated by Thomas Dewey. He went to bed thinking he had lost the election and was awakened at 3 a.m. to learn that he had been reelected. The famous photo of him gleefully holding an early copy of the *Chicago Daily Tribune* carrying the blatant headline "Dewey Defeats Truman" was taken in front of the Elms Hotel.

The original tile floor and the huge "walk-in" fireplace in the lobby, as well as the art deco designs and stained glass in the Monarch Room, make this magnificent hotel worth a visit. It is, of course, on the National Register of Historic Places.

Boxer Jack Dempsey used the hotel as a training center. Now a complete fitness center on the grounds has tennis courts, riding stables, jogging and walking trails, a gazebo large enough to hold a good-size wedding party, mountain biking, and, of course, an outdoor pool and hot tub. Indoors is a gorgeous turquoise-blue pool cradled in rustic stone walls. The newly renovated spa—an expansive 28,000-square-foot facility—offers a place where you can spend your days with pampering spa treatments. The quartz table experience soothes aching muscles and stimulates the immune and lymphatic system. You can enjoy a massage or salt rub, too. The Grotto is a modern twist on a Roman bath. There's also a steam room, sauna, hot tubs, the indoor European paperclip-shaped lap pool, and a 24-hour fitness room.

The hotel offers 24-hour room service and concierge service. A gourmet shop features coffee, espresso, cappuccino, entrees, and homemade ice cream, and the beauty salon offers hair and scalp treatments, facials, manicures, pedicures, and makeup.

strange as it sounds

Mormon travelers on the old trails left legends and stories. There is still a site inside the Excelsior Springs city limits that is visited by pilgrims. Mormons were being chased from the country and took refuge in an old church; such a storm came up that it spooked their pursuers' horses, the river rose, and the pursuers gave up and went home, leading the Mormons to believe they had been delivered by a miracle.

The beautiful little stone church across the street from the Elms, at the corner of Regent and Kansas City Avenues, is the *Church of St. Luke, the Beloved Physician.* The Episcopal congregation began having services in Excelsior Springs as far back as 1905, but it was 1933 when the church was built on property donated by Major W. A. J. Bell of Blechingly, England. The church is built in the English style, similar to the Church of St. Mary the Virgin of AD 1090 in Bell's home parish. It was built of stones quarried on Major Bell's property nearby. The inside of this remarkable church is so lovely that it is often requested for weddings. Guests at the Elms are frequently visitors on Sunday mornings. You will be most welcome, so sign the guest book and plan to stay for coffee and refreshments in the undercroft. Be sure to visit the quiet and beautiful little memorial garden out back.

Right down Kansas City Avenue at Chillicothe Street (beside the Elms Hotel) is an old depot where trains brought guests from Chicago and Kansas City to the hotel. Now it is the **Wabash BBQ** (646 S. Kansas City Ave.; 816-630-7700; wabashbbq.com). The meats smoked in the old brick garage out back are very good and so is the secret barbecue sauce. Jim McCullough and his wife,

Taking the Waters

Excelsior Springs has long been famous for its waters. Native Americans were aware of the benefits of the springs, but the settlers called them poison (or PIE-zen, as they pronounced it). The medicinal uses of the waters were responsible for the founding of the town in 1880. There are five categories of mineral water, and each has a medicinal purpose. Excelsior Springs is one of only six cities in the world to have all five of them—one of two in the US—and you can still experience most of them at the Hall of Waters there.

First is iron manganese, which as the name suggests is a source of iron; then there's sulfo-saline, which is a very, very strong laxative (given a 2-ounce cup, people were told not to drink it in the elevator but to wait until they got to their rooms—no joke!). The next is soda bicarbonate, which is naturally carbonated and was used to settle a queasy stomach. The fourth category used to be the last—the neutral waters, which could be drunk in unlimited amounts—until it was discovered that they had very different compositions and served different purposes. These were calcium and lithium waters. The lithium water had properties that soothed depression (the most famous and best-tasting water in the world was Blue Rock Lithia), and, of course, the calcium water, which is the only water still bottled today in Excelsior Springs, is an excellent no-calorie source of calcium.

Back in the 1980s when I was on the city council, I suggested that the city bottle the calcium or Blue Rock Lithia water as a source of income. The other councilmen said, "Who would drink bottled water?" and voted no. Isn't hindsight fun? Who drinks bottled water? Just about everyone, now.

Cheri, have restored the building to its 1925 charm. After its days as a depot, which ended in 1933, new owners converted it into a dairy, delivering milk to the residents of Excelsior Springs. The dairy sold milk shakes and burgers, too, and Jim—whose family goes back six generations in town—remembers hanging out here in the 1960s. He and Cheri looked at the walk-in coolers that once held cans of fresh milk and knew they would be perfect for slabs of meat, the big garage fine for smoking. On summer weekends you can enjoy music out on the patio. The barbeque here gives any place in KC a run for its money.

There are plenty of artists in this little town. **Molly Robert's Studio** (253 E. Broadway; 816-900-1028) is an eclectic little spot that is stuffed to the rafters with art you'll want to touch and take home with you—and Molly is a prize-winning artist. If you love rocks and crystals, incense, smudge, intricately carved wooden boxes, and blank journals with pizzazz, this is the place to find them. Check out the funky purses, totes, and weekender bags, too.

Bohemian Sage Gallery (106 E Broadway; 816-651-7328) boasts an eclectic mix of artists and local and crafted gifts and goodies. It's also the destination for art classes and workshops. From oils, acrylics, and watercolors to exquisite painted gourds, wall hangings, jewelry, and intricate handwoven baskets, you'll find the perfect thing. Artist Kat McKown and her partner, Laurie Ahart, own this spot in Excelsior Springs.

Other Trails (othertrails.com) is a coffeehouse on Broadway, just one door west of the Hall of Waters, surrounded by historic architecture. Enjoy fresh-baked treats as well as the signature coffees. Don't miss the pumpkin bars or the ooey-gooey butter cake. As you might guess from the name of the place, owners are big on the outdoors, and you'll find books and maps and other trail-related goods on the shelves. Open Mon through Sat 6:30 a.m. to 2 p.m.

Willow Springs Mercantile (249 Broadway; 816-630-7467; shopthemerchantile.com) has the largest selection of Missouri wines in the world, as well as an enormous collection of Missouri craft beers and bottles from 15 Missouri distilleries. You'll find great shopping for crafts and unique gifts (chocolate-dipped wine glasses?), gourmet foods, coffee, and tea. There is often live music in the basement bistro, too.

Jim and Daphne Bowman started "The Merc," as locals call it with affection, in 2005, born of their love of cooking, but it soon developed into a delightful gathering of good food, local honey, wines, ciders, and a fun place to meet up with friends. You might even catch Jim playing his guitar on a quiet, rainy afternoon. Hours are Tues through Fri 10 a.m. to 6 p.m. (lunch served 11 a.m. to 3 p.m.), Sat 11 a.m. to 5 p.m. (lunch 11 a.m. to 3 p.m.), and Sun noon to 5 p.m. (lunch all afternoon).

ariverruns through

When I was the mayor, I was praising our town at a city council meeting and said, "How many cities have a river running through them?" The newspaper editor smirked and began scribbling. There was a moment of silence, then everyone started calling out the names of cities, big cities. Almost every city was founded *because* it was on a river. Of course, I made front page the next day and everyone had a good laugh at my expense. Small town humor—you gotta love it.

If you love the outdoors, you'll want to explore the many parks. Overlooking the town is ***Siloam Mountain Park,*** complete with three shelter houses and winding trails. Below that park—and hugging the Fishing River, which runs through the town—you'll find the ***Fishing River Linear Trail*** on the north side of the river, and East Valley Park on the south. Originally designed by George Kessler, the famous landscape architect and city planner in the late 19th and early 20th centuries, there are still signs of the original trails and stonework.

But wait, the best is yet to come. Tucked into the limestone bluffs and forested slopes on the southeast end of the park, you'll discover **Isley Park Woods,** a designated Missouri Natural Area. Here you'll find many species of trees, birds, mammals, and a tremendous display of wildflowers every spring. Two shelter houses in the larger park and a paved walking trail invite you to explore.

The remaining mineral water well is on the north side of the river; it's spectacular. The paved trail through the park will take you right up an impressive set of stairs back up to Siloam Mountain and around again.

The Inn on Crescent Lake (1261 St. Louis Ave.; 816-630-6745; crescentlake.com) is a three-story Georgia colonial mansion on 22 acres. The home was built in 1915, and the crescent-shaped moat for which it was named still encircles the estate. The guest rooms all have private baths (some have whirlpool tubs) and individual temperature control and cable television. Edward and Irene shared a dream of having the perfect country inn where people could unwind. The swimming pool is a fine spot for cooling off, and the ponds are great for fishing. Paddleboats are available for tooling around the little lakes, and you may see geese and ducks swimming peacefully nearby. There is even a fishing boat to use. Breakfast is served in the sun-filled solarium. The Inn on Crescent Lake has been featured on *Restore America* with Bob Vila and was named "Missouri's Most Romantic Getaway" by *Policygenius Magazine.*

Mill Inn Restaurant (415 St. Louis Ave.; 816-637-8008) looks vaguely south-of-the-border. Inside you'll find wonderful cinnamon rolls (if you can beat the local farmers to them!), peanut butter pie, and on Wednesday and Saturday only, homemade bread pudding. This place has been here forever and will never go away, with any luck.

Dubious Claims Brewery (451 S. Thompson Ave.; 818-900-1882; dubiousclaimsbrewingco.com), just east of the Elms Hotel on Thompson Avenue, boasts its own artisanal beers, great food, and good company. Check out how the brews are made, right there on the premises. Why "Dubious Claims," by the way? The town's spa facilities thrived until a national media exposé of dubious claims dried up the mineral-water business. You can no longer drink the mineral waters, so Dubious Claims asks you to "let our beer be the cure for what 'ales' you."

Right next door is **Wood Chux Axe Throwing** (455 Thompson Ave.; 816-900-2489), where you can throw axes to your heart's content. It's a good way to flush pent-up emotions and burn that resentment and anger, but it is also good for the ego as you get better at it. In addition to axe-throwing, this family-friendly place offers indoor cornhole, foosball, darts, and many more games. There are lounges for relaxing, bars for refueling, and a stage for live music and photo-ops.

Just around the block is another new place. Sometimes you wait a long time for a building in an old town to find new life . . . 30 years in the case of the Hope Funeral Home at 216 Spring St. Finally, someone with vision and the necessary resources have given this beautiful stone building a new life. It's now the **Casa de Vite** (816-288-3187), a wine-tasting venue and more that makes perfect use of the place. It's the 2023 winner of the Preserve Missouri award. New owner Susan Blaser fell in love with its historical charm and purchased it. The building now houses a chapel for weddings, bridal party dressing rooms, tasting rooms, and event space. There's even a garden patio for outdoor dining, sipping, and chatting.

Excelsior Springs also has one of the most beautiful old golf courses in the Kansas City area in **Excelsior Springs Municipal Golf Course** (excelsiorgolf. com), and since it is a municipal course, it's affordable. Rolling hills, big trees, and surrounding woodlands make it challenging; watered fairways and paved cart paths make it pleasant year-round. It is an "English-type" course, unique because it has no sand traps or bunkers, which keeps play moving smoothly (so leave your sand wedge in the car). If you go into the Golf Hill Grille in the newly built clubhouse for a meal or for a cold drink, don't miss the tiny 1830 log cabin tucked inside. It's one of the original structures in this old town and lets you see how Missouri settlers once lived. The Battle of Fredericksburg,

Payne's Jailhouse Bed & Breakfast

The **Payne's Jailhouse Bed & Breakfast** (426 Concourse Ave.) is the pride of Mark and Anna Sue Spohn. Their home was formerly home to the police chief from 1926 to 1953. The chief built the jailhouse onto the back portion of his own home to have a place to keep the shackled prisoners so that he could sleep in his own bed at night. They didn't have a jailhouse in town back then. But the rooms are so very nice now—big-screen TV, fireplace, and huge walk-in shower. When we stayed there, it was the day before Christmas, meant to be spent with my family in Excelsior Springs. We caught the COVID-19 virus on the plane coming into KC and started feeling sick the second day in town. We ended up quarantined at Payne's. It was -3 degrees and snowing. We had a warm fire and football on the big-screen TV, and my family brought dinners and left them outside the door (and waved to us through the glass). Mark brought breakfast for Christmas morning. What could have been a Christmas disaster was saved by genuine Midwestern hospitality and a warm comfy room with a stash of muffins and sandwiches that Mark kept replacing. We left to fly back home after seven days, and no one in my family caught the virus from us, including my 99-year-old aunt. It's a family memory we can laugh about now: I can hear my grand-daughter Molly saying, "Remember that Christmas Grandma spent in jail?" But we are truly grateful to have been staying at Payne's.

a Civil War skirmish, was fought along the southwest sector of the course, and a monument commemorating the event stands near the 15th tee.

Interesting that this small city has two trolleys that take folks on winery tours and to historic sites. So, let's talk about wineries. **Fence Stile Vineyards and Winery** (816-500-6465; fencestile.com) belongs to Shriti Plimpton, who invites you to "follow the grape to the glass" by touring the vineyards and caves where the wine is aged. The tours are $35 and space is limited, so call for reservations. The candlelight wine tasting is extra special. For a nice change, taste handcrafted rums and brandy for $2 a pour. Blackberry rum and rum cocktails are available to enjoy in the tasting room. Summer and winter hours change, so it is best to call ahead.

March 1 marks the opening of **Dari-B Drive In,** a classic drive-up ice-cream parlor. You may see a line clear around the building on opening day (March 1), even if the snow is kneecap deep. It's been a family tradition since 1954, and home of the Sangria Shake. Hours are 11:30 a.m. to 9 p.m. every day during the season; the Dari-B closes for winter on October 31.

South down Highway O off Highway 10 and just east of Excelsior Springs a few miles is the **Sundance Ranch KC** (12607 Hwy. O; 816-701-9535; www .sundancekc.com). Ever wanted to spend the night in a tree house? You may see deer or a vixen (that's a female fox) pass by right below the deck. No? There are also two comfortable lake cabins, a glamping site, a place overlooking a serene lake atop a hill, and the "Hole in the Wall" luxury guest suite. Trails roam throughout the property, inviting exploration. The owners started their dream in 2018 after discovering the perfect location and soon began construction of their first lodging, the Robbers Roost Treehouse, offering rustic elegance in a serene forest setting surrounded by beautiful Bethany Falls limestone bluffs and an ephemeral stream. The nearby 15-acre rock-lined lake offers bountiful fishing, kayaking, and swimming opportunities.

Shamrock Ranch (12300 Shoemaker Rd.; 816-377-2313; theshamrock-ranch.com), a bit east of Excelsior Springs, now carries wines from the original Four Horses and a Dog Vineyard and Winery. You'll find the event center tucked away among rolling hills and rock bluffs down Shoemaker Road—it's quiet and private and beautiful, and large enough to handle most events.

From Excelsior Springs go east on Highway 10, turn left on Highway M, then right onto Highway U, then right onto Crowley Street/Highway C (still with me?). Follow Highway C and what a surprise to find, just east of Excelsior Springs in the tiny town of **Rayville,** a winery and really good pizza. **Van Till's Winery** (13986 Hwy. C; 816-776-2720; vantillfarms.com) does wood-fired pizza in a semi-outdoor oven. There's a tasting room and wine shop open Tues through Thurs 11 a.m. to 5 p.m. and Fri and Sat till 9 p.m. Pizza hours are Fri and Sat noon to 9 p.m. They boast of farm-to-table goodness from their own huge garden near the heated patio in the peaceful countryside. It's worth the trip just to see the oven and greenhouses. This is a great spot for private parties, too. Van Till's has a new wine-tasting venue back in Excelsior Springs called **Pairings by Van Till** (415 S. Thompson Ave.; 816-900-0012; pairingsbyvantill.com)—the baked brie is delightful. Pairings serves boards with a variety of charcuterie choices, cheese, vegetables, and desserts paired exclusively with wine from Van Till Family Farm Winery.

By the Yard Fabrics (16587 Hwy. C; 816-470-6703) is north of Rayville on Highway C . . . just keep driving. The shop has an incredible array of beautiful prints for quilts and other projects—or buy one of its gorgeous quilts while you're there. Hours are Tues through Sat 10 a.m. to 4 p.m.

Also from Excelsior Springs, follow the signs to the **Watkins Woolen Mill State Park and Historic Site,** west off US 69 onto Highway 92 near Lawson, and get ready to walk back in time. The decades fall away like leaves as you wander down the footpath from the parking area. You pass deep Missouri woods, then a tiny stone-walled cemetery where the gravestones are encrusted with lichen. Farther along the path a brick giant rises to your right, and a graceful mansion crowns the hill to your left. A young belle could make quite an entrance down the lovely curved walnut staircase in the entryway—and probably did, more than once.

Waltus Watkins built his empire here around 1850, in the years before the Civil War. Quite an empire it was: The three-story brick mill employed dozens, providing woolen fabrics to the area. The milling machinery, from washing vats to looms, is still intact, providing pristine examples of early industrial ingenuity. The house and its outbuildings reflect a gracious life—the reward for hard work and hardheaded business sense.

Before it became a state park, the mill seemed destined for destruction. The family was selling it after more than a century of occupancy, and the place was on the auction block. Representatives from the Smithsonian were on hand to bid on rare equipment—but the day was saved, along with the integrity of the mill complex, when private individuals bought the site lock, stock, and barrel (and there were a few of those about). Eventually they were able to pass the mill complex along to the State of Missouri, and now you can tour the mill and the elegant home on the hill, participate in living-history weekends (try not to miss the Victorian Christmas), or watch an ongoing archaeological dig intended to discover still more about day-to-day life in the 19th century. Tours are given Mon through Sat 10 a.m. to 4 p.m. and Sun 11 a.m. to 4 p.m. Winter hours are 11 a.m. to 4 p.m. Special events are usually free. An interpretive center acts as museum and buffer between now and the 19th century.

Call (816) 580-3387 or visit mostateparks.com/park/watkins-mill-state-park for more information.

A brick church and an octagonal schoolhouse are nearby, both restored to their original condition. The Watkins children and those of mill workers and local farmers attended to their readin,' 'ritin', and 'rithmetic here. See the schoolhouse when it's open, if you can; call (816) 296-3357. The ventilation system of windows high in the octagonal clerestory turret is ingenious. Sunlight reflects softly around the white-painted walls inside; not much artificial light would have been necessary, with the tall windows on every side.

The park also has a 5-mile bike path through the woods as well as a sandy beach for swimming in the lake. Riding trails for horses are also a feature of the park. There are 98 campsites with hookups. Check the park website for special events held during the spring, summer, and fall months.

During spring, summer, and fall, stop by the **Corner Kitchen & General Store** (26017 CR RA; 816-368-1132) on the way into the park for groceries, tackle, bait, drinks, snacks, fresh cinnamon rolls or a heartier breakfast, or a quick sandwich to take with you. Look for the little stagecoach out front. There's "Pickin' on the Porch" at the store every fourth Saturday starting at 6:30 p.m. (bring your own lawn chairs . . . there's pickin' on the porch and sittin' out front).

If you're taking Highway 92 westward to Kearney, you will have passed the turnoff to Watkins Mill State Park, but if you're still in the mood for natural beauty, heads up! A bit farther west from the turnoff to Watkins Mill, you'll find the turn for **Tryst Falls Park,** which was once a popular meetup for young lovers, hence the name (shhhh, it still is). Check out the beautiful waterfall and natural amphitheater with picnic tables. On the south side of the small park there are shelter houses, playground equipment, and flush toilets (which are locked up in winter).

Going to **Lawson**? Look for the **Candyman** at 202 W. 6th St. (816-296-7231; candymancorp.com). The store carries just about every kind of candy you can imagine. It's a kiddie's dream come true. Chocolate, jelly beans, and for heaven's sake, try the bacon-filled chocolate piggies! It's all here, but what is most important is that it's your center for home-making candy; you can buy the coatings, molds, recipes, and tools you will need. Call or order online.

If you find yourself in need of home cooking in a little cafe where everyone treats you like a regular, look for **Catrick's Café,** right on the small downtown main street at 410 N. Pennsylvania Ave. (816-580-4177). Who can resist something called the Sugar-Daddy Burger? The **Nutmeg Bakery & Cafe** is nearby at 310 N. Pennsylvania Ave. (816-301-7023). Snag some biscuits and gravy for a hearty start to your day, but there are also cinnamon rolls, or whatever your goodie-loving heart desires. It's open for breakfast and lunch.

For a surprise out in the country, **Lamp Family Farms** has opened an old-fashioned candy store, the **Lamp Country Farm Store** (660-358-4017), with hard candies in bulk that you may remember in a "penny-candy store" from days gone by. The walls are lined with shelves full of jams and jellies, an array of seasoning salts and herbs, homemade soaps, gifts, gardening advice, workshops, and other goodies. Don't forget your four-legged family members—there are bacon-flavored bone-shaped doggie treats, too. Pony rides? Petting zoo? Why not?

Feeling outdoorsy? **Lawson City Lake** (19799 N. Raum Rd.), on 111 rolling acres just north of the town, is a great place to picnic, camp, fish, boat (electric motors only, or canoes and kayaks), sketch, watch birds, or play disc golf. It's acres of fun in nature. The city has just recently created the Lakeview Campground and RV Park with all the amenities, and there's also a new event center and gazebo. A 1.7-mile trail goes around the lake and features several benches and exercise stations.

A modern fishing dock was recently added. The Missouri Department of Conservation stocks the lake with bluegill, channel catfish, and largemouth bass; properly managed, these species provide great fishing and good eating (state fishing regulations apply). Use the website at lawsonmo.gov/city-lake or call (816) 675-2205 for more info or to reserve your favorite camping spot, complete with RV and trailer hookups.

History buffs should look for the **Jesse James Farm Historic Site** (816-736-8500; jessejamesmuseum.org), just off Highway 92 on Jesse James Drive, between Excelsior Springs and **Kearney** (watch for signs). The white house with its gingerbread trim and cedar roof sits just over a rise, a little way back from the road; the new asphalt drive and path make the place wheelchair accessible. The original part of the house is a log cabin, which was rescued from a precarious slide into decay. The cabin contains, among other things, the remains of Jesse's original coffin, which was exhumed when the body was moved to nearby Kearney (pronounced CAR-ney); the family originally buried him in the yard to keep the body from being disturbed by those bent on revenge or looking for souvenirs. The coffin is odd by today's standards; there was a glass window at face level—presumably for viewing the body, not for providing a window on eternity for the deceased!

The newer section of the house was a Sears & Roebuck mail order. Mrs. James decided that the old place was getting too rundown—not to mention crowded—and she sent for the two-room addition, assembled on the spot. It still sports the original wallpaper.

This is the famous outlaw's birthplace, the place where his father was hanged and his mother's arm was lost to a Pinkerton's bomb. Enjoy the on-site museum, which includes a gift shop full of James memorabilia, books, and local crafts, or stick around in August and September for the play *The Life and Times of Jesse James*. Brother Frank was there at the farm, too. Admission to the museum and home is $9 for adults, $8 for seniors, and $5.50 for children. Hours are Mon through Sat 9 a.m. to 4 p.m.

July 17, 1995, was a big day in Kearney. The body buried in Jesse's grave was exhumed for DNA testing to finally settle the debate about who exactly was buried in the James family plot. Jesse's descendants offered DNA samples, and another man who claims that his grandfather is buried in Jesse's grave also offered his DNA for testing. People who believe that James died in 1950 at a very old age as well as people who believe it is Jesse's body in Mt. Olivet Cemetery brought folding chairs that morning to watch. "You goin' to the digging?" was the question asked at the local cafe when it opened early that morning. By closing time, lots of people were wearing "We Dig Jesse" T-shirts. Oh, you want to know about the DNA test, do you? It was Jesse, all right.

And if you've ever wanted to lay a flower on the outlaw's grave, it's located in **Mt. Olivet Cemetery** on Highway 92, a half mile east of I-35 in Kearney. Look for it near the cedar trees at the west end of the cemetery, which is open during daylight hours year-round.

Legend has it that Jesse, Frank James, and/or Cole Younger visited darn near every fallen-down log cabin in this part of Missouri—not to mention the surrounding states. The James gang would have had to be in three places at once, the way their exploits were reported, but no matter. That's the fun thing about legends: They're much more elastic than the truth.

Slivinskis' Bakery in Kearney (196 W. SR 92; 816-903-2245) is where Jason Miller bakes scrumptious muffins and other decadent delights. Get there very early if you want to try the white chocolate raspberry muffin and a cup of great coffee. Early means 5 a.m. Tues through Fri. You can sleep in on Sat and Sun, when the place doesn't open until 6 a.m. Everything is gone by noon every day, which is when he closes. You can call manager Terry Kinney and have a few goodies saved for you.

On the same path, but in the historic downtown area, is **Trash & Treasure** (109 E. Washington; 816-628-6119), where new and used clothing, toys, office supplies, tools, *whatever!* can be found. Hours are Tues through Thurs 10 a.m. to 5 p.m., Fri noon to 5 p.m., and Sat 10 a.m. to 3 p.m. Jeanette Montgomery's shop is also online at stores.ebay.com/trashandtreasure.

Now you can slip into **Mojo's to Go** (100 E. 6th St.; 816-902-6656), which according to locals is the best little coffee shop in town. Great coffee and great people who, a recent visitor said, make you feel so welcome you feel like a native—a chocolate-filled native, at that. It's open Mon through Fri 6 a.m. to 6 p.m.

Gino's Italian Cuisine (123 E. Washington; 816-903-4466; ginosinkearney.com) has the old-world charm of Italy. Family-owned by George (Gino) and Julie Disciacca, Gino's features authentic Sicilian and northern Italian cuisine. One of Gino's signature entrees is Pasta Gino. So very good. Try the Steak Mediterranean—a 5-ounce filet topped with a red cream sauce, shrimp, and crabmeat. Your meal will be accompanied by lovely romantic music, and you can enjoy the full wine list. Hours are Mon through Thurs 11 a.m. to 9 p.m. and Fri and Sat till 10 p.m.

Kearney may be a small town, but it does not lack diversity. **LaFuente Mexican Restaurant** (750 Watson Dr.; 816-903-9922; lafuentemexrest.com) serves authentic specialties. Try the *chilaquiles Mexicanos* with green tomatillo sauce or the chiles rellenos with a cold Dos Equis. The service and food are both excellent. Open seven days a week for lunch and dinner, hours are Sun through Thurs 11 a.m. to 10 p.m. and Fri and Sat till 10:30 p.m.

Want to visit a real working farm with foods you can trust? Head south on Highway 33 from Kearney to **Barham Family Farm** (16800 NE 128th St.; 816-365-2445; barhamfamilyfarm.com), through rolling hills, pastures, and meadows. Black Angus beef are raised on this 100-year-old family farm, happily grazing on pastures ripe with brome, fescue, foxtail, dandelion, and clover. The meats are non-GMO, with no added antibiotics or growth hormones. Love pork, chicken, turkey, duck, or processed goodies like brats, sausages, and delicious bacon? Barham has it, along with eggs, cheeses, fresh goat milk soaps, jams, jellies, BBQ rubs, salts, and more in the farm store. If you're a devotee of hard-to-find organ meats, pure lard, or other specialties (oxtail soup in the winter), call ahead; they'll either have them on hand or will save some back for you. You'll want to visit with the quirky, attention-loving goats at the farm, too. The store on the farm is open Thurs and Fri 10 a.m. to 6 p.m. and Sat 9 a.m. to 3 p.m., but Kenny Barham and family will also deliver right to your door if you sign up for their scheduled deliveries. You can also find them at the huge **Liberty Farmers Market** spring through fall.

Head north on I-35 from Kearney and take the off-ramp at **Cameron.** Nearby is one of the most charming small Missouri parks, **Wallace State Park** (10621 MO-121; 816-632-3745; mostateparks.com/park/wallace-state-park), with rustic shelter houses of wood and stone, trails, limestone-bedded creeks, and a jewel-like little lake you can easily walk all the way around. Discover a wonderful little campground tucked among the trees on top of the bluff towering over the lake. There are four hiking trails to explore, scattered picnic areas, and fishing in Allaman Lake. In winter, you can see down across the lake far below, but the feeling of magical privacy really shines in the summer when the leaves are out. There's more room for camping at the far end of the park, with showers, electrical plug-ins, and more.

Kingdom Coffee Roasting (402 E. Evergreen St.) in nearby Cameron will make your mouth water when you catch the scent of warm coffee beans in the air. There are all kinds of straight-up and fancy coffees; dine in or drive through, it's your choice. It's open every day 6 a.m. to 6 p.m. *Robyn's* (115 E. 3rd St.; 816-632-1155; robynsofcameron.com) is a family-style restaurant with rustic booths and brick walls. Dine in or carry-out; it's home-style and plenty of it. Or try *Dino's Diner & Family Restaurant* (402 E. Evergreen; 816-632-4455). Best hash browns ever!

Highway 9 will lead you to the charming little college town of *Parkville,* just 20 minutes from Kansas City. This is a bustling yet pedestrian-friendly crafts and antiques center that moves at a leisurely pace, with longtime shops interwoven with new establishments. Wear comfy shoes and a warm coat in cool weather, and enjoy the brisk walk between shops.

Just past the shopping complex is quiet *English Landing Park* on the banks of the Missouri. Look for the historic Waddell "A" truss bridge, built in 1898, one of only two left in the country. It was salvaged and moved to its present location. Now it's the focal point of the park, providing a walkway across a small feeder creek leading to the big river. Keep going past English Landing and you'll find *Platte Landing Park,* complete with a boat ramp on the big river that slides by the town, a dog park, walking trails, and a big roomy shelter house.

Just before English Landing Park, turn off to the right and find *Fabric Chic* (170 English Landing Dr., Ste. 111; 816-982-9191), an astoundingly complete fabric and quilt shop. Seriously, it's like a rainbow mated with an aloha shirt and this shop is their baby. Twelve hundred bolts of fabric will dazzle your eyes and get your creative juices flowing. Just across the parking lot at 173 English Landing Dr. is *La Bottega Parkville Vintage Antique Mall* (parkvilleantiquemall.vpweb.com), which is stuffed to the rafters with treasures. There are some real bargains hidden away in this place. It's open 10 a.m. to 5 p.m. seven days a week.

If you find yourself suddenly in need of a treat to keep your strength up, you're in luck. *The Old Fashioned Candy Store, Deli and Antique Shop* is handy at 122 S. Main St. (816-912-2022); you'll feel like a kid again. At *River's Bend Gallery* (106 E. Main St.; 816-587-8070) you will find a collection of fine arts and crafts, delicate mobiles, and other beautiful things. Hours are Tues through Thurs 10 a.m. to 5 p.m., Fri and Sat 10 a.m. to 6 p.m., and Sun noon to 5 p.m.

Downtown Parkville is loaded with places to shop, so it is a fine day trip from Kansas City. You can taste wine at **Wines by Jennifer** (405 Main St.; 816-505-9463; winesbyjennifer.com), which gives lots of choices when it comes to wine, mostly from small boutique wineries around the world. Sample wines in the tasting room Tues and Wed 3 p.m. to 8 p.m. and Thurs through Sat noon to 8 p.m. There are cheeses from Osceola Cheese Company, local fresh breads, fruit, meats, crackers, and other foods that complement wine. Do a little shopping, too, for wine racks, decanters, and openers as well as cheese plates and more.

Then head for **Stone Canyon Pizza** (15 Main St.; 816-746-8686; stonecanyonpizza.com). A favorite here is the Verdura pizza: fresh mushrooms, artichoke hearts, sun-dried tomato, sweet roasted red peppers, mozzarella, and fresh basil. This is not just a pizzeria, though; it has plenty of other choices as well. The tequila-lime chicken comes to mind. It is a cozy, rustic place with lots of small-town friendliness. Hours are Mon through Fri 11 a.m. to 9 p.m. and weekends till 10 p.m. (till 11 p.m. on weekends in the summertime).

Frank's of Parkville (100 Main St.; 816-746-8282; franksofparkville.com) is one of the best Italian restaurants around, in business since 1931. On the small, intimate side, Frank's is a welcoming oasis after a busy afternoon. Check out classic Italian dishes on its $12 lunch specials. Exposed brick walls, original paintings, and a colorful mural on the back wall add to the old-world atmosphere. You can also choose to dine on the patio or book the party room with a reservation.

The Craic (12 Main St.; 816-599-4012) is just down the street from Frank's, so if you're in an Irish mood and dying for some fish-and-chips, shepherd's pie, or a Dublin coddle with a nice Guinness, this is the place for you. Naturally, there's music and fun, as well—that's what "craic" is, after all. It offers curbside and delivery as well as dine-in, but if at all possible you'll want to be there for the craic.

Jason and Kathy have opened their circa 1885 mansion to visitors as **Main Street Inn B&B** (504 Main St.; 816-272-9750; mainstreetinnparkville.com). It's handy to MCI Airport, and downtown KC is only minutes away. There are three guest rooms, all with private baths. It was voted the best B&B north of the river.

Parkville Nature Sanctuary (parkvillemo.gov/nature-sanctuary) is the place to go when you've had enough and need to walk off some emotions. Here you'll find 115 unspoiled acres of mixed forest with nearly 3 miles of walking trails, limestone bluffs, and wildlife. Don't miss Old Kate's Trail, which goes past a little waterfall. You park at the trailhead and walk in through loess bluffs and mixed forest that feel almost primeval. It's a treat whatever the season.

Take Mill Street to NW River Road out of town and onto I-435 and head north. Then merge onto I-29 (exit 31) and follow it to **Platte City.** A former millionaire's estate on 73 acres is now the **Basswood Resort** (15880 Interurban Rd.; 816-858-5556 or 800-242-2775; basswoodresort.com). This 1935 lakeside home has six suites—each with two bedrooms and a mini or full kitchen, some with fireplaces, and all in country French decor. Besides the lodge itself, there are cabins, RV sites, and campgrounds.

There are lots of cool old buildings in the main part of town, as well as just off the square, so wander around a bit to see what's what. And while you're there, wander a bit more to find **Iowker Creek Vineyards & Winery** (16905 Jowler Creek Rd.; 816-858-5528; jowlercreek.com), the area's first "green winery." It is owned and operated by Jason Lacy and Kit Lacy, Kansas City born and raised siblings. Take a look at all the sustainable practices they've put in place from the grape to the glass to make delicious wines you can feel good about drinking. "We try and do everything we can to care for our land, our people, and our animals to sustain the business for generations to come." Try all eight samples, with a warm baguette—you won't be sorry. They often host events with live music. Open Thurs noon to 5 p.m., Fri noon to 9 p.m., Sat 11 a.m. to 9 p.m., and Sun 11 a.m. to 5 p.m.

Just off Highway 45, **Weston** is a beautiful town tucked between rounded hills, its past shaped as much by the nearby Missouri River and its thread of commerce as by the orchards, vineyards, distilleries, and good tobacco-growing soils here. After the signing of the 1837 Platte Purchase, it attracted settlers who recognized its rich soil—and appreciated the low prices.

Historic preservation in Weston has been a high priority for many years; the place exudes charm as a flower exudes scent. A beautiful old Catholic church overlooks the town, and tobacco and apple barns stand tall on many of the surrounding hills. It has a foursquare flavor that just feels historic—and in fact, Weston bills itself as the Midwest's most historic town. There are more than 100 historically significant homes and businesses from before the Civil War alone. Book a tour of the homes (advance reservations are required for the tour; call 816-640-2650 and ask to arrange a mini-tour for groups of 15 or more of two of the homes), or visit the **Weston Historical Museum** (601 Main St.; 816-386-2977; westonhistoricalmuseum.org). Hollywood has discovered Weston, and it's not unknown for movie cameras to roll on Main Street. Life in Platte County goes way back, long before these neat homes were built or the first still was cranked up; the museum will take you from prehistoric times through World War II. Hours are Tues through Sat 1 to 4 p.m. and Sun 1:30 to 5 p.m. (closed Jan and Feb). This one is a bargain; admission is free, and it's a day trip all by itself.

The **Halfway House & Stone Basement** historic site is located on the old toll road from Platte City and Weston. In 1849, the Weston to Platte City toll road was completed, and John Floersh operated the Halfway House as well as served as the toll collector. Later, pro-slavery owners operated a tavern and holding area for slaves. The remaining stone basement once displayed rings in the ceiling where slaves were chained; they have been removed but the stone building remains as a reminder of our sad past. If you're on Highway 273 going toward Weston from Platte City, you'll find it just after Bee Creek, before the Wilkerson Cemetery. There is a little side road that goes off to the right called Vaughn Lane, which leads to a construction site now. it's worth the sobering side trip.

Green Dirt Farm Creamery (1099 Welt St.; 816-386-2156; greendirtfarm. com/creamery) is well worth finding. Green Dirt makes and serves artisan sheep cheeses that are so good (bonus—a lot of people who can't handle cow's milk products do fine with sheep or goat milk) and also offer mixed milk artisan cheeses and cow's milk ice cream made on this sustainable farm. You'll find a selection of foods and crafts from local small-batch makers, too. Green Dirt Farm founder, Sarah Hoffmann, wanted to raise her kids where they could run around in the fresh air and experience the joy and life lessons that happen when you grow up on a farm. She decided to leave her job as a successful academic physician to start a new life on the farm. And give others delicious, wholesome food, sustainably made.

Weston's **Holladay Distilling Company** (816-640-3056; holladaydistill-ery.com) is a rare treat, 1.25 miles south of town on Highway JJ. They say this is the oldest continuously active distillery in the country—or at least west of the Hudson River. It was founded in 1856 by stagecoach and Pony Express king Ben Holladay. It was known as McCormick Distilling Company for many years but recently went back to its original founder's name. Today it is still making real Missouri bourbon from the same limestone spring that Ben Holladay dis-covered. Tours are available (reservations required), where you can taste the bourbon and learn how it is distilled on-site. Hours are Mon through Sat 10 a.m. to 5 p.m. and Sun 12:30 to 5 p.m.

Buy a bottle of fine bourbon and then head to 357 Main St. to **Weston Tobacco** (816-386-4086; westontobacco.com), the place to go if you are really into good cigars. Take a tour of the walk-in humidor and look at and sniff the hand-rolled Black Ribbons as well as 600 other types of cigars. Buy a cigar, take your bottle of bourbon, and sit in the smoking lounge (the lounge is BYOB) and enjoy a good old-fashioned drink and smoke. It's open daily 10 a.m. to 8 p.m.

Be sure to visit the **McCormick Country Store** (420 Main St.; 816-640-3149) in Weston. You can find mugs, T-shirts, and other gift items as well as a fine line of cigars. There's a tasting room in which you can taste the products of the distillery for 25 cents.

If you love things Irish, don't miss the **Celtic Ranch** (404 Main St; 816-640-2881; celticranch.com). Imported Irish tweeds and knits for men and women, "newsboy" flat caps, gifts, stunning sterling silver jewelry, and so much more—including Utilikilts. The owners take trips to the Auld Sod often and bring back such an amazing array of goods, you'll think you just stepped off the train in County Cork. Put your feet up and enjoy "The Whiskey Snug" at the ranch, which carries over 1,100 Irish whiskeys, single malt scotches, unusual bourbons, ryes, and an extensive offering of international spirits. You can purchase samples by the shot or take home a bottle to enjoy.

Pirtle's Weston Vineyards Winery (502 Spring St.; 816-640-5728; pirtlewinery.com) is one of Missouri's most interesting wineries, located in the former German Lutheran Evangelical church. Jesus made wine, so why not Pirtle's? Owner Elbert Pirtle's striking stained-glass windows depict the winery's logo and a wild rose—the math professor from the University of Missouri–Kansas City is quite the Renaissance man.

Northern Platte County soil is conducive to some fine viticulture; taste the products of these rolling hills Mon through Sat 10 a.m. to 6 p.m. and Sun 11 a.m. to 6 p.m. The Pirtles love to talk wine and vines. Try the mead, a honey-based beverage once thought to be a "love potion." It's sweet and smoky because it's aged in Holladay Distilling oak barrels. They say that originally the church was upstairs and a cooperage was in the basement, where barrels were made to serve northwest Missouri. The winery now has a wine garden where you can take a basket of cheese, sausage, and bread to enjoy with your wine.

The **American Bowman Restaurant** ("where the Past is Present"), at 500 Welt St., is the oldest continuously operating pub in Weston at 150-plus years old. Owners Mike Caokley and Corey Weinfurt offer Irish-style food and entertainment, pewter mugs, and kerosene lamps on the tables. O'Malley's 1842 Pub, the Post Ordinary, the Heritage Theater, and malt and hops cellars are in the same building. There's an actual brewery here in a cozy brick arch-roofed room. Be advised, though, it's a narrow corridor down a couple of levels to get there, and if stairs are an issue, you may prefer the restaurant upstairs. They call it "your trip to Ireland without the airfare," and that it is, laddie. At Christmas try the Dickens Dinner; during other seasons, 1837 Dinners, Civil War Dinners, and 19th-Century Irish Banquets are yours for the ordering. For reservations call (816) 640-5235. Visit the website at westonirish.com. Open seven days a week 11:30 a.m. to 9 p.m.

If you're in the mood for something a bit more upscale, the circa 1847 ***Avalon Café*** (816-640-2835; avaloncafeweston.com) perches invitingly above the main drag, at 608 Main St., across the street from the museum. It offers an excellent beef tenderloin with a bourbon sauce—kind of a salute to Weston's distillery history—but tender and flavorful. There is a nice selection of wines. Owner-chefs Kelly Cogan and David and Lisa Scott grill a fine salmon and offer an entire wild-game section on the menu. Hours are Tues through Thurs 11 a.m. to 2 p.m. and 5:30 to 8 p.m., Fri and Sat 11 a.m. to 3 p.m. and 5:30 to 9 p.m., and Sun 10 a.m. to 2 p.m. (with brunch option). There is a side entrance without stairs on the left side driveway for either walking in or dropping off or picking up.

You can choose a B&B or the renovated 1845 ***St. George Hotel*** (500 Main St.; 816-640-9902; westonirish.com/stgeorge-hotel), which has 26 guest rooms that have seen steamboat captains and traveling salesmen from long ago. The hotel bar features Weston-made beer, wine, and whiskey as well as coffee and soft drinks. The rates are reasonable. Come on a Saturday night, when Weston is lively.

If you prefer a B&B, "steamboat gothic" describes the circa 1898 ***Benner House Bed and Breakfast*** (645 Main St.; 816-640-2616; bennerhouse.com). With its double-deck wraparound porch and gingerbread trim, the jaunty, turn-of-the-20th-century mansion looks as if it could steam away like the nearby riverboats. Brass beds and baths with pull-chain water closets are mixed with Jacuzzi tubs to add to the interior decor and to your mood. There is a private bath for each room. The view from the second-floor rooms is spectacular, with the wide Missouri visible across the floodplain. The candlelit breakfasts star delightful little pastries and secret-recipe muffins. A hot tub has been added that guests may use.

The ***Missouri Bluffs Boutique*** (512 Main St.; 816-640-2770; missouribluffs.com) is full of quirky, unique clothes, jewelry, and handmade purses. It's like a maze, with rooms opening off rooms, but the clothing is delightful and the art is worth the search. The owner obviously enjoys shopping to stock the boutique. Hours are Mon through Sat 10 a.m. to 5 p.m. and Sun noon to 5 p.m.

Take a short jaunt west of Weston back on Highway 45 to see a view worth going way out of your way for. ***Weston Bend State Park*** is one of Missouri's newest, and the scenic overlook that spreads a panorama of the Missouri River and rolling fields, wooded loess hills, and Leavenworth clear across the river in Kansas is simply not to be missed. There's also camping, picnicking, hiking, and bicycling, if that's your pleasure. Call (816) 640-5443.

Snow Creek Ski Area (816-640-2200; skisnowcreek.com), just north of Weston, is open seven days a week through the cold months. There's plenty of man-made snow (up to 4 feet), lifts, ski rentals, and a cozy lodge for après-ski. Normal costs include a snow pass (a lift ticket), plus rental equipment if needed. (Yes, there is downhill skiing in Missouri; the big hills near the Missouri River are satisfyingly steep, if not long. You can still break a leg if you're so inclined.) Snow passes are sold 30 minutes before each session. Beginning in early January every year, there is a special midnight-madness ski on Fri and Sat 10 p.m. to 3 a.m. The regular rates vary so much that calling (816) 640-2200 and listening to the recording is a good idea. Snowboards are available, too. To reach Snow Creek from the north, take I-29 south to exit 20 (Weston), then go to Highway 273 and drive about 5 miles. When you reach a flashing red light at Highways 273 and 45, turn right onto Highway 45 and go 8 miles north. Snow Creek is on the right. There is a restaurant and bar, so you can stay for dinner. Lessons are available.

Iatan Marsh near the water treatment plant is the place to be in winter if you're a birder. The warmer waters here attract flocks of migrant waterfowl; who knows what you might spot. Nearby *Bean Lake* and *Little Bean Marsh* catch the birds—and birders—year-round, too. You may see rails and bitterns, yellow-headed blackbirds, green herons, and egrets along with the ducks and geese. An observation tower makes sighting easier; Little Bean Marsh is the largest remaining natural marsh in Missouri, a remnant of our wetlands heritage. All that bird-watching make you thirsty? You'll want to discover nearby *Riverwood Winery* (22200 Hwy. 45 N.; 816-579-9797), near the little town of Rushville. The service, the staff, and the wines get glowing reviews. It's just off Highway 273.

If you've read Lewis and Clark's journals, you'll remember the description of an oxbow they dubbed "Gosling Lake." This is now thought to be Sugar Lake in *Lewis and Clark State Park* (816-579-5564; mostateparks.com), just off US 59. There's a huge fish hatchery here; you can see anything from fry to fingerlings to lunkers.

St. Joseph ("Where the West Officially Started Getting Wild") is a river town that lost the race to Kansas City when KC was first to bridge the Muddy Mo with the Hannibal Bridge. Still a big and bustling town, it has plenty for the day-tripper to do and see. Consider this: St. Joe has eight museums.

The *Albrecht-Kemper Art Museum* (2818 Frederick; 816-233-7003 or 888-254-2787; albrecht-kemper.org) has a collection of some of the finest American art in the country, including works by Mary Cassatt, William Merritt Chase, George Catlin, and Missouri's own Thomas Hart Benton. Housed in an old Georgian manse, the museum has been in operation since 1966. Hours are Tues 9 a.m. to 4 p.m., Wed through Fri 10 a.m. to 4 p.m., Sat and Sun 1 to 4 p.m. Entry fees are $10 for adults, $8 for seniors, and $7 for students.

Then of course there's the 1858 **Patee House** at 12th and Penn, St. Joseph's only National Historic Landmark. The magnificent old hotel was the original headquarters for the Pony Express. It houses a tiny village inside a downstairs room, plus a steam engine that almost pulls into the rebuilt "station." Admission is $8 for adults, $7 for seniors (60+), $5 for students (6–17), and age 5 and under free.

Also at 12th and Penn is the **Jesse James Museum** (816-232-8206), and the **Robidoux Row Museum** is at 3rd and Poulin. Admission to each is $2. The **Pony Express Museum** (914 Penn St.) chronicles the history of these early mail runs. It is open Mar through Oct, Mon through Sat 9 a.m. to 5 p.m. and Sun 11 a.m. to 4 p.m. In the winter, the hours are a bit shorter; the museum closes at 4 p.m. on weekdays.

There's a morbid fascination to this next one, the **Glore Psychiatric Museum,** at (3408 Frederick Ave.; 816-232-8471; stjosephmuseum.org), 1 mile west of I-29 exit 47. The museum is housed in an old, rather forbidding wing on the hospital grounds and features 20 display rooms of arcane treatments for psychiatric disorders, from prehistoric times to the recent past. (What did cavemen do, you ask? Knocked a hole in your skull to let out the evil spirits.) Admission is free.

As long as we are on the subject of museums, here's a bizarre one that might interest you: **The Heaton-Bowman-Smith & Sidenfaden Funeral Museum** (3609 Frederick Blvd.; 816-232-3355 or 816-232-4428) in St. Joseph displays the state's oldest funeral home, circa 1842, belonging to the state's first licensed funeral director. The museum is full of creepy things like old coffins, the small basket Jesse James's body was carried to the undertaker in, old cooling boards (yuck, don't even think about it!), as well as lots of photos and newspaper clippings. Please remember that this is a working funeral parlor, so be respectful of the families there. It is free, but you have to call first.

Did we neglect dinner? Oh dear! For a hearty, German-style dinner, with its piquant flavors and rich sauces, there's one nearby at **The Cabbage Roll** (2641 Lafayette St.; 816-233-4444). It's an old-school, family-run restaurant featuring traditional German dishes and daily specials. If customer ratings are any indication—and they are—it rates 4.7 out of 5.

For some good Cajun cuisine, also in a historic brick building downtown, find **Boudreaux's Louisiana Seafood & Steaks** (224 N. 4th St.; 816-387-9911; boudreauxsstjoe.com), and *Laissez les bons temps rouler* ("Let the good times roll"). If you like Cajun food, you will love this menu. The Cajun and Creole dishes are wonderful—jambalaya, red beans, anything blackened—but

Boudreaux's is also a full steak house with excellent-quality meat. The seafood is outstanding as well.

If a juicy steak with all the fixings is your thing, **Hoof & Horn Steak House** (429 Illinois Ave.; 816-238-0742; hoofandhornsteakhouse.net) has been grilling steaks to perfection since 1896. It must be doing something right to be in business that long. Outdoors the building looks as if it hasn't changed a bit since the 19th century when drovers, trappers, riverboat men, and travelers dined there. Open Wed through Fri 11 a.m. to 9 p.m. and Sat 4 p.m. to 9 p.m.

Stay at **Whiskey Mansion** (1723 Francis St.; 816-676-1529; whiskeymansion1885.com), a historic 1885 mansion that has been restored in St. Joseph's historic center. The rooms are quiet and full of antiques, and are reasonably priced. Or move from whiskey to beer and step into the wealthy world of the **Shakespeare Chateau Inn & Gardens Bed & Breakfast** (809 Hall St.; 303-232-2667; shakespearechateau.com). This incredible mansion must be seen to be believed. It is in the Hall Street Historic District downtown. The spooky-looking old mansion is a perfect setting for murder mystery dinners, which are always fun, but the home isn't spooky at all. It is a luxury bed-and-breakfast furnished with pricey antiques. There are beautiful gardens for weddings, and a gourmet breakfast. The rooms each have Wi-Fi, a Jacuzzi tub, a private bath, and a plasma big-screen HDTV.

Book lovers will rejoice in finding **Books Revisited,** a used bookstore at 1906B N. Belt Hwy, owned by the Rolling Hills Library. You're sure to find something to pique your interest, at affordable prices. There are comfy chairs here and there to sit and browse before you make your purchases. Do bring a nice big bag to take them home in. No one walks out with just one book. The store gets fresh inventory all the time but also features local authors and history books. Visit stjomo.com for a complete listing of everything going on in town.

The man *Rolling Stone* called "The King of Hip Hop," rapper Eminem, the multiplatinum-record and dozen–Grammy Award winner is from St. Joseph. Eminem, aka Marshall Bruce Mathers III, was born here in 1972.

In 1981, when Ronald Regan became president of the United States, Jane Wyman, a native of St. Joe too, became the "first ex-wife" of an American president.

For sheer spectacle visit **Loess Bluffs National Wildlife Refuge** near **Mound City** (660-442-3187; fws.gov/refuge/loess-bluffs) during the fall migration. You may see up to 350,000 snow geese fill the air like clouds. These clouds, though, are full of thunder; the sound of that many wings is deafening. Snow, blue, and Canada geese, migrating ducks, and attendant bald eagles (as many as 150 representatives of our national symbol), plus coyotes, beavers, muskrats, and deer, make this a wildlife lover's paradise. At least 268 species of birds have been recorded on the refuge. It's an essential stop on the flyway for migratory waterfowl, as it has been for centuries; this area was described in the journals of Lewis and Clark. There are now 7,193 acres on the refuge just off US 159; watch for signs. Unusual loess hills that look like great dunes, reddish and fantastically eroded, are threaded with hiking trails.

Audrey's Motel (1211 State St.; 660-442-3192; audreysmotel.com), off I-29, is an old-style motel, and clean as a new penny. An hour and a half north of KC, it's handy to both travelers and wildlife watchers. It overlooks the Loess Bluffs Wildlife Refuge in the valley below—it's in the town of *Mound City*—and it's a great place to stay after a long day of wildlife-watching. The rooms on the backside have big picture windows that allow you to watch the flocks come in to feed in the evening or rise in great clouds in the morning. Sunsets are spectacular here, plus there's a continental breakfast. Audrey's is pet-friendly on the lower level, if your dog or cat also enjoys a nice outing. Hunters find this a handy spot to stay, too, with freezer facilities and experienced guides.

Hungry for a delicious, hearty meal? Locals and visitors alike love *Quackers Steakhouse* (660-442-5502) in downtown Mound City at 1012 State St. (you won't need a GPS; this is a small town.) From pulled pork to prime rib, fried chicken to tenderloins to burgers, and an array of salads and desserts, you'll find something to fill that hollow space. It's open Mon through Thurs 10:30 a.m. to 10 p.m. and Fri and Sat till midnight; happy hour is from 3 p.m. to 6 p.m.

If you're jonesing for Mexican, you can't go wrong with *Señor Barrigas* (515 State St.; 660-442-0176). The place has a cozy atmosphere and gets great reviews both for the food and the service, and is so much cooler than fast food.

At *R Farm Distilling* (16755 Hwy. 59; 660-442-1006; rfarmdistilling.com) in Mound City, they plant, harvest, and distill the corn, wheat, and rye that create signature whiskey spirits from field to finish. Tour and tasting times are Thurs and Fri 1 and 3 p.m. and Sat noon, 1:30, 3, and 4:30 p.m. A Missouri favorite seems to be the Gooey Butter Cake Cream Liqueur made with R Farm whiskey. You can taste the bourbon and whiskey that is currently aging but not yet for sale—good things take time—and there are snacks and specialty desserts. Any of the vodka cocktails on the menu can be made into mocktails for those who don't drink but love to sit on the patio and feel the clean Missouri air. Enjoy the tour and the day and get your **Missouri Spirits Expedition** stamp, too.

Now let's head to *Maryville.* Go east on US 159, then north on US 59 to Highway 113. Follow it east to Highway 46 and east into Maryville, home to *5 Mile Corner Antique Mall* (30622 US 71 S.; 660-562-2294). Five thousand square feet of antiques are waiting for you to peruse. Hours are Mon through Sat 10 a.m. to 5 p.m. There's more to do in Maryville than just shop, of course.

For instance, you can visit the Mary Linn Performing Arts Theater to hear a concert or watch a play performed by the Missouri Repertory Company.

A little farm in Maryville was the birthplace in 1888 of author and lecturer Dale Carnegie, who ended up teaching everyone *How to Win Friends and Influence People* in a big way.

If you are ready for a bit of quiet, retreat from the world at **Conception Abbey** (conceptionabbey.org) at the junction of US 136 and Highway VV in **Conception Junction.** Benedictine monks run the **Printery House** (800-322-2737), where they make greeting cards and colorful notes (ask for their catalog) when they are not going about their real work. Benedictines consider their true work to be prayer—but the work of their hands is prayer, too. Stay over at the 1,000-acre retreat, 900 of which is productive farmland; visit with "the weather monk," or learn along with the seminarians. The Romanesque Basilica of the Immaculate Conception (1891) adjoining the monastery has examples of Beuronese art. Tours can be arranged by calling the guest center (660-944-2809) to make a reservation.

If you love charming old historic districts, don't miss **Maysville,** just west of I-35 on Highway 6. You can compare its main historic district with a wonderful old photo from the 1920s taken from the same spot and feel as if you've stepped back in time. All that's missing are the Model-T Fords.

Hungry for some good Mennonite cooking? The **Old Cook Stove** tucked into the edge of Maysville (119 SE Rosa Rd.; 816-449-2285) is a spot you won't want to miss. In addition to a broad range of choices on the menu, it offers pre-packaged country cheeses in the cooler, along with a variety of old-fashioned deli meats, bulk foods, specialty coffees, breads, and mouthwatering baked goods, especially those luscious Mennonite-style fried pies. It's open Tues through Fri 7 a.m. to 5 p.m. and Sat 8:30 a.m. to 2 p.m.

How about a real Italian soda in cherry or cranberry, or a selection of teas you won't find just anywhere? **Lot Community Coffee** (212 W. Main St., Ste. C; 816-306-6538) has all of that and more. Open Mon to Fri 7 a.m. to 2 p.m. And look for the big, happy piggies in the storefront windows (can't miss it) at **Jim Bob's Backyard BBQ** (110 W. Main St.; 816-306-8070). It is your typical Missouri BBQ with checkered tablecloths and good smoked beef. Don't miss it. Closed Mon.

In nearby **Osborn** you'll find the **Shatto Milk Company** (9406 N. Hwy. 33; 816-930-3862), a wonderful dairy that offers fun events and farm tours, as well as delicious flavored milks, non-dairy drinks, cheese, butter, and ice cream in addition to regular milk and cream. And do read the labels; they're quirky and hilarious.

Heading roughly toward Smithville Lake? Why not take the back roads and small highways and explore? Leaving Lawson, you can take Highway PP toward Holt. What's that motorcycle sculpture silhouetted against the sky? Check it out. It's **Walnut Creek Winery** (90 N. Main St.; 816-776-8847; walnutcreekwine. com), with a wall of wines for your delectation—enjoy a variety of tastings and pairings. The decadent made-from-scratch crème brûlée makes this place a definite magnet.

But that's not all. On the south side of the main drag is **Angle Acres** (619 Oak St.; 816-269-1562; angleacres.com) in **Lathrop,** a delightful find in this era of fast food and convenience stores in every small town. Molly Angle used to go to all the farmers' markets in the area with her honey and other things, gathering up her goods and her home-schooled kids and driving all over the region, but then decided to open her own store close to home. This general store is fully stocked with bulk herbs and spices, teas, Molly's honey (some infused or otherwise flavored, such as cinnamon honey, pepper honey, and just imagine the garlic honey as a marinade—all of which you can sample), BBQ supplies, jams, jellies, apple butter, beeswax candles, local meats, and more. Open Wed through Fri 11 a.m. to 6 p.m. and Sat 8 a.m. to noon.

Hop on over to **Enchanted Frog Antiques** (7950 E. Hwy. 116; 816-740-6933). It's a short jaunt east on Highway 116—keep going to discover a huge, well-kept inventory that will have you hanging out for hours. Owner Joyce Steinbuch will be glad to answer all your questions or aim you in the right direction.

Visiting during berry season? Lathrop is a great growing area for these luscious, sweet treats. Check out **Mule Barn Berries** (223 NE Mule Barn Rd.; 877-487-3778; mulebarnberries.com) and enjoy a day on the farm as you pick. You can pick blackberries, raspberries, corn, and tomatoes depending on the season.

Head north on Highway 33 and turn west onto Highway 116/33, and you'll find **Plattsburg,** the county seat of Clinton County and home of some gorgeous murals. **Sugar Whipped Bakery** (107 N. Main St.; 816-930-0014) is so good they run out of goodies regularly and must close up early. It looks tiny from the street, but it packs a huge wallop of yummy sweetness.

Leaving Plattsburg on Highway C, you'll end up near Smithville Lake, having made yet another loop.

Smithville is near the intersection of US 169 and Highway 92, and if all you know about the place is that it used to flood, you're in for a nice surprise. **Justus Drugstore** (106 W. Main St.; 816-532-2300) is the place to stop and order the grilled Berkshire port rib eye and smoked crispy shoulder on chestnut risotto. What! In a drugstore? It's been reviewed in the *Kansas City Star, Bon*

President for (Less Than) a Day

The Greenlawn Cemetery in Plattsburg is the final resting place of a man who served as president of the US for one day—Sunday, March 4, 1849. Outgoing vice president George M. Dallas had already resigned from office the Friday before. The term of President James K. Polk expired at noon on the fourth. The incoming Zachary Taylor refused to take his oath on the Sabbath, waiting until 11:30 Monday morning. For that 23 1/2-hour period, the nation had no elected chief executive. The Succession Law of 1792 stated that the head of the Senate automatically became president should the top two offices be vacant. David Rice Atchison was that man. They say the president slept through much of his term of office. There is no presidential library here, but there is a statue of Atchison at the entrance of the Clinton County Courthouse in Plattsburg.

Appétit, and *Time* magazine in the past few years. So trust me on this or check it out yourself at drugstorerestaurant.com. Dining hours are Wed through Thurs 5:30 to 10 p.m., Fri and Sat till 11 p.m., and Sun till 9 p.m.

The town is close by **Smithville Lake** for summer fun, and there are plenty of shops to browse in. Smithville Lake is a fairly recent addition to Missouri's array of man-made lakes. Constructed by the US Army Corps of Engineers to control the flooding that Smithville residents have lived with since there was a Smithville, the lake is also a magnet for water-lovers. Turn north off Highway 92 (between Kearney and the town of Smithville) for sailing, fishing, boating, or just messing around.

Also at the lake is Missouri's own **Woodhenge,** a re-creation of a Woodland Native American site that may have been used as an astronomical observatory around 5,000 years ago. The original location of Woodhenge was uncovered during the building of the lake, and dredging was halted until archaeologists could study the area. It was important enough that the present site was reconstructed as an aid to further study; scientists from Woods Hole, Massachusetts, have come here to observe the solstice and equinox.

Near the dam at Smithville Lake, one of the largest glacial erratics in the area squats like a patient dinosaur under an accretion of graffiti. A large, pink Sioux-quartzite stone, this elephant-size monster was brought here by the last glacier some 15,000 years ago. It may have been an important landmark for the Paleo-Indians who lived in the area.

At the **Jerry Litton Visitor Center** (16311 DD Hwy N.; 816-532-0174), also near the dam, you can find out about these earliest inhabitants, about visits by Lewis and Clark as they came through on the nearby Missouri River, about the pioneer settlers, and about the birds and animals that make this area home. Admission is free.

Places to Stay in Northwest Missouri

KANSAS CITY

Holiday Inn
11130 Ambassador Dr.
(airport)
(816) 891-9111
Inexpensive

NORTH KANSAS CITY

Marriott at the Airport
775 Brasallia Ave.
(816) 464-2200
Moderate

LIBERTY

Days Inn
209 N. 291 Hwy.
(816) 781-8770
Inexpensive

Fairfield Inn
8101 N. Church

(816) 792-4000
Inexpensive

JAMESPORT

Jamesport Inn Motel
305 W. Auberry Grove
(800-884-5946)
Inexpensive

Places to Eat in Northwest Missouri

KANSAS CITY

Cascone's Italian Restaurant and Lounge
3733 N. Oak Trafficway
(north of the river)
(816) 454-7977
Moderate

Trezo Mare
4105 N. Mulberry Dr.
(Briarcliffe Village north of the river)
(816) 505-3200
trezomare.com
Expensive

Majestic Steakhouse
931 Broadway (downtown)
(816) 471-8484
majestickc.com
Expensive

Stroud's
5410 NE Oak Ridge Dr.
(north of the river)
(816) 454-9600
stroudsrestaurant.com/
north.html
Moderate

LAWSON

Catrick's Cafe
410 N. Pennsylvania Ave.
(816) 580-4177
Inexpensive

FINDING HELPFUL VISITOR INFORMATION

Excelsior Springs
exspgschamber.com
(816) 630-6161

Jamesport Community Association
jamesportmissouri.org
(660) 684-6146

RIVERSIDE

Corner Cafe
4541 NW Gateway Dr.
(816) 741-2570
thecornercafe.com
Inexpensive

WESTON

Weston Red Barn Farm
16300 Wilkerson Rd.
(816) 386-5437
westonredbarnfarm.com
Inexpensive

Northeast Missouri

North of St. Louis the land changes. Hills are gentler; they are thske legacy of a wall of glacial ice that smoothed rough edges and brought with it tons of rich, deep soil some 15,000 years ago. Thanks to that gift, quintessentially mid-American towns are dotted with the docile shapes of cows; barns are large and prosperous-looking; fencerows blossom with wildflowers; and bluebirds and meadowlarks sing.

Northeast Missouri is rich in history as well. That consummate storyteller Mark Twain was born here; he has endowed us with more colorful quotations than any writer before or since. You've heard of Mark Twain Cave and his boyhood home in Hannibal, but did you know that near Florida, Missouri, you can explore Samuel Clemens's birthplace? General Omar Bradley's birthplace is in this area, too, along with General John J. Pershing's boyhood home and a monument to General Sterling Price.

The Civil War raged from St. Louis to the Iowa border, where the Battle of Athens took place. Tiny Palmyra was the site of an atrocity that Presidents Abraham Lincoln and Jefferson Davis called the worst of war crimes.

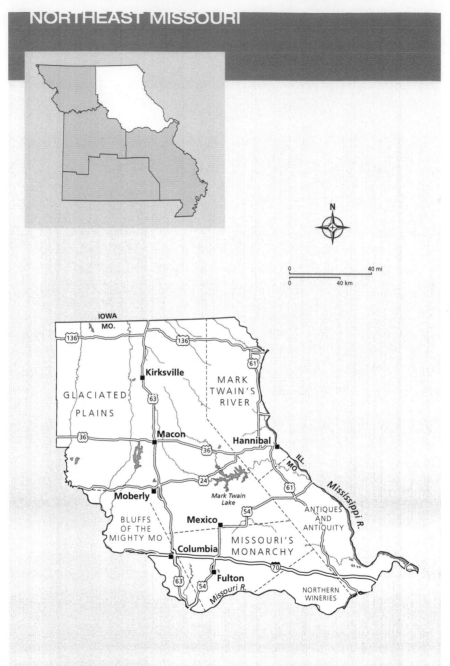

All along the Missouri River valley are tiny, picturesque towns, many with a German heritage, and many with wineries where you can taste the best the US has to offer. (Mount Pleasant's port won the gold in international competition.) Lewis and Clark passed by these town sites on their way to the Northwest Passage and remarked on them in their journals.

The mighty Mississippi is busy with commerce, as it has been for more than 200 years. Barges churn by, and the power of that mile-wide channel vibrates under you as you stand on a riverboat deck. The Great River Road, which runs along the Mississippi from New Orleans to its source, is so picturesque that plans are afoot to make it a National Scenic Byway.

missouri borders

Missouri borders eight states (Nebraska, Iowa, Illinois, Kentucky, Tennessee, Arkansas, Oklahoma, and Kansas). Only Tennessee touches as many neighbors.

Bald eagles feed along both rivers in winter, drawn by open water and good fishing below the locks and dams. Amish communities, college towns, museums, eateries, petroglyphs, wildlife refuges—whatever your interest, you'll find it satisfied in northeast Missouri, where literally everything is off the beaten path.

Antiques and Antiquity

Just north of St. Louis is **St. Charles** (mile 39.5 on the KATY Trail). Missouri's first capitol is located at 208–216 S. Main St. (636-940-3320); legislators met here until October 1826, when the abandoned buildings began to settle slowly into decay. In 1961 the State of Missouri began a 10-year restoration project that sparked the revitalization of St. Charles. Shops, restaurants, and delightful little surprises abound. Take a walking tour of history; the St. Charles Convention and Visitors' Bureau (636-946-7776; historicstcharles.com) can get you started.

You should have collected a batch of stamps for your **Missouri Spirits Expedition** log by now, but there are a few more distilleries coming up in this section. Let's start with **St. Louis Distillery** at their new address 825 South Main St. in historic Old Town in St. Charles (314-805-0867; stldistillery.com), voted the Best Craft Vodka Distillery in the USA by Readers' Choice. If you want to taste a pure, smooth vodka, try the single-batch Cardinal Sin Vodka. There are other Cardinal Sins, you know: There's Envy, a rye whiskey; Wrath, with cinnamon and chili pepper; Pride, an American single malt; and Greed, Imperial Whiskey—and OMG this brown sugar whiskey is surely the greatest sin of all. The tasting room is open Wed and Thurs 12 to 5 p.m., Fri and Sat 12 to 7 p.m.

Boone's Lick Trail Inn (1000 S. Main St.; 636-947-7000; booneslick.com) is an 1840 Federal-style home on the Boone's Lick Trail, right where the trail has crossed Main Street for more than 155 years. It is also right by the ***KATY Trail*** and pet-friendly, so bring your four-legged hiking buddy. Seven guest rooms are decorated in regional antiques, and there are two gathering rooms. It is close to the airport and the Ameristar Casino.

The city is the state's largest National Register Historic District, with 10 blocks of mid-1800s buildings authentically restored. Stroll along cobblestone streets, watch the river flow by, and enjoy fine dining, antiquing, and history.

Both of our big rivers have claimed more than their share of casualties. Steamboats sank with dismal regularity, and to this day—locks and dams notwithstanding—riverboat captains watch their charts and take their soundings much as Samuel Clemens did when he sang out, "Mark twain!" The channels of both the Missouri and the Mississippi are graveyards for boats, from tugs to stern-wheelers; the rivers are not to be taken lightly. Our Lady of the Rivers Shrine, a lighthouse-like monument at Portage de Sioux, is a reminder that brave travelers needed all the help they could get.

That said, it's time to board the ***Ameristar Casino St. Charles*** (1 Ameristar Blvd.; 855-680-3239). The station is off I-70 just 10 minutes west of Lambert Airport and gives you two action-packed casinos. The casino on the boat is open Sun through Thurs 8 a.m. to 5 a.m. and 24 hours Fri, Sat, and holidays. Take the 6th Street exit (229A) just across the bridge.

New on the block is the ***Schlafly Bankside*** (920 S. Main St.; 314-241-2337; schlafly.com), a brewpub next to the Missouri River. It is the kind of place where friends and neighbors come to gather around a pint, and is just a few steps from where the famed Lewis and Clark Expedition began. It opens every day at 11 a.m. and stays open until 9 p.m. on weekdays and 10 p.m. on weekends (Sun till 8 p.m.).

trivia

The Missouri River flows north—the wrong way and against all natural order—along St. Charles County. It flows north for several miles, then turns east to join the Mississippi River. This is one of the few places in the Western Hemisphere where a major river flows north.

This is an area with more than 100 quaint shops and restaurants plus many art, craft, and historical festivals offered throughout the year. Be prepared to spend at least a day here. St. Charles is also right on the KATY Trail. If you didn't bring your bike, you can rent one at the ***Touring Cyclist*** (11816 Saint Charles Rock Rd.; 314-739-5183; touringcyclist.com) in ***Bridgeton.*** The shop will provide bikes, tours, transportation, or anything a cyclist needs to do the KATY Trail. Susan Schneider, Sean

Maiscott (loves mountain biking), and Dan Lindsay, the mechanic who knows it all about biking and the KATY Trail, are here to solve your problems and give you good advice.

Winfield, Clarksville, Louisiana—the names are strung like beads along the Great River Road (now scenic Highway 79) between St. Louis and Hannibal. These little towns harbor more antiques shops than you will know what to do with. There are so many, in fact, that we have room to include only those towns that have additional attractions. Don't let that stop you, though; Missouri is a mecca for affordable goodies. If you can't find what you're looking for, you just haven't found the magic spot yet, and isn't the search as much fun as the finding?

Little **Eolia** has **St. John's Episcopal Church** and cemetery, the oldest Episcopal church west of the Mississippi.

Bowling Green features antiques shops along Business US 61. **Honeyshuck** (207 E. Champ Clark Dr.; 573-324-5224) is the restored front-gable-and-wing frame home of House Speaker James Beauchamp "Champ" Clark, who was elected to the US House of Representatives in 1892 and went on to become minority leader in 1909. Clark was a frontrunner for the Democratic nomination for president but lost it to New Jersey governor Woodrow Wilson on the 46th ballot. The house got its name from the yard's honey locusts, whose shucks fall to the ground.

Several miles outside Bowling Green on Highways Y and M is a thriving Amish community. It is filled with talented craftspeople who carry on the traditions passed down to them by their parents. Several families make and sell handmade crafts and bakery goods. A woodworking shop creates beautiful handmade furniture and cabinets. You can arrange for a tour of the area by calling the Bowling Green Chamber of Commerce at (573) 324-6800.

If your sweet tooth needs satisfying while you're in Bowling Green, be sure to visit **Bankhead Candies** (810 N. Bus. US 61; 573-324-2312; bankheadcandies.com). They've been making hand-dipped chocolates since 1919, and

TOP RECOMMENDATIONS IN NORTHEAST MISSOURI

Buck's Ice Cream	Mount Pleasant Estates
Hannibal	Poppy
KATY Trail	Rocheport
Les Bourgeois Vineyards	St. Charles

experience does make a difference! Four generations are involved, and owner Laura Portwood says most people tell her that candy is an impulse item, not a destination. "Not with us!" she says with a laugh. The candy is still prepared in large copper kettles, poured onto a marble table, cut, and hand-dipped. Chocolates can be ordered online but will not be mailed in the summertime, when they would melt.

snakingfrolics

Clarksville was called Appletown by river men because of the huge quantity of apples it shipped on the river each fall. But "Snakeville" would have been more accurate, because the really big feature of the town was its rattlesnake population. During its early years Clarksville was a choice place for a popular sport called "snaking frolics." The record was set by the town constable, who along with others in town killed 9,000 rattlers on one of the town's annual spring hunts.

Lock and Dam No. 25 on the Mississippi is a fine place to watch the eagles feed in the winter. Or take the old Winfield Ferry across the river to Calhoun County, Illinois. (Don't worry, you can come right back if you're not through antiques hunting.)

If you fancy a bit of wilderness about now, a short detour west on Highway 47 will take you to spectacular *Cuivre River State Park* (636-528-7247; mostateparks.com). More than 31 miles of trails will let you discover one of the state's most rustic parks. The rough terrain is more like the Ozarks than the rest of glacier-smoothed northern Missouri, and like the Ozarks, it encourages many plants found only farther south, such as flowering dogwood, Missouri

TOP ANNUAL EVENTS IN NORTHEAST MISSOURI

FEBRUARY
True/False Film Festival
Columbia
Documentary film festival; bands play at screening and directors chat with audiences.
(573) 442-8783

JULY
National Tom Sawyer Days
(and National Fence Painting Contest)
Hannibal
(573) 221-2477 or 1-TOMANDHUCK
(866-263-4825) (toll-free)

Annual Demolition Derby
Macon
maconmochamber.com

AUGUST
Fork & Cork Artisan Folk Festival
Macon

SEPTEMBER
Great Forest Park Balloon Race
greatforestparkballoonrace.com
Columbia

orange coneflower, and dittany. Frenchman's Bluff overlooks the Cuivre River valley. The Lincoln Hills region, where Cuivre River State Park is found, formed millions of years ago when intense pressures caused the earth to buckle. Erosion cut even deeper; the resulting springs, sinkholes, and rocky cliffs make this an outdoors-lover's paradise. Archaeologists speculate that the region was home to prehistoric humans as early as 12,000 years ago; a 1937 dig unearthed a stone chamber containing a skeleton and pieces of a clay pot.

Clarksville is finding its way back—but back toward the past. With about the same population that it had in 1860, this spic-and-span town has new life in its old veins. A historic preservation effort mounted in 1987 has saved many of the delightful buildings in record time. Age-old traditions of quilting, stained glass, blacksmithing, and furniture making are found in Clarksville. Many small businesses closed in 2022 due to flooding, but much of the town is on the National Register of Historic Places, and it has a good museum.

The town commands an 800-square-mile view of the valley of the Big Muddy from an aerie on the highest point overlooking the Mississippi. Surprisingly, barge traffic on the river below is constant. See ice-formed drumlins (those are hills) in this panoramic view.

Clarksville is a great place to observe wintering eagles; the **Missouri Department of Conservation's Eagle Days,** held here the last weekend of January, can swell the town's normal population of 500 to more than 5,000. Bald eagles can number from the hundreds to the thousands, depending on the weather. (The colder the winter has been, the more eagles gather here.) The **Clarksville Eagle Center** offers information, a museum, and spanking-clean restrooms. Call (573) 242-3132 or check out seatriverroad.com/hannibal/hanevents/eagledays.htm.

Visit clarksvillemo.org for more information on the town.

The entire business district of downtown **Louisiana** is on the National Register of Historic Places. It is what a wealthy river town looked like in the mid-1800s and is well known for its antiques shops along Georgia and Main Streets. It is filled with beautiful antebellum homes and the occasional paddleboat going by on the Mighty Mississippi. Close your eyes and imagine. But most interesting is the fact that it has the most intact Victorian streetscape in the state. Dozens of historic homes line Georgia and Main Streets, and it still, of course, has a town square. The **Louisiana Historical Museum** is at 304 Georgia St. (573-754-5550). Also worth a visit, perhaps, is the old **Gates of Peace Jewish Cemetery** off US 54.

There is some good antiquing in Louisiana. At 515 Georgia St. is **Kate's Attic Antiques and Mini Mall** (573-754-4544), with 40 booths to browse through. Hours are 10 a.m. to 4:30 p.m. every day.

The ***Eagles Nest Inn*** is in a beautifully restored and renovated building at 217 Georgia St. (573-754-9888; innateaglesnest.com). The inn is over a winery and European-style bakery, and breakfast is served in the bakery every morning. What a grand way to wake up. ***Great River Road B&B*** is high on a bluff with a panoramic view overlooking the Mississippi River at 403 N. Main St. (573-725-5136). This 1860s Victorian home offers incredible sightings of eagles, not just a view of the countryside. Beverly and Charlie Cogar are the hosts.

Mark Twain's River

For tourists, ***Hannibal*** is not exactly "off the beaten path." Half a million people annually come through this picturesque little town. Everybody knows about the Mark Twain Boyhood Home. Everybody's seen that fence—or at least pictures of it—where Tom Sawyer tricked his buddies into doing his work for him. There is also a fine dinner cruise on the Mississippi riverboat the *Mark Twain*. So we'll let you find them on your own.

But did you know that right across the street, at 211 Hill St., is the ***Becky Thatcher House***? Actually Becky was Laura Hawkins, who lived here in the 1840s and attended school with young Sam Clemens. She was his childhood sweetheart, immortalized in print as Tom Sawyer's Becky Thatcher. The upstairs parlor and bedroom of the home are restored and are open to the public at no charge. The main floor features a bookshop carrying the largest selection anywhere of books by or about Mark Twain. First editions and out-of-print books are sometimes available. It's owned by the Mark Twain Museum (573-221-9010; marktwainmuseum.org).

Stop at ***Becky's Old Fashioned Ice Cream Parlor & Emporium*** (318 N. Main; 573-221-0822; beckythatcher.com), which is right around the corner from the Mark Twain Boyhood Home, for a cool ice-cream treat. The back third of the shop has a collection of Mark Twain books and other children's classics as well.

While you're in the historic district, look for ***Ayers Pottery*** (308 N. 3rd; 573-221-6960; ayerspottery.com), half a block from the Mark Twain Museum. Steve Ayers does beautiful work, using primarily Missouri clays, and the shop is set up to encourage your involvement. There's a hall around three sides of the workshop, so you can see every step in the process. He also stocks a selection of beautiful kites, porcelain jewelry, baskets, and hand-forged things—goodies he picks up while on the craft-show circuit. Even when Steve's out of town, the shop is open Mon through Fri 7 a.m. to 3:30 p.m.

Steve has opened another shop in Hannibal, aptly named ***Java Jive Coffee House*** (211 N. Main St.; 573-221-1017), where, along with pottery, he also carries coffee beans in many flavors. If you want to try some of them, there is a delightful cappuccino bar in the back of the store. Hours are Mon through Sat 7 a.m. to 8 p.m. and Sun till 6 p.m. Steve is involved in a project to list all of the artists living along the river route. While you sip your espresso, he can give you directions to many other craftspeople to visit along the way.

If elegant Victoriana is your weakness, stay in gingerbread heaven at the **Garth Woodside Mansion** (11069 New London Gravel Rd.; 573-221-2789; garthmansion.com). This one's on the National Register of Historic Places, and it deserves to be. Mark Twain was often a guest of the Garths. Built in 1871, this stunning Victorian summer mansion is on 39 acres of gardens and woodlands that retain the feel of early Hannibal countryside.

You won't believe the three-story flying staircase with no visible means of support; you might not trust it, either, though they say it's quite safe. Enter the walnut-lined library through 9-foot doors, or check out the extra-wide hostess's seat in the dining room. (No, the hostess wasn't that wide; it accommodated the voluminous petticoats of the era.) The eight bedrooms still have the discreet opulence of Twain's era, though innkeepers Mary and Kevin Hackmann say that the new featherbeds make people sleep later. The aroma of freshly baked pastries and muffins draws you to the dining room, where the eight-leaf walnut table is just as it was then. You can spend the day rocking on the veranda or watching deer or fox from the library window and spend the evenings leisurely near a fire. Christmas is an especially fine time to visit, when the mansion becomes a fairyland of authentic Victorian decorations.

Don't miss the mansion where Mr. Clemens addressed the cream of Hannibal society on his last visit here in 1902. It's **Rockcliffe Mansion** (1000 Bird St.; 573-221-4140; rockcliffemansion.com), a wonderfully quirky place full of art nouveau decor, which was a breakaway style from the established Victorian. It, too, is on the National Register of Historic Places.

If you're at all Irish (and who isn't, at least one day of the year?), don't miss **St. Patrick,** the only town in the world (with a post office) named for everybody's patron saint. If you like, send a package of mail containing stamped, addressed envelopes to Postmaster, St. Patrick, MO 63466, to get the special St. Paddy's Day cancellation. It's more fun to visit the post office, though. The letter boxes are antique, and the hospitality is the old-fashioned kind you'd expect in a town of 14 souls.

The **Shrine of St. Patrick** is fashioned after the Church of Four Masters in Donegal, Ireland; the style is ancient Celtic. There's a round bell tower with a circular staircase of the kind used on the Auld Sod. Dublin-made stained-glass windows are patterned after the famous illuminated manuscript, the Book of Kells; the most unusual has St. Patrick surrounded by the symbols of Ireland's four provinces: Ulster, Leinster, Munster, and Connaught. Perhaps you are beginning to catch the flavor of the place.

Oh, yes, there's another unusual attraction: geodes. What's a geode, you may ask? You must not be a rock hound, if you are wondering. A geode is a rather undistinguished blob that looks like a rounded river rock. But inside— ah, inside—there is magic. Beautiful crystal formations fill the hollow center of a geode like a Fabergé egg; they're considered gemstones.

trivia

The word *twain* means "two" when used as a mark or measurement of the depth of the water. *Mark twain,* therefore, means "two fathoms."

Some of the world's finest geodes are found in this small area. You can buy one at **Buschling Place,** 3 miles north of Dempsey; the Buschlings specialize in country crafts, turquoise, and, of course, geodes. Or you can find your own at **Sheffler Rock Shop and Geode Mine** (26880 Outer Road 27; 319-795-5013) in **Alexandria** (located 2 miles south of Way- land on US 27). A new highway has gone in here and the old rock shop has been demolished. The new one is a little harder to find, but follow me: Go to the intersection of Highways 27 and 61, then get on the access road going north; stay on it for about 6 blocks and the rock shop will be on the west side of the road. This is the only geode mine in the US that is registered with the US Bureau of Mines. Watch for the round rock building made entirely of 60 tons of mineral specimens. This shop is open year-round and has been selling minerals, agates, and jewelry-making supplies for more than 30 years. If you come to dig your own geodes, bring a rock hammer and a bit of muscle; these treasures don't come without sweat equity. The mine is usually open in the winter from 9 a.m. to 5 p.m., but all manner of conditions affect a mine—cold temperatures, rain-induced flooding—so best to call and see what's going on when you plan to visit. Someone will be there to help you. There is a $25 fee, but you can carry out 50 pounds of geodes. The shop has been expanded to include a huge collection of fossils.

Bethel is the kind of place you dream about when you're feeling nostalgic for the "good old days," when things were simpler and the world was more easily understood, when people could meet one another's eyes directly and a handshake meant everything. Bethel old-timers say, "When you get it right, why change?" And here, they've pulled it off.

It's not all old-time ambience and down-home goodies. Bethel has a thriv- ing art colony. Thousands of people flock here for the **World Sheep and Wool Festival** (ouch! a pun!). Other festivals throughout the year draw folks for antiques, fiddlers, music, and Christmas in Bethel. If you see a line on the sidewalk downtown, likely it's for the family storefront bakery that opens only during festivals. Breads, cinnamon rolls—they've got it.

Founded as a utopian religious colony in 1844, the whole town is listed on the National Register of Historic Places.

Northern Wineries

Take a different loop to see the **Missouri River** and the little wineries that sprout like vines along its banks. There's a lot of history along the Missouri; whatever your interest, you'll find plenty to see and do.

Take Highway 94, for example. It's for people who don't like their roads straight and flat: mile after mile of two-lane blacktop that curves and winds from St. Charles to Jefferson City. It is one of the most beautiful and exhilarating drives in the state and is a practical route to mid-Missouri for those of us who don't enjoy the mind-numbing 70 mph of the interstate. Since you have this book with you, the assumption can be made that you like to drive, so Highway 94 is a "must-do" trip. Cross US 40 outside St. Charles, go a mile, and turn into the **August A. Busch Memorial Wildlife Area.** This 7,000-acre preserve has nature trails, hunting areas, shooting ranges, and 32 lakes for fishing. It features a self-guided tour of native prairie, pine plantation, and farming practices that benefit wildlife. In the spring and fall, thousands of migrating birds can be seen at the shorebird and waterfowl preserve.

Missouri River State Trail, Missouri's part of the KATY Trail following the old MKT Railroad right-of-way, meanders through here, and on weekends large crowds of bikers and hikers wander along the 26 miles of trail from US 40 at Weldon Springs to Marthasville. If you have a bike on the roof, convenient parking can be found all along the trail. There are plenty of places to get a meal or rent bikes if you didn't bring your own, and even a bed-and-breakfast and a winery for a picnic lunch along the trail.

trivia

Defiance is so named because the local townsfolk were so defiant in gaining a stop for their community when the railroad was being built through the area.

There's a spectacular view of the river beyond the outskirts of St. Louis on Highway 94. There are so many good destinations along this route. This road will challenge the best Grand Prix wannabe with its collection of diamond-shaped signs warning of another set of sharp curves. But slow down and watch for wild turkey and deer. Enjoy the tidy farmhouses and pretty churches as you aim for towns such as Augusta, Dutzow, and Hermann that wait along the route.

Missouri Vintners—1800s and Beyond

Winemaking isn't new to the state. The first designated wine district in the country was actually here in Missouri—not California! In the 1800s the wine business thrived here and the wines were internationally acclaimed. By the late 19th century, the entire nation's wine manufacturing and distribution was centered in St. Louis, and Missouri was producing 2 million gallons a year. It was second only to California in wine production. Then Prohibition shut down the wineries, and the state's wine industry all but disappeared for more than four decades. Only one winery continued to operate during the 1920s: St. Stanislaus Winery, located at a seminary, made sacramental wine for religious orders.

You will enjoy **Defiance**'s (mile 59.1 on KATY Trail) little shops and taverns and be amazed to learn that this whole town was under water during the Great Flood of 1993. History buffs will want to take a 6-mile detour from Highway 94 down Highway F to the Daniel Boone Home.

This is a chance to get another stamp on your **Missouri Spirits Expedition** log. Here in **Defiance** is the **Judgment Tree Distillery** (125 Boone Country Ln.; judgmenttree.com). Chris Lorch and Scott Koziatek are the guys who make the fine distilled spirits.

You could also stop in for a visit to the **Sugar Creek Vineyards & Winery** (125 Boone Country Ln.; 636-987-2400; sugarcreekwines.com) to taste some of Missouri's wine. Becky and Ken Miller will show you around. Take Highway 40/61 and turn south onto Highway 94, travel 12 miles along the Lewis and Clark Trail, and watch for the sign. It's the first winery on the Weinstrasse overlooking the Missouri River valley and the KATY Trail. Hours are 10:30 a.m. to 5:30 p.m. every day. All the wineries are closed Thanksgiving, Christmas, and New Year's Day.

Somehow you would imagine a log cabin—or a sod hut, maybe—to have housed Daniel Boone. This beautiful stone house with ivy clinging to its double chimneys, crisply painted shutters, and ample back porch is not what you'd expect at all. Built in 1803, the **Daniel Boone Home** (1868 Hwy. F; 636-949-7535; sccmo.org) is ruggedly elegant and comfortable. Add a DVD player and a microwave, and you could move in tomorrow. Boone lived to a ripe old age. The naturalist John James Audubon described him as a "stout, hale, hearty man." He died here in 1820 at age 86.

Here are Daniel's powder horn and his long rifles, his writing desk, and the very bed where his long career on the American frontier ended. It's a small bedchamber; the four-poster bed looks as if it were just made up with fresh sheets and a clean white counterpane, ready for the man himself to come in from a hard day of hunting, settling the frontier, and making history. Daniel kept a coffin he had made for himself under the bed and periodically tried it out. Alas, he grew too big for it and had to give it away.

The kitchen is cozy, with low beams and a huge fireplace. Mrs. Boone's butter churn sits nearby, and you can almost see the family gathered here, waiting expectantly for that rich, yellow butter to spread on hearth-baked bread. Your tour guide will point out where the whole foundation of the house moved thanks to an earthquake. A chapel, summer kitchen, and spool house have been added on the grounds, and down in a little valley are a number of historic structures that have been moved to the property. A small chapel done in blue and white still hosts weddings set to its 1860 organ music. Check the website for tour times, which are seasonal.

Leaving Defiance, you'll enter the Missouri River valley wine region. There are more wineries along Highway 94 than anywhere else in the state, with a wide choice of places to sample wine and have a meal. You can visit **Montelle Winery** (201 Montelle Dr.; 636-228-4464; montelle.com) at **Osage Ridge,** a half mile east of Augusta on Highway 94. Owner Tony Kooyumjian says the secret to his wine is the vineyards. This part of the state has the first recognized vineyards in the country—before California even—but thanks to Prohibition that all changed. The fact remains that this area has a unique soil, microclimate, and history. This 11 square miles of Missouri farmland is perfect for grapes. Montelle continues to make wines recognized for their unique taste and quality. There is also a distillery here. The Klondike Café at the winery offers lunches to enjoy with the wine. All of the wineries along the river offer wine tasting and sales as well as great spots to enjoy a bottle of wine with a picnic lunch.

Just down the road a piece from Dan'l's house you'll find the little German wine-producing town of **Augusta** (mile 66.4 on the KATY Trail). More than 150 years ago it was a self-sufficient town with a cooperage works, stores, and a German school. Before Prohibition, when Missouri was the second-largest wine-producing state in the nation, there were 13 wineries located in Augusta's valley, beyond the bluffs above the southernmost bend of the river. Deep, well-drained soil and freedom from spring frosts were perfect for viticulture. This is recognized as America's first official wine district and the first in the New World to bear an official "Appellation Control" designation. Today, there are four wineries on the **Augusta Wine Trail:** Augusta Winery, Montelle Winery, Balducci Vineyards, and Noboleis Vineyards.

Augusta still deserves its reputation. **Mount Pleasant Estates** (5634 High St.; 800–467-WINE (9463); mountpleasant.com), at I-44 at the Highway UU exit, 2 miles east of Cuba, was purchased in 1966 by Lucian and Eva Dressel (it's now owned by MPW Inc.). A short 20 years later, the Dressels' 1986 Vintage

Port took top port honors in the International Wine and Spirit Competition in London, England, making theirs the first Missouri winery since Prohibition to win an international gold medal, from a field of 1,175 wines and more than 20 countries. Mount Pleasant's 1987 Jour de la Victoire Ice Wine also won a silver medal, the highest award given to an American ice wine. *Appellation Cafe,* on-site at the winery, is a casual little cafe with fresh-made wraps and sandwiches. It closes in winter.

Augusta Winery is at 5601 High St. (636-228-4301; augustawinery.com). It is a scenic drive through the Missouri River valley, and the winery has a wine and beer garden to bring picnic baskets to; in the summertime (Apr through Nov) there is live music.

If you appreciate lovely wooden sculptures and vessels with an elegant, contemporary feel, you'd hardly expect to find them in the backcountry. But at *Michael Bauermeister Studio,* craftsman Michael Bauermeister is full of surprises. He works with Missouri woods to create delicate, finely designed pieces that would grace the best of homes.

Michael's shop is in an old-fashioned store building in Nona, which isn't a town anymore. It's just Michael's house and shop and a few other buildings. Follow High Street west, which turns into Augusta Bottom Road, 3 miles to the shop on the left side of the road. Shop hours are unpredictable because special orders and commissions keep the craftsman hopping. Call (636) 228-4663 to make sure your trip won't be for nothing. Visit the website at michaelbauermeister.com. He prefers e-mail to make an appointment to visit his studio: michael@bauermeister.com.

trivia

Mount Pleasant Estates' sparkling wine Genesis was used to christen the aircraft carrier USS *Harry Truman* in 1996. At first the shipbuilders sent the bottles back because they wouldn't break, so the people at Mount Pleasant just rebottled the wine in cheaper, thinner bottles for the occasion.

Augusta is a town worth the visit. Go to augusta-missouri.com to get the grand tour. There you will find a link to *Gallery Augusta* (5558 Walnut; 800-748-7638), a family-owned gallery for over 36 years. Framed artwork by well-known artists such as Thomas Kinkade and Jesse Barnes, as well as work by many local artists, Michael Bauermeister for one, are on display. Beautifully hand-carved early American furniture can also be viewed. New artists are added all the time. Hours are Mon through Sat 10 a.m. to 5 p.m.

There are several bed-and-breakfasts in Augusta. The most luxurious is the 1885 *H.S. Clay House* (219 Public St.; 313-261-3244; hsclayhouse.com). The owners give 100 percent to making guests feel like royalty, including a gourmet breakfast. Take-and-go lunches can be made available in the fridge for you to carry with you on your adventures, and dinners made specially by a local chef can be ordered in advance to enjoy in the dining room of the B&B. Visit the website for more about this beautiful home surrounded with 1,600 feet of deck.

A one-lane bridge followed by a 90-degree turn leads you to **Dutzow** (mile 74 on the KATY Trail). If you found Augusta charming, Dutzow is downright quaint. This historic Dutch town, founded in 1832 by Baron Von Bock, was the first German settlement in the Missouri River valley. In the mid-19th century, "Missouri's Rhineland" attracted immigrants who were inspired by enthusiastic accounts of natural beauty and bounty; among the most convincing was Gott-fried Duden's *Report on a Journey to the Western States of North America*, pub-lished in 1829, which contributed to the settlement of these lovely little enclaves all up and down the Missouri River. The town offers several antiques shops.

The severe floods of 1993 and 1995 were setbacks for **KATY Trail State Park,** which runs along the river for more than 200 miles. This long, skinny state park snakes along connecting towns from the St. Louis area to Clinton. The finely crushed gravel trail allows biking or hiking for 45 miles, from St. Charles west to Treloar. You cross bottomland forests filled with migratory birds, wetlands, fields of wildflowers, and dolomite bluffs. The small towns along the way welcome trail users. You can stop for wine tastings at Defiance and Marthasville and lunch at Augusta.

Blumenhof Vineyards and Winery, at 13699 S. Missouri in Dutzow (636-433-2245; blumenhof.com), takes its name from the Blumenberg fam-ily's ancestral farm in the Harz Mountains of Germany; *blumenhof* translates as "court of flowers." Enjoy the winery's Teutonic decor and the welcome invitation to stop and smell the flowers—along with the bouquet of the wine. Blumenhof produces wines from the finest American and European varietal grapes. There's a full range of wines, but dry table wines are a tour de force. (The Vidal Blanc won a gold medal in international competition.) This is a small family farm winery using locally grown grapes from Missouri. Open every day year-round except Easter, Thanksgiving, Christmas, or New Year's. Enjoy the patio in warm weather, then come inside by the tasting room fireplace in winter. Local live music is in the Brathaus Grill in spring, summer, and fall.

Marthasville (mile 77.7 on the KATY Trail) has a covered bridge that takes you back to a time when life was simpler. When you are ready for dinner, find **Cori's Gables** (101 N. Hwy. 47; 636-433-5048); with a nice warm meal—breakfast, lunch, or dinner—or some nighttime fun—live music Fri, Sat, and Sun—this is the place to be. It is a "family tavern," as locals describe it, a casual place with a full bar where children are welcome. From the KATY trailhead the cross-street is One Street, go south on One about 0.3 mile to Highway 47/94.

Bluffs of the Mighty Mo

Highway 94 winds over steep hills set with ponds and quiet, picturesque farms. Small and almost picture-postcard pretty buildings nestled in the trees are clearly visible in winter and half-hidden in summer. The highway follows the river through a series of tiny towns that give you a taste of Missouri past—Rhineland, Bluffton, Steedman, Mokane—each is as inviting as the last. You may find a great little cafe here or a hidden mine of antiques.

Plan to stay awhile in *Columbia.* It's a great base camp for some far-flung exploring—that is, once you can tear yourself away from the town itself.

Columbia is home to the *University of Missouri,* which has a beautiful campus that houses a number of disciplines. If you have an interest in antiquities, don't miss the *Museum of Art and Archaeology* (115 W. Bus. Loop 70), which boasts a collection from six continents and five millennia. The museum, in Pickard Hall at the corner of University Avenue and 9th Street, is on the historic Francis Quadrangle. Built in 1894, it's on the National Register of Historic Places. You'll find artwork by Lyonel Feininger, Lakshmi, Francken the Younger, and many well-known classical and contemporary American artists.

future anchors— takenote!

The University of Missouri–Columbia was the first state university west of the Mississippi. The first school of journalism was founded and the first degree in journalism in the world was awarded at the University of Missouri–Columbia in 1908.

Archaeology has long been a strong field of study at the university, which offers bachelor's, master's, and doctoral degrees as well as courses in museum studies. The museum's collections reflect almost a century of work by students and faculty in places as diverse as Africa, Egypt, South Asia, Greece, and the American Southwest. Pre-Columbian and Oceanic works round out the collection. The museum is wheelchair accessible, and tours for the visually impaired are available without prior notice. Other guided tours can be arranged by calling (573) 882-3591 (at least two weeks in advance for groups). See the website at maa.missouri.edu.

The *Museum of Anthropology* (115 W. Bus. Loop 70; 573-882-3573) was extensively renovated and has displays of Native America that are most interesting. Included in the displays are an Arctic fishing village and a pre-pioneer Midwest settlement—a one-room prairie cabin and a fur trader's canoe filled with beaver pelts and ropes of tobacco.

A Place to Call Home

The *Devil's Icebox* is a unique sinkhole in Rock Bridge Memorial State Park near Columbia. It is the only habitat worldwide for a small flatworm called the pink planarian. This park is known for its many sinkholes, caves, underground streams, and small springs. These are all characteristic of a topography known as "karst." Devil's Icebox Boardwalk leads visitors over the rock bridge to Devil's Icebox, by a sinkhole, past Connor's Spring, and back through the 125-foot-long natural tunnel. The Devil's Icebox is pretty cool, literally, because cooler air flows through along the underground stream. Devil's Icebox Cave, upstream, is closed except to those who register in advance for daylong wild cave tours, which are worthwhile.

While the museums are easy to find, a well-guarded secret on the university campus is **Buck's Ice Cream,** in Eckles Hall (1400 E. Rollins St.; 573-882-1088; cafnr.missouri.edu), part of the food and nutrition service. Ice cream and frozen yogurt are made here daily, and it is wonderful stuff. Try the special Tiger Stripe ice cream. (Just because the nutrition service makes this wonderfully sinful treat doesn't mean it isn't high in butterfat. It is. But what the heck, it is sooooo good.) Hours are noon to 5 p.m. Mon through Fri and on Sat during warm weather. (Buck's is closed between semesters.)

Looking for a unique experience in Columbia? There are some very unusual, actually unique, shops at the corner of 5th and Walnut (500 E. Walnut St.) where **The Shops at Sharp End** has opened with 19 entrepreneurs launching businesses in an old parking garage. Interesting history here: This used to be the center of business for Columbia's Black community from 1900 to the 1960s. Then, as happened in so many communities, urban renewal swept in and tore it all down. Since segregation was in full swing, there was no place for residents to go. Everything just disappeared. A high- rise parking garage was built. This is a brand-new effort to support minority entrepreneurs. Start-up businesses have space to become successful. And what interesting businesses they are: The **Black Tea Bookshop** features books by Black authors and a place to talk about them, **Designs by Neisha** offers custom T-shirts, while **Raw Roots Turmeric** is all about ayurvedic herbs and the information as to why you need them. **Fudge Brand, Mya's Gourmet Popcorn,** and **Vital Apparel** are obviously must-find shops, too. Also to be found are bath and body items, candles, clothing, foods, holistic natural items, and stuffed animals. These are only some of the places in this "retail incubator," which will try to stay true to the original idea by having at least 51 percent minority-owned shops with total space for about 40 shops. Grants are available for business to help with start-up costs. For more information call (573) 801-5662, Wed through Sat from 10 a.m. to 6 p.m.

The **Flat Branch Pub and Brewery,** downtown at 115 S. 5th St. (573-499-0400; flatbranch.com), needless to say, is very popular with students here. (They love the homemade root beer and ginger ale.) You can tour the brewing area or have lunch in the pub or on the patio, weather permitting. Hours are Sun through Thurs 11 a.m. to 9 p.m. and Fri and Sat till 10 p.m.

Columbia has an active and varied crafts community. **Bluestem Missouri Crafts** (573-442-0211; bluestemcrafts.com) showcases the work of more than 80 Missouri artists and craftspeople. Whatever your particular weakness, from wrought iron to weaving, from folk-art whirligigs to fine jewelry, you'll find it at Bluestem (named after the native prairie grass). The shop is located at 13 S. 9th St. and is open Mon through Sat 10 a.m. to 6 p.m. and Sun noon to 5 p.m.

Another source for handmade and unusual items in Columbia is **Poppy** (920 E. Broadway; 573-442-3223; poppymadebyhand.com). Whether you are looking for a gift or just browsing around, this is a place with personality, upbeat and colorful. The owners work directly with the artisans, who do what they do for a living—professionals—as you can tell from the high quality of their work. The store features hand-blown glass, pieces shaped in clay or created from fiber, and a line of exquisite—and expensive—jewelry. Although there is some two-dimensional art, it is mostly a gallery of fine crafts. The shop is open Mon through Sat 10 a.m. to 6 p.m. and Sun noon to 5 p.m.

Carol Leigh Brack-Kaiser is the talent behind two businesses: **Carol Leigh's Specialties** and **Hillcreek Fiber Studio** (hillcreekfiberstudio.com). Carol Leigh's Specialties was created to market products made by Carol's own hands: handspun yarns and fabrics colored with natural dyes, woven shawls, blankets, and wall hangings. Hillcreek Fiber Studio is for teaching. It all began with a spinning class at the nearby university. Spinning led to weaving and then to dyeing, which led to advanced studies in fiber arts. Carol began to take her work to living-history and rendezvous events, where people appreciated the labor and old-world methods of her handmade textiles. Now she sits by her adjustable, triangular loom, which she and her son, Carl Spriggs, patented and now manufacture at her home at 7001 Hillcreek Rd., just outside Columbia.

Carol has several classes in spinning special fibers, in floor loom, and in the ancient methods of inkle and tablet weaving. She also conducts classes in Navajo-style weaving and offers a designer's yarn class. Standing over a simmering vat of wool dye, she produces vibrant colors from indigo; Osage orange (also called hedge apple), which gives vibrant yellows and golds; brazilwood for red, purple, plum, maroon, and burgundy; logwood for lavender and black; cochineal, a bug from Central and South America, for bright reds; madder root for orange-red; and other natural dyes. Carol Leigh asks that you call before you visit: (573) 874-2233 or 800-TRI-WEAV (874–9328). The shop is open Tues through Saturday 9 a.m. to 5 p.m.

One more gustatory note—okay, two: truffles and chocolate pizza. You'll find these and too many other rich temptations to mention at the *Candy Factory* (701 E. Cherry St.; thecandyfactoryonline.com). These folks call themselves "your hometown candy makers," but the good news is that even if Columbia isn't your hometown, they'll be glad to ship anything you want, nationwide. Use the special order number: (573) 443-8222. You can even buy sugar-free chocolates for those people on restricted diets who still need a treat.

Formosa Restaurant is upstairs at 3301 W. Broadway Business Park Ct., Ste D (573-449-3339; formosacolumbia.com) and serves seven styles of Chinese cooking with full bar service. While this little spot is sort of hidden away, plenty of people know about it. Open Mon through Thurs 10:30 a.m. to 10 p.m., Fri and Sat 10 a.m. to 11 p.m., and Sun 11 a.m. to 10 p.m.

Six-Mile Ordinary (700 Fay St.; 573-673-6974; sixmileordinary.com), near Columbia College, was under construction at the time of this writing but should be open by the time you read this. Just the names of the products are worth a trip to buy your Christmas/Chanukah gifts: Deep Six Vodka, El Diablo Tequila, Slick Whistle Whiskey, Old Plank Rum, and Sticky Wicket Gin, plus you can get a stamp on your **Missouri Spirits Expedition** log.

Woodsmen Distilling is at 7239 Hwy. A (660-456-7610; drinkwoodsmen. com). There are corn whiskeys and bourbons and ryes here, but try the Pecan Barrel Whiskey, which is aged six months in white oak barrels, then three years in a pecan barrel. All the flavor comes strictly from the barrel; there are no added pecan flavorings or syrups. This is the only place in the state to find coconut rum. This is the best reason to be doing the **Missouri Spirits Expedition,** isn't it? To find unusual and wonderful spirits to raise your spirit.

Rocheport is a good spot to sample the KATY Trail (mile 178.3) through Missouri's middle; the trail is among the longest of the nation's growing network of rail-trails and stretches more than 200 miles from Machens just north of St. Louis to Clinton, 75 miles southeast of Kansas City. The *KATY Trail* follows the old Missouri-Kansas-Texas Railroad bed that curves along the north bank of the Missouri River, and one of the most scenic parts of the trail rolls from Rocheport southeast to Jefferson City along a wooded band between the river and the cliffs—sheer limestone walls rising 100 feet above the Muddy Mo. The compacted rock pathway is easy riding even for thin racing tires, the canopy of oak and sycamore trees offers brilliant color in the fall, and the trail is flowered with dogwood and redbud in the spring. Summertime rides lead through kaleidoscopic colors of wildflowers and trumpet vine blossoms fluttering with hummingbirds.

Rocheport and many other small mid-Missouri river towns invite modern-day explorers to follow in the footsteps of Lewis and Clark. In the middle of Rocheport is a popular trailhead for the KATY Trail State Park, so whether you choose to follow Lewis and Clark's journey by river, by bike, by foot, or by car, Rocheport is a good place to begin. Missouri's **KATY Trail State Park** is the longest nonmotorized public portion of the entire Lewis and Clark Trail. The trail travels along the Missouri River for much of its 238-mile distance across the state. The scenery is beautiful, and it is the perfect place to find solitude with Mother Nature along the Mighty Mo. For more information about the KATY Trail, contact the Department of Natural Resources at (800) 334-6946 and order your free color brochure. For general trip planning, call the Missouri Division of Tourism at (800) 877-1234 or visit visitmo.com.

Rocheport (rocheport.com) is an interesting hamlet; it is so historic that the whole town was placed on the National Register of Historic Places. It basks in the sun on the banks of the wide Missouri River and still has dirt streets, which is fine with the bicyclists who flock there to ride the KATY Trail.

If you are on the KATY Trail, then you must be a cyclist or a hiker. Look for **KATY Trail Bed & Breakfast** (at the 178.5 mile marker (101 Lewis St.; 573–698-BIKE [2453]; katytrailbb.com) in Rocheport. This historic Adirondack-style house is on the trail and has five guest rooms, plus a separate cottage. It is also the home of the KATY Boxcar, converted to a comfy room that sleeps eight with full bath and mini kitchen with microwave and coffeemaker. Kids love it. It would be ideal for a group doing the trail. There is even an outdoor hot tub, and you will be sent off with a fine breakfast.

The **Meriweather Café and Bike Shop** (701 1st St.; 573-698-1222) is a good spot to rent a bike if you want to do just part of the KATY Trail and didn't bring your own gear. For a little extra you can rent a kid trailer, so no one gets tired and wants to quit. The café offers "simple scratch cooking" with breakfast all day. Lunch and dinner run the gamut from beautiful salads to battered fries (with dip). You do need your energy for the ride, right? Cafe hours and bike rentals are Sun through Tues and Thurs through Sat 8 a.m. to 4 p.m.

If it's not telling tales out of school, you may want to enroll for a term at the **School House Bed and Breakfast** (504 3rd St.; 573-698-2022; schoolhousebb.com). Innkeepers Chandrika Collins and Andy Hickman run this big foursquare edifice at 3rd and Clark Streets and made it more inviting than any school we've ever seen. The three-story school was built in 1914 and served as the area's cultural center for more than 60 years. There are now 10 guest rooms, each with its own style, featuring antique bathtubs, sinks, and toilets.

The Teacher's Pet Suite contains a two-person Jacuzzi. The garden courtyard invites relaxation. There is also the ***Clark Street Lodge*** for bigger groups: families, cycling groups, or "girlfriend-get-aways." The ***Dorm House*** is next to the schoolhouse and has two private rooms.

The family-owned winery ***Les Bourgeois Vineyards*** (12847 W. Hwy. BB; 573-698-3401; missouriwine.com) welcomes visitors. Admire the spectacular view of the Missouri River at the Bluff Top Restaurant for Sunday brunch and watch the barges float by. Sample Bordeaux-style wines—plus a generous charcuterie of Missouri sausage, cheese, and fresh fruit. The sunsets are divine here. The A-frame wine garden is open seasonally, but the winery and sales room are open every day of the year 11 a.m. to 6 p.m. Good food—everything from burgers to steak au poivre—is served Thurs through Sat at the ***Bluff Bistro*** (14020 W. Hwy. BB). Call the bistro at (573) 698-2300 for seasonal hours.

On Hwy 240 headed to Glasgow you will pass through the small town of Slater, where the highest-paid star of his time, Steve McQueen, was born in 1933.

All this driving makes a body thirsty, so how about an old-fashioned cherry phosphate? Or maybe a thick, rich malt made with hand-dipped ice cream? Stop by tiny ***Glasgow,*** where you'll find ***Henderson's*** (523 1st St.; 660-338-2125), a fifth-generation drugstore on the main drag. Staff will fix you the fantasy float of your dreams.

Glasgow's narrow, two-story city hall has a surprised expression; the round-topped windows look like raised eyebrows. But there's nothing too shocking in this historic little town unless you discover that the old bridge on Highway 240 is the world's first all-steel bridge, built in 1878. Eight hundred tons of steel were used in construction at a cost of $500,000; it costs more than that to salt the wintry streets of a small city today.

Near Fayette is the only spot in the entire Western Hemisphere—that's hemisphere, folks—where you'll find inland salt grass. ***Moniteau Lick,*** near the more familiar Boone's Lick, is the place. This area was once important for naturally occurring salt; there are more than 80 place names in Missouri containing the words "salt" or "saline."

Glaciated Plains

Marceline is where Walt Disney grew up. The man who brought us Disneyland and Walt Disney World and Mickey Mouse and brightened our childhoods is remembered here at the ***Walt Disney Hometown Museum*** at 120 E. Santa Fe. Hours are Tues through Sat 10 a.m. to 4 p.m. and Sun 1 to 5 p.m. Admission is $10 for grownups, $5 for kids, and kiddies under 6 get in free.

From here, a short jaunt north and west will take you to **Laclede** and the **General John J. Pershing Boyhood Home.** The rural gothic building is a National Historic Landmark and is as ramrod straight as the old man himself, softened with just a bit of gingerbread. The museum highlights Pershing's long career. Only 3 miles away is **Pershing State Park** (mostateparks.com/pershingsite.htm), with the largest remaining wet prairie in Missouri, Late Woodland Indian mounds, and the War Mothers Statue. Also, the **Locust Creek Covered Bridge State Historic Site** is just north of Pershing's home at 16952 Dart Rd. The bridge was built in 1868 and is the longest of Missouri's four remaining covered bridges, at 151 feet.

You are now in what is known as the Glaciated Plains. A good example of the huge Laurentide ice-sheet movement is the **Bairdstown Church Erratic,** a huge, pink, lichen-covered granite boulder that stands 10 feet high, 20 feet wide, and 24 feet long and is estimated to weigh the same as a Boeing 747 (768,000 pounds). It sits in the middle of a pasture on the Dunlop family farm near Milan. Over the years these huge gifts from the north have been cut by pioneers for millstones or converted to monuments. This one remains untouched. It came to the state when the glacier pushed its way from Canada 175,000 years ago. It is obviously a very strange visitor to this flatland.

Open farmland dominates Highway 5 North; the rolling hills recall the prairie that covered much of presettlement Missouri. East of Milan on Highway 6, discover busy **Kirksville** and environs. There's a lot happening in Kirksville, as always in a college town. Kirksville is home to Truman State University and T. Still University of Health and Science, so it offers the kinds of places young people enjoy. For example, there is the **Del & Norma Robinson Planetarium** at Truman State University (100 E. Normal Ave., Ste. 2100; 660-785-7827), which is open to the public. Less educational but fun is the **Ville Escape Room & Axe Throwing** at 116 S. Franklin St. (thevilleescaperoom.com). Each escape room has a story (e.g., the FBI is in need of help to solve a mystery involving an agent gone missing), and you have 60 minutes for your team to figure it out. Call (660) 851-4346 to make reservations for your group. The axe-throwing lanes are a great venting activity, but you must be over 13 years old and wear shoes with toes. Seriously. The town is also the home of the **Kirksville College of Osteopathic Medicine** (atsu.edu/kcom)—lots of lively young people running around here, having fun, eating out, and just generally being college kids.

Is your family doctor an MD or a DO? If they are a Doctor of Osteopathy (DO), their profession got its start right here in Kirksville when Andrew Taylor Still established the first school of the osteopathic profession, in 1892, in a one-room schoolhouse. The college has grown; today there are 15 buildings (including two hospitals) on a 50-acre campus, and the student body numbers more than 500. Former US Surgeon General C. Everett Koop delivered the 1988 commencement address.

Visit the ***Andrew Taylor Still National Osteopathic Museum*** (800 W. Jefferson; 660-626-2359). It's a three-building complex that includes the log cabin birthplace of Dr. Still, the tiny white clapboard cabin that served as the school, and the museum itself, with its impressive collection of osteopathic paraphernalia. One of the most interesting is the entire nervous system of the human body taken from a cadaver and placed behind glass to see. Hours are Mon through Fri 10 a.m. to 4 p.m. and Sat by appointment. Admission is free.

Buildings of many architectural styles, from Romanesque and Renaissance revival to Italianate and Victorian, from art deco and art nouveau to beaux arts and prairie, strut their stuff on the walking tour of Old Towne Kirksville. Begin the grand tour at Old Towne Park (Elson and Washington Streets) and follow the signs, or pick up a map at any of the businesses marked with a red flag. It's only 1.5 miles by foot—but well over 100 years if you're traveling in time.

When the nightlife gets too much for you in hoppin' Kirksville, head out of town to ***Thousand Hills State Park.*** This part of Missouri was sculpted by glaciers; rich, glacial soil is the norm, not the exception, and the streams and rivers that cut through this deep soil formed the "thousand hills." The park straddles the Grand Divide. Like the Continental Divide, this geologic landform is an area where high ground determines the direction of surface water drainage. It always seems as if you should feel the difference as you cross, but you don't. This mini-mountain ridge runs along US 63 from the Iowa-Missouri border to just south of Moberly; western streams and rivers flow into the Missouri River, eastern waters into the Mississippi.

Much of the park is remnant prairie—look for big bluestem, rattlesnake master, blazing star, and Indian grass, which are maintained by periodic burning. Because of the cooler climate here, you'll find plants not found in other parts of the state, such as the lovely interrupted fern in the deep ravines of the park. There is a natural grove of large-toothed aspen, a tree common to northern states but quite rare in Missouri. In Thousand Hills State Park, you can also find our grand-champion aspen.

If prehistory interests you more than natural history, don't miss the petroglyphs near camping area number 3. Archaeologists believe these crosses, thunderbirds, sunbursts, and arrows were scratched into the sandstone by peoples who inhabited the site between AD 1000 and 1600. They may have been reminders of the order of the ceremonial rituals passed along by the Middle Mississippi culture, which were in use for a long period of time. Many glyphs appear to have been carved by hunters of the Late Woodland culture between AD 400 and 900. The site is listed on the National Register of Historic Places;

it's nice to know this list contains more than the usual antebellum mansions and Federal-style courthouses we seem to expect.

Visit **Weathervane Antiques,** at 2214 US 63 in **Macon** (660-385-2941; weathervaneantiques.com) for a walk down memory lane. It's open seven days a week from 10 a.m. to 5 p.m.

Tiny **Ten Mile** just north of Macon doesn't even show up on the map; it's an Amish community near Ethel. Watch for little yard signs; many of these places have tiny shops on the farmstead where baked goods, yard goods, homemade candy, baskets, or quilts are sold.

Take the grand tour through **Paris** (no, not the long way around; this is Paris, Missouri). Tiny **Florida** is the closest town to the **Mark Twain Birthplace State Historic Site** (573-565-3449) and **Mark Twain State Park,** which offers camping, swimming, and river recreation. Visit mostateparks/twainpark.htm. The two-room cabin where Samuel Clemens came into the world reminds you of something; it could have come straight from one of his books. A bit of Twain was Tom Sawyer and Huck Finn (you remember Huck, that red-haired scamp who lived life to the hilt, devil-take-the-hindmost). If you've read *The Adventures of Huckleberry Finn,* this won't come as a big surprise.

What is a surprise is that the two-room cabin is totally enclosed in an ultra-modern museum, which houses first editions of Clemens's works, including the handwritten version of *Tom Sawyer* done for British publication. Sit in the public reading room to conduct personal research—or just to get in touch with the old wag. For example, Twain once wrote, "Recently someone in Missouri has sent me a picture of the house I was born in. Heretofore I always stated that it was a palace but I shall be more guarded now." Open Apr through Oct, Tues through Sat 10 a.m. to 4 p.m.; Nov through Mar, Fri and Sat 10 a.m. to 4 p.m. There is an admission charge.

ancienttrees

If you are interested in antique trees, look at the bicentennial tree in Paris at 710 Cleveland. This oak tree is more than 300 years old. There is a California redwood tree also in Paris at 406 W. Monroe that was brought by covered wagon from California in 1832. I hope they are still alive when you decide to search them out!

On the second full weekend of August each year, the US Army Corps of Engineers, the Missouri Department of Natural Resources, and the Friends of Florida sponsor the Salt River Folklife Festival in the tiny town of Florida.

Although this is not Madison County, 5 miles west of Paris and 3 miles south on County Road C, you'll find a different kind of nostalgic symbol, the **Union Covered Bridge.** It is the only Burr-arch covered bridge left in the state. Named for the Union

Where to Winter If You're a Canada Goose

Southeast from Chillicothe (take US 65 to Highway H) is a "birders" detour not to be missed. Swan Lake National Wildlife Refuge (fws.gov/refuge/swan_lake) is the wintering grounds for one of the largest concentrations of **Canada geese** in North America. This 10,670-acre refuge also attracts more than 100 bald eagles each winter. The main entrance is 1 mile south of Sumner on County Road RA. Photography and bird-watching are permitted, and there is a 0.75-mile habitat trail and observation tower.

Church, which once stood nearby, this 125-foot-long, 17 1/2-foot-wide bridge was built in 1868. It is now a state historic site. You can almost hear the clatter of horses' hooves and the rumble of wagon wheels through the old wooden tunnel. (You'll have to use your imagination; the recently restored bridge is open to foot traffic only—it's blocked to vehicles.)

After a picnic at the covered bridge, continue west on US 24 to Highway 151. (Pay attention now.) Go south to Highway M, and after a few miles you will come to Highway Y. A drive south on Y will take you through another Amish community. There are no retail shops along the route except **Sam's Store,** which has no sign out front—you have to ask for directions—but there are signs in the yards offering a variety of handmade goods, including home-made candy, quilts, and furniture. Fresh garden produce, eggs, and honey are also sold. You can get off the highway and take many small buggy roads to explore the community. Small schools, like the one named Plain View, dot the landscape, and buggies leave dust trails on the roads. This is Middle America in its simplest form.

There are some pretty exotic destinations around here, aren't there? Milan, Paris—and now **Mexico,** south of "gay Paree." (Oh, the places you can say you've been!) Mexico is called "Little Dixie" because of its strong Southern sympathies during the Civil War; now you can visit the Little Dixie Wildlife Area nearby.

In Mexico is the **Graceland House Museum** (501 S. Muldrow; 573-581-3910), a stately antebellum mansion housing the Audrain County Historical Society. It is located in the 11-acre Robert S. Green Park, which has a playground, picnic area, and gracious lawn. It is one of the oldest homes in the county, built in 1857. This Greek Revival home is listed on the National Register of Historic Places. You can experience the lifestyle of the era with wedding dresses, an extensive doll collection, china, silver, and antique furniture as well as antique tools. Hours are Wed through Sat noon to 4 p.m. Admission is $5 for adults and $3 for children.

The *American Saddlebred Horse Museum* is also at 501 S. Muldrow. Here is a fine-art exhibit including works by artists George Ford Morris, Gladys Brown, and B. Beaumont, and saddlebred primitives by Audrain McDonough from the 1920s. Many famous horses are featured in the photographs and paintings. This museum is the oldest saddlebred museum in the nation, established to complement Graceland while commemorating Mexico's longtime renown as the Saddle Horse Capital of the World. There is an extensive collection of saddle horse memorabilia. Hours and admission are the same as for Graceland.

The *Audrain Country School,* also part of this complex, was constructed in 1903 and is furnished with authentic items used in country schools—slate blackboards, desks, games, and other memorabilia saved from rural schools in the county. An outhouse behind the school adds to the authenticity of the setting. Open Wed through Sat 10 a.m. to 4 p.m.

Call (573) 581-3910 or visit audrain.org for information on all three places.

Notice all the redbrick buildings in the Mexico/Vandalia area? The land is underlaid with a type of refractory clay that makes great bricks; there are still four brick plants in Audrain County.

A 14-mile jog back east from Mexico will take you to *Centralia.* Don't miss it if you enjoy "kinder, gentler" countryside. *Chance Gardens* includes a turn-of-the-20th-century mansion, home of the late A. Bishop Chance. Built in 1904, its onion-domed turret, gracious porticoes, and ornate woodwork invite visitors with an eye for elegance. A gift to the public from the A. B. Chance Company (the town's largest industry), it's been Centralia's showplace for years.

The gardens that surround the home say something about the kind of luxury money can't buy. It takes time to plan those masses of color that bloom continuously through the seasons and lead the eye from one brilliant display to another—time to plan and time to maintain. That's a luxury most of us don't have.

While you are there, you will want to visit the *Centralia Historical Society Museum* (319 E. Sneed St.; 573-682-5711; centraliamuseum.org), in a house built in 1904 and dedicated to preserving and exhibiting artifacts that document the history of the area. In the fall the museum is host to a quilt show, and hundreds have been showcased here. It's all free—no admission charge, just a donation bucket. It's open May through Oct, Wed and Sat and Sun 2 to 4 p.m.

Tiny *Clark,* a hoot and a holler from Centralia, is the birthplace of General Omar Bradley. There's an active Amish community in the Clark area; watch for those horses and buggies. Some sport bumper stickers, much easier to read at this speed than on the interstates. "I'm Not Deaf, I'm Ignoring You" and "I May Be Slow, But I'm Ahead of You" seem to be local favorites. You'll want to slow down yourself to admire the clean, white homes and commodious barns of the Amish.

There's a little town called **Higbee** nearby, population 568 at last census. Barrel-making companies A&K Cooperage and Barrel 53 are here, but the real reason to find Higbee is to get another stamp on your **Missouri Spirits Expedition** log and try some high-quality whiskey, bourbon, or moonshine at **Skullsplitter Spirits** (603 Hwy B; 660-456-7660; facebook.com/Skullsplitterspirits). Open Mon through Fri 10 a.m. to 4 p.m. and Sat 11 a.m. to 5 p.m.

Moberly is home to the **Blissfully Yours Sweet Shoppe & More** (619 Concannon St.; 660-353-0756), which is filled with fudge, truffles, clusters, and 72 flavors of jelly beans. Call it sugar-coated nostalgia and add 34 flavors of hand-dipped ice cream, too. On a more grown-up note, one of the hidden gems in town is the **Evelyn E. Jorgenson Fine Arts Gallery** (101 College Ave.; 660-456-4100, ext. 11626). It is on the Moberly Area Community College's campus. Hours are Mon through Thurs 7 a.m. to 8:30 p.m. and Fri till 4 p.m.

Missouri's Monarchy

Winston Churchill journeyed to **Fulton** to address Westminster College in 1946 just after he had been defeated for reelection as England's prime minister. Churchill delivered the most famous speech of his life, the "Iron Curtain" speech. "From Stettin in the Baltic to Trieste in the Adriatic, an iron curtain has descended across the Continent. Behind that line lie all the capitals of the ancient states of Central and Eastern Europe."

The invitation to speak at Westminster College had a handwritten note at the bottom in a familiar scrawl: "This is a wonderful school in my home state. Hope you can do it. I'll introduce you. Best regards, Harry Truman." The president and his respected friend arrived in Fulton on March 5, 1946. The Cold War is over now and the Iron Curtain lowered, but the ties between the college, the town, and Great Britain remain unbroken.

In the 1960s Westminster president R. L. D. Davidson wanted to honor those ties. The resulting plan was bold and perfect—if not as well-publicized as the move of the London Bridge to Arizona. The college acquired the centuries-old Church of St. Mary the Virgin from Aldermanbury, England, and dismantled it stone by stone. The edifice was shipped across the Atlantic and cross-country to Fulton, where it was reconstructed on the Westminster campus (Harry Truman himself turned the first spade of earth in 1964), and rededicated in 1969. It now houses the **Winston Churchill Memorial and Library**

Biscuits and Gravy—the Ultimate Test

I have been writing since 1985, and as I read my notes and journals, it seems that most of my memories revolve around food. So it doesn't surprise me that I gain weight with each book I write. I have photos to remind me of the Eiffel Tower, but when someone asks, "Best meal of your life?" my memory of sweetbreads in champagne sauce take me back to Paris, the world's most beautiful city.

And so it is with Missouri. I remember strolling along Washington's Front Street and watching the river amble by, hearing the trains approaching along the track that parallels the river, but if someone asks, "Best biscuits and gravy?" I remember a little diner in town. The waitress heard me say I had never had biscuits and gravy. So she gave me no other breakfast option. I would have biscuits and gravy. They were wonderful: soft, flaky biscuits covered with thick, sausage-filled gravy. Since that fateful day I have ordered B&G at hundreds of restaurants, and it has never been the same. Hockey pucks covered with Elmer's glue—bland, dry, tasteless attempts at a meal fit for the gods. It is my ultimate test of an eating establishment that claims to serve breakfast.

Fried chicken—now there's another test. The best pan-fried chicken in the state is at Stroud's in Kansas City. Served family style on big platters with green beans and mashed potatoes covered with pan gravy, it is an all-you-can-eat-and-take-the-rest-home heaven. Oh my, is it any wonder you have to get there before they open to line up for a seat?

When I wrote about Arkansas, it was fried catfish and hamburgers (in honor of President William Jefferson Clinton) I searched out, but none of the hamburgers matched the tiny burgers at Hayes Hamburgers in suburban Kansas City.

In Kansas it was fried chicken and muffins (it seems that most of the B&Bs in Kansas make delightful muffins that are soft and warm and huge) that drew my attention. And while Missouri is famous for its steak and barbecue, there was a cold smoked-trout dish at the Blue Heron in Osage Beach that has lingered in my memory for years.

Say what you will about scenic highways, backroad museums, and shopping; what is really important is the answer to the age-old question: "Where should we eat?"

(501 Westminster Ave.; 573-592-5369; nationalchurchillmuseum.org), currently the only center in the US dedicated to the study of the man and his works. Churchill's original oil paintings (the very public man had a private side, and enjoyed relaxing with his paints), letters, manuscripts, family mementos, and other memorabilia are on display, in addition to the fire-scarred communion plate rescued from the ruins of the church after World War II.

The church itself is deeply historical; built in 12th-century London, it was redesigned in 1677 by Sir Christopher Wren, one of the finest architects of the period. Damage caused by German bombs seemed to signal its end until

Westminster College stepped in to rescue the building. It is open from 10 a.m. to 4:30 p.m. seven days a week. Tours are available.

The Berlin Wall fell in 1989, and a piece of it, marked with angry graffiti of the past, was made into a sculpture by Churchill's granddaughter, Edwina Sandys. She cut out simple but powerful shapes of a man and a woman as openings in the wall and called it *Breakthrough*. That piece now stands on campus. In 1992 Mikhail Gorbachev spoke at Westminster, further symbolizing the end of the Cold War.

strangeas itsounds

If you can, find Founder's Cemetery on the north edge of Paris. It is listed in *Ripley's Believe It or Not!* because it is the home of possibly the only tombstone in the world to list three wives of one husband.

As long as you are searching out cemeteries, find the Walnut Grove Cemetery and take a good look at the caretaker's building. Its architecture is Little Dixie Victorian, and it was constructed around 1870. The round turret originally enclosed a water tower for water storage.

The *Auto World Museum* (200 Peacock Dr.; 573-642-2080; autoworldmuseum.com) has rare cars (among them the shiny black 1931 Marmon, a 16-cylinder car that gangsters made infamous), vintage fire trucks (including a 1922 Ahrens Fox Pumper), tractors, and buggies. It is the dream come true of Bill Backer, who has been collecting and restoring old cars for more than 50 years. When the local Kmart left town, Bill had the opportunity to grab 37,000 square feet of work space. When he moved in he thought he would open a museum for a month or so to show off his cars. It became so popular that he decided to divide the area and use the front as a museum and the back as a workroom.

The rare cars were a hit—cars such as a Stanley Steamer, a DeLorean, and a 1986 Pulse (not old, but only 60 of these motorcycles-become-cars were made). They are right there with the Edsel and Studebaker as unique collectibles. Bill also has an 1875 Haynes, the only one in the US in private hands (there is one in the Smithsonian in Washington, DC). If you want to see a great collection of more than 100 vehicles, from horseless carriages to solar cars, this is the place. There is also a gift shop with local artisans contributing military memorabilia, railroad collectibles, fine china and crystal, and a little bit of flea market. In addition, there's a large display of Kennedy memorabilia. Open Apr through Dec, 9 a.m. to 5 p.m. daily; you can make an appointment for a tour in the winter, too.

Experience historical charm and warm hospitality in one of the five beautiful guest rooms at *Logonberry Inn* (310 W. 7th St.; 573-642-9229; loganberry-inn.com) in Fulton. Each guest room at the inn has a private bath, luxury linens, and an electric fireplace and is furnished with both modern and period antiques and reproductions designed to honor the history of this 1899 Victorian home. Free Wi-Fi is available throughout. Each morning includes breakfast prepared by chef and owner, Nanette. Guests can easily walk to the historic downtown Brick District to enjoy art galleries, fine dining, great shopping, and interesting museums. Just a half a block away you'll find the National Churchill Museum and Westminster College, as well as William Woods University down the road. Fulton is located just a short drive from wineries, Columbia, and Jefferson City. No matter the reason for your travels, it is a welcome alternative to hotel lodging, with personal touches for a memorable stay.

thekingdom ofcallaway

Callaway County in effect seceded from both North and South and stood independent briefly as the *Kingdom of Callaway* when federal troops deposed Governor Claiborne Jackson and established a provisional government in Jefferson City during the Civil War. Early in October 1861, 600 federal troops came to subdue Rebel Callaway County. Former state representative Jefferson Jones gathered 600 troops to defend the county from the federal invasion. Equipped with shotguns and hunting rifles, they tried to look like a trained army. They even painted logs black and hid them in the brush with wagon wheels to look like artillery. The federal commander, General John Henderson, agreed not to advance against this "well-trained force of men" and allowed Callaway County to negotiate a treaty with the federal government. The treaty recognized the county's independence and granted Callaway the right to govern itself. And so, Callaway County became "the Kingdom of Callaway." After the war ended, the "kingdom" still refused to be reconstructed and governed by outside forces.

Beks Restaurant (511 Court St.; 573-592-7117) offers upscale dining for medium prices. This charming eatery is housed in the historic Brick District in a circa 1880 building and serves imported beer, steaks (no, not just steaks, but filet with blue cheese crumbles), and seafood. Try the salmon or shrimp Alfredo or some of the other specialties, such as pepper-crusted elk rib loin. See the complete menu at beksshop.com. Restaurant hours are Tues through Fri 11 a.m. to 2 p.m. and 4:30 to 8 p.m., and Sat noon to 9 p.m.

The **City of Fulton Walking Trail** is a 3-mile walking and biking trail that connects three parks. The trail runs along Stinson Creek, crosses a covered bridge, and passes below "Lover's Leap" cliff.

The **Fire Fighter's Memorial of Missouri** (5599 Angel Dr.) in **Kingdom City** features a bronze statue that is identical to the one donated to the city of New York after the terrorist attack of 9/11. Here tribute is paid to all the brave firefighters who have given their lives in the line of duty.

Wood Hat Spirits (489 Booneslick Rd.; 573-835-1000; woodhatspirits.com) is in **New Florence.** Gary Hinegardner, owner and distiller, makes whiskey that is fermented, distilled, and aged on-site using the only wood-fired still in the country. Tastings are available anytime during business hours; tours are by reservation only. Tasting room hours are Mon, Thurs, Fri, and Sat 10 a.m. to 5 p.m. and Sun noon to 5pm. (closed Sun Jan through Mar). Come in and try the bourbon, corn whiskey, black walnut liqueur, and especially the persimmon cordial. This delicate essence of local, wild persimmon is infused with cardamom, cinnamon, and jaggery—it is a delicious aperitif. Get your **Missouri Spirits Expedition** stamp. Try the Flight of Five—five shots for $5.

While *Crane's Country Store* (10675 Old US 40; 573-254-3311; cranes-country-store.com) in *Williamsburg* may look like an old-time general store, once inside you find it is a real working store. Many antiques and memorabilia are on display. Have a sandwich and an ice-cold bottle of pop while you browse.

From the Kingdom of Callaway, thence hie thyself back east along I-70 to *Graham Cave State Park* (573-564-3476) near *Danville.* (Oops, this royalty stuff gets to you!) Graham Cave is a huge arch of sandstone that dwarfs its human visitors. This rainbow-shaped cave is shallow, so the tour is a self-guided one. Spelunkers, don't let that put you off. Although this is not a deep-earth cave with spectacular formations, artifacts were found here dating from the area's earliest human habitation, some 10,000 years ago. Before the Native Americans formed themselves into tribes, Graham Cave was an important gathering place. Spear-type flints, made before the bow was invented, were found here, along with other signs of human use. The dig itself is fenced to prevent finds from being removed, but you can admire these fine examples of the earliest Show-Me State inhabitants in the small museum in the park office. Take the Danville/Montgomery City exit off the interstate and follow Outer Road TT 2 miles west; it dead-ends at the park, so you can't go wrong. Check in at the park office to pick up a map to the cave. Check the park's website for the cave's seasonal hours at mostateparks.com/grahamcave.htm.

Places to Stay in Northeast Missouri

HANNIBAL
Quality Inn & Suites
120 Lindsey Dr., US 36
(573) 221-4001
Inexpensive

COLUMBIA
Holiday Inn
2200 I-70 Dr. SW
(573) 445-8531
Inexpensive

LOUISIANA
River's Edge Motel
201 Mansion St.
(573) 754-4522
Inexpensive

ST. CHARLES
Red Roof Inn
I-70 and Zumbehl Road 3
(636) 947-7770
Inexpensive

MOBERLY
Best Western
1200 E. Hwy. 24
Junction of US 63/US 24
(660) 263-6540
Inexpensive

KIRKSVILLE
Days Inn
3805 S. Baltimore
US 63 S./Route 6
(660) 665-8244
Inexpensive

MACON
Super 8 Motel
203 E. Briggs Rd.
Junction of US 36/US 63
(660) 385-5788
Inexpensive

MEXICO
Budget Inn
1010 E. Liberty
(573) 581-1440
Inexpensive

KEARNEY
Super 8 Motel
210 Platte Clay Way
(816) 628-6800
Inexpensive

BETHANY
Family Budget Inn
4014 Miller St.
I-35, Exit 93
(660) 425-7915
family-budget-inn-bethany.
business.site
Inexpensive

CAMERON
Econo Lodge
220 E. Grand
(816) 632-6571
Inexpensive

Places to Eat in Northeast Missouri

COLUMBIA
Booches Billiard Hall
110 S. 9th St.
(573) 874-9519
Inexpensive

Shakespeare's Pizza
225 S. 9th St.
(573) 449-2454

FINDING HELPFUL VISITOR INFORMATION

Kirksville
visitkirksville.com
(816) 665–3766

Marceline
marcelinemo.us/tourism.htm
(660) 376–3528

Paris
parismo.net
(660) 327–4450

Plattsburg
plattsburgmo.com
(816) 539–2649

Smithville
smithvillemo.org
(816) 532–3897

shakespeares.com
Inexpensive

KIRKSVILLE

Rosie's Northtown Cafe
2801 N. Baltimore
(660) 665-8881
Inexpensive

KINGDOM CITY

Iron Skillet
3304 Gold Ave.
I-70 and US 54
(573) 642-0676
Inexpensive

MARYVILLE

A&G Restaurant
208 N. Main St., Business
71
(660) 582-4421
agrestaurant.com
Inexpensive

INDEX

1220 Artisan Spirits, 8
4J Big Piney Horse
  Camp, 60
5 and 10 Antiques, 136
5 Mile Corner Antique
  Mall, 178
66 Drive-in Theatre, 69

A
Adam-Ondi-Ahman
  Shrine, 154
Adrian's Pioneer
  Kitchen, 150
Affäre, 96
Afterward Tavern &
  Shelves, 95
Akers, Tom, 61
Albrecht-Kemper Art
  Museum, 175
Alexandria, 192
American Bowman
  Restaurant, 172
American Dwelling, 136
American Jazz
  Museum, 93
American Saddlebred
  Horse Museum, 208
Ameristar Casino St.
  Charles, 186
Andrew Taylor Still
  National Osteopathic
  Museum, 205
Angle Acres, 179
Anna Marie's Teas, 146
Anna's Bake Shop, 151
Annie Gunn's, 18
Anvil, The, 40
Appellation Cafe, 196
Arcadia, 33
Arcadia Valley, 33
Arcadia Valley Academy
  and Thee Abbey
  Kitchen, 33

Arcadia Valley
  Bungalows, 34
Arri's Pizza, 119
Arrow Rock, 116
Arthur Bryant's
  Barbecue, 90
Arvin Gottlieb
  Planetarium, 101
Assumption Abbey, 67
Audrain Country
  School, 208
Audrey's Motel, 177
Augusta, 195
August A. Busch
  Memorial Wildlife
  Area, 193
Augusta Winery, 196
Augusta wine trail, 195
Auto World
  Museum, 211
Ava, 67
Avalon Café, 173
Avilla, 69
Ayers Pottery, 190

B
Back Home Again, 24
Bairdstown Church
  Erratic, 204
Bankhead Candies, 187
Barham Family
  Farm, 167
Barnett, 132
Bass Pro Shops Outdoor
  World, 53
Basswood Resort, 170
Bastille Day, 39
Battle of Lexington State
  Historic Site, 115
Battle of Wilson's
  Creek, 54
B.B.'s Lawnside
  Bar-B-Que, 91
Bean Lake, 174

Becky's Old Fashioned
  Ice Cream Parlor &
  Emporium, 190
Becky Thatcher
  House, 190
Beks Restaurant, 212
Bella Italia
  Ristorante, 43
Bellefontaine
  Cemetery, 7
Bellvoir Winery, 146
Benner House Bed and
  Breakfast, 173
Berger, 21
Best of Kansas City, 95
Bethel, 192
Bias Vineyards &
  Winery, 21
Big Cedar Lodge, 82
Big Creek Café, 136
Big Creek Country
  Music Show, 136
Big Dick's Halfway
  Inn, 133
Big Oak Tree State
  Park, 47
Big Spring, 63
Billy Gail's Cafe, 79
Bixby, 33
Black Archives of
  Mid-America, 94
Black Madonna
  Shrine, 17
Blackshire Distillery, 23
Blissfully Yours Sweet
  Shoppe & More, 209
blossom rocks, 37
Blueberry Hill, 11
Bluebird Bistro, 104
Blue Owl Restaurant
  and Bakery, 30
Blue Springs, 123
Bluestem Missouri
  Crafts, 200

Bluff Hole, 62
Bluff View Marina, 35
Blumenhof Vineyards
    and Winery, 197
Bohemian Sage
    Gallery, 158
Bolduc House, The, 39
Bollinger Mill, 42
Bone Hill View
    Distillery, 115
Bonne Terre, 32
Bonne Terre Mines, 32
Bonnots Mill, 24
Books Revisited, 176
Boone's Lick Trail
    Inn, 186
Boonville, 117
Bothwell State Park, 121
Boudreaux's Louisiana
    Seafood &
    Steaks, 175
Bourbon, 28
Bowling Green, 187
Branson, 76
Branson Cafe, 78
Branson Scenic
    Railroad, 78
Branson Zipline and
    Canopy Tours, 77
Bridgeton, 186
Brix Urban Winery &
    Market, 40
Broadway Cafe, 105
Broadway Roasting
    Co., 105
Brookside Toy &
    Science, 106
Broussard's Cajun
    Restaurant, 44
Brown's Vintage &
    Variety, 135
Buckner, 115
Buck's Ice Cream, 199
Burfordville, 42
Burfordville Covered
    Bridge, 43

Burroughs Audubon
    Society Library, 123
Buschling Place, 192
Bushwhacker
    Museum, 137
Bynum Winery, 126
By the Yard Fabrics, 163

C
Cabbage Roll, The, 175
Calvary Cemetery, 7
Camden, 150
Camdenton, 134
Cameron, 168
Canada geese, 207
Candy Factory, 201
Candyman, 164
cannoli, 13
Cape Girardeau, 43
Carol Leigh's
    Specialties, 200
Carthage, 68
Casa de Loco
    Winery, 135
Casa de Vite, 161
Cassville, 73
Castello's Ristorante, 47
Catrick's Cafe, 165
Cave Vineyard Winery &
    Distillery, 41
Celedonia, 35
Celtic Ranch, 172
Central Dairy, 119
Centralia, 208
Centralia Historical
    Society Museum, 208
Chabom Tea and
    Spices, 53
Chance Gardens, 208
Chances 'R', 133
Charlecote, 106
Charley's Buffet, 131
Charlie Gitto's on the
    Hill, 12
Chateau on the Lake, 82
Cherokee removal, 45

Children's Peace
    Pavilion, 113
Chillicothe, 150
Christopher Elbow
    Artisanal
    Chocolate, 95
Church of St. Luke,
    the Beloved
    Physician, 157
Circus Flora, 10
City Market, 97
City Nights, 101
City of Fulton Walking
    Trail, 212
Civil War Museum, 68
Clark, 209
Clark Street Lodge, 202
Clarksville, 189
Clarksville Eagle
    Center, 189
Classic Cup, 105
Claycomo, 148
Clifty Creek Natural
    Area, 26
Clinton, 135
Clinton's, 108
Club 60, 68
Cockrell Mercantile
    Company, 124
Coldwater Ranch, 64
Cole Camp, 127
College of the Ozarks,
    The, 80
Colonial House Historic
    Reproductions, 69
Columbia, 198
Commerce, 44
Community of Christ's
    International
    Headquarters, 112
Conception Abbey, 178
Conception
    Junction, 178
Concordia, 127
Concordia Area Museum
    and Historical
    Society, 127

Concordia Fall
Festival, 127
Cooky's, 138
Cool Beans Coffee
House, 150
Cooley Lake, 149
Cooley Lake River
Access, 149
Copper Mule, 23
Copper Run
Distillery, 80
Cori's Gables, 197
Corner Kitchen &
General Store, 164
Corporal Blue 's
Smoothie Shack, 150
Country Club Plaza, 90
Country Colonial Bed
and Breakfast, 153
Country Cupboard
Restaurant, 153
Courthouse
Exchange, 108
Craic, The, 169
Crane's Country
Store, 213
Creighton, 115
Cross Country Trail
Rides, 63
Crossroads Art
District, 96
Crown Candy Kitchen, 8
Cuivre River State
Park, 189
Culture Boutique
Hotel, 57
Cunetto's House of
Pasta, 12
Custard's Last
Stand, 124

D
Daniel Boone's
Home, 194
Daniel Boone State
Park, 28

Danny Edwards Blvd
BBQ, 91
Danville, 214
Dari-B Drive In, 162
Dauphine Hotel, 24
Davisville, 37
Dawt Mill, 66
Defiance, 194
Del & Norma Robinson
Planetarium, 204
Depot, The, 33
Devil's Icebox, 199
Devil's Kitchen Trail, 74
Dick's 5&10 Cent
Store, 78
Dillard, 37
Dillard Mill State
Historic Site, 37
Dino's Diner & Family
Restaurant, 168
Dobyns Restaurant, 80
DogMaster
Distillery, 200
Dogwood Canyon
Nature Park, 84
Dorm House, 202
Dorothea B. Hoover
Historical
Museum, 70
Downhome
Collectibles, 152
Downtown Café, 121
Dr. Hertich's House, 40
Dubious Claims
Brewery, 160
Dutch Bakery and Bulk
Food Store, 120
Dutch Country
Store, 132
Dutch Valley, 127
Dutzow, 197

E
Eagles Nest Inn, 190
Edelbrand Pure
Distilling, 24
El Acapulco, 47

El Dorado Springs, 137
Elements, 150
Elephant Rocks State
Park, 37
Elms Hotel, 155
Eminence, 61
Eminence Canoes,
Cottages & Camp, 64
Emme's Attic, 129
Enchanted Frog
Antiques, 179
Endangered Wolf
Center, 14
English Landing
Park, 168
Eolia, 187
Eureka, 17
Evelyn E. Jorgenson
Fine Arts Gallery,
The, 209
Ewe's in the
Country, 139
Excelsior, 132
Excelsior Book
Store, 132
Excelsior Fabric, 132
Excelsior Harness
Shop, 132
Excelsior Springs, 154
Excelsior Springs
Municipal Golf
Course, 161

F
Fabric Chic, 168
Far West, 154
Fence Stile Vineyards
and Winery, 162
Fernweh Distilling, 22
Fiorell's Jack Stack
Barbeque, 102
Fire Fighter's Memorial
of Missouri, 212
Fishing River Linear
Trail, 159
Fish Market in
Liberty, 148

Flat Branch Pub and Brewery, 200
Fleming Park, 123
Flint Creek Inn, 117
Float Stream Cafe, 65
Florida, 206
Florissant, 16
F.O.G. Cycles & Knucklehead's Saloon, 104
Forest Park, 10
Formosa Restaurant, 201
Fort Davidson State Historic Site, 33
Fort Leonard Wood, 60
Fort Osage, 113
Frank's of Parkville, 169
Fred Restaurant, The, 118
Freight House, 102
French Colonial America, 39
Frisco Highline Trail, 57, 58
Fulton, 209
Furniture Solutions, 143

G
Gallery Augusta, 196
Galloway, 58
Garozzo's Ristorante, 100
Garrison, The, 85
Garth Woodside Mansion, 191
Gary R. Lucy Gallery, 19
Gates and Sons Bar-B-Q, 90
Gates of Peace Jewish Cemetery, 189
Gateway Arch, 4, 6
Gateway Riverboat Cruises, 6
Gem Theater Cultural and Performing Arts Center, 94

General John J. Pershing Boyhood Home, 204
Genghis Khan Mongolian Barbecue, 103
Georgetown, 122
Georgetown Country View Estate, 121
George Washington Carver National Monument, 71
German Table, The, 127
Gigi's Boutique, 114
Gingerich Dutch Pantry and Bakery, 152
Ginger Sue's, 146
Gino's Italian Cuisine, 167
Glade Top Trail, 51
Glasgow, 203
Glenn House, 43
Glore Psychiatric Museum, 175
Golden, 83
Golden City, 138
Golden Ox Restaurant, 89
Golden Pioneer Museum, 83
Golden Prairie, 138
Golden Rule General Store, 35
Good Ole Days Country Store, 33
Gooey Louie's, 10
Graceland House Museum, 207
Graham Cave State Park, 213
Grain Valley, 125
Grand Falls, 70
Grand Gulf State Park, 65
Graniteville, 37
Gravois Mills, 133
Gray/Campbell Farmstead, 55

Great Murals Tour (Cape Girardeau), 43
Great River Road B&B, 190
Green Dirt Farm Creamery, 171
Green Ridge, 128
Greenwood, 126
Greenwood Antiques and Country Tea Room, 126
Grinders Pizza, 96
Gruhlkes, 21
Grünauer, 102

H
Ha Ha Tonka State Park, 134
Half-Crocked Antiques, 29
Halfway House & Stone Basement, 171
Hallmark Crown Center, 95
Hall of Waters, 154
Hamilton, 154
Hammons Black Walnut Emporium, 137
Handel Haus Tea Room, 127
Hannibal, 190
Harley Park, 118
Harry S Truman's Birthplace, 137
Hawthorne Inn, 129
Hayes Hamburgers, 143
"Heatherly War" of 1836, 149
Heartland Antique Mall, 59
Heaton-Bowman-Smith & Sidenfaden Funeral Museum, The, 175
Heinrichshaus Vineyards and Winery, 28
Henderson's, 203

Henry County
Museum, 135
Hereford House, 107
Hermann, 21
Hermannhof Winery
Festhalle, 23
Hermann Visitors'
Information
Center, 21
Hermann Wurst
Haus, 22
Herzog Mansion, 23
Hidden Log Cabin
Museum, 65
Hidden Valley
Resort, 18
Higbee, 209
Hillcreek Fiber
Studio, 200
Historic Commercial
Hotel, 138
Historic Liberty Jail, 146
H & M Country
Store, 152
Hodge Park, 144
Hodgson Water Mill, 66
Holladay Distilling
Company, 171
Hollister, 82
Holy Grounds Coffee &
Book Shoppe, 146
Home of Sliced
Bread, 150
Honeyshuck, 187
Hoof & Horn, 176
Hotel Frederick, 118
H. S. Clay House, 197
Huey's Café, 146
Hunter-Dawson Home
and Historic Site, 49

I
Iatan Marsh, 174
Iggy's Diner, 69
Imperial, 29
Independence, 108

Inn on Crescent Lake,
The, 160
Inn on Main, 115
Inn St. Gemme Beauvais
B&B, 40
Iowker Creek Vineyards
& Winery, 170
Iron Spike Interactive
Model Train
Museum, 20
Ironton, 34
Isley Park Woods, 160

J
Jackson, 42
Jaegers Subsurface
Paintball, 145
Jamesport, 151
Java Jive Coffee
House, 190
Jayder's, 150
J.C. Penney Memorial
Library and
Museum, 154
Jefferson City, 119
Jerry Litton Visitor
Center, 180
Jesse James Bank
Museum Historic
Site, 146
Jesse James Farm
Historic Site, 165
Jesse James
Museum, 175
Jewell's Stocksdale Art
Gallery, 147
J. Huston Tavern, 117
Jim Bob's Backyard
BBQ, 178
Johnny's Pit BBQ, 27
Johnson's Shut-Ins, 35
Jolly Mill, 73
Joplin, 70
Joplin Historical and
Mineral Museum, 70
Joplin Museum
Complex, 70

J. Rieger & Co., 104
Judgement Tree
Distillery, 194
Junie Moon Cafe, 17
Justus Drugstore, 179

K
Kansas City, 89
Kansas City Museum,
The, 103
Kate's Attic Antiques
and Mini Mall, 189
KATY Trail, x, 122,
186, 202
KATY Trail Bed &
Breakfast, 202
KATY Trail State Park,
197, 202
Kauffman Center for the
Performing Arts, 96
KC Power and Light
District, 97
KC Streetcar, 95
Kearney, 165
Kehde's Barbeque, 121
Kelly's, 105
Kimmswick, 30
Kimmswick Bone
Bed, 30
Kingdom Coffee
Roasting, 168
Kingdom of
Callaway, 212
King Jack Park, 73
Kingsville, 123
Kirksville, 204
Kirksville College
of Osteopathic
Medicine, 204
Knot Hole Woodcarving,
The, 136
Kozy Kaboose, 18

L
Labadie, 17

La Bottega Parkville
Vintage Antique
Mall, 168
Laclede, 204
LaFuente Mexican
Restaurant, 167
Lake Jacomo, 123
Lake Lotawana, 125
Lake of the Ozarks, 129
Lake Wappapello
Outdoor Theatre, 46
Lamar, 138
Lambert's Cafe, 45
Lampe, 84
Lamp Family Farms, 165
Landers, 57
Lathrop, 179
Laumeier Sculpture
Park, 12
Laura Ingalls Wilder–
Rose Wilder Lane
Museum and
Home, 68
Laurie, 133
Lawson, 164
Lawson City Lake, 165
lead fields, 22
Lebanon, 59
Leedy-Voulkos Art
Center, 96
Lee's Summit, 123
Le Fou Frog, 99
Leila's Hair
Museum, 112
LeMeilleur house, 39
Lemp Mansion
Restaurant & Inn, 14
Les Bourgeois
Vineyards, 203
Lesterville, 34
Levee, 103
Lewis and Clark State
Park, 174
Lexington, 114
Liberty, 146
Liberty Farmers
Market, 167

Lidia's, 102
Linn, 120
Little BBQ Joint, A, 110
Little Bean Marsh, 174
Lock and Dam No.
25, 188
Locust Creek Covered
Bridge State Historic
Site, 204
Loess Bluffs National
Wildlife Refuge, 177
Logonberry Inn, 212
Lohoman, 120
Lone Jack, 126
Long Creek Herb
Farm, 83
Lot Community
Coffee, 178
Louisiana, 189
Louisiana Historical
Museum, The, 189
Lyceum Repertory
Theatre, 117

M
Maclay House, 120
Macon, 206
Main Street Inn
B&B, 169
Manny's, 101
Mansfield, 68
Mansion Hill, 32
Margaret Harwell Art
Museum, 46
Marina Grog and
Galley, 125
Mark Twain Birthplace
State Historic
Site, 206
Mark Twain National
Forest, 36, 66
Mark Twain State
Park, 206
Marshal's Home and
Museum, 110

Martha Lafite
Thompson Nature
Sanctuary, 148
Marthasville, 197
Maryville, 177
Mastodon State Park, 29
Maysville, 178
McCormick Country
Store, 172
Mel's Hard Luck
Diner, 77
Meramec Farm Cabins
and Trail Riding
Vacations, 28
Meramec State Park, 29
Meriweather Café and
Bike Shop, 202
Mexico, 207
Michael Bauermeister
Studio, 196
Midwest Genealogy
Center, 124
Mill Inn Restaurant, 160
Milo's Tavern & Bocce
Garden, 12
Mina Sauk Falls, 36
Miner Indulgence Bed
and Breakfast, 26
Mingo National Wildlife
Refuge, 46
Miniature Museum of
Greater St. Louis, 14
Mission Taco Joint, 96
Missouri Bluffs
Boutique, 173
Missouri Botanical
Garden, 4
Missouri Department of
Conservation's Eagle
Days, 189
Missouri Expedition
Log, 186
Missouri Meerschaum
Company, 21
Missouri Mines State
Historic Site, 33

Missouri Ridge
Distillery, 80
Missouri River, 149, 193
Missouri River State
Trail, 193
Missouri Spirits
Expedition, 3
Missouri Spirits
Expedition Log,
194, 201
Missouri's
Stonehenge, 26
Missouri State Fair, 121
Missouri statehood, 26
Missouri Town
1855, 123
Missouri Wildflower
Nursery, 119
Mizumoto Japanese
Stroll Garden, 56
Mojo's to Go, 167
Molly Robert's
Studio, 158
Moniteau Lick, 203
Montelle Winery, 195
Moon City Pub, 53
Moonrise Hotel, 6
Morrel Ranch, 153
Mound City, 176, 177
Mound Grove
Cemetery, 111
Mountain Grove, 68
Mr. Ed's, 58
Mr. Ed's drive-in, 58
Mt. Olivet Cemetery, 166
Mule Barn Berries, 179
Munger Moss Motel, 58
Museum of
Anthropology, 198
Museum of Art and
Archaeology, 198
Mutual Musicians'
Foundation, 93
Myrtle's Distilled
Spirits, 72
Myrtle's Place Backalley
BBQ, 47

N
Naked Spirits, 13
National Frontier Trails
Center, 108, 111
National World War I
Museum at Liberty
Memorial, 95
Nearly Famous Deli &
Pasta House, 54
Nebo Hill, 149
Negro Leagues Baseball
Museum, 93
Nelle Belle's Diner, 148
Nelson-Atkins
Museum, 89
Nevada, 137
New Madrid, 48
New Madrid Fault, 48
New Madrid Historical
Museum, 48
Newtonia Civil War
battles, 71
Nobletons Distilling
House, 21
Noel, 69
North Kansas City, 143
Northland Fountain, 93
Nutmeg Bakery &
Cafe, 164

O
Oktoberfest, 21
Old Bank Museum, 155
Old Brick House, 39
Old Cathedral
Museum, 6
Old Cook Stove, 178
Old Fashioned Candy
Store, Deli and
Antique Shop,
The, 168
Old Jail Museum
Complex, 25
Old McKendree
Chapel, 42
Old Ozarkian
Distillery, 17

Old Stagecoach Stop, 60
Old St. Ferdinand
Shrine, 16
Oliver House, 42
Onondaga Cave, 28
Ophelia's Restaurant
and Inn, 109
Orrick, 150
Osage Beach, 132
Osage Ridge, 195
Osborn, 178
Osceola, 138
Osceola Cheese
Shop, 139
Other Trails, 159
Ozark, 84
Ozark Heritage
Festival, 66
Ozark National Scenic
Riverways, 62
Ozark Trail, 36, 64

P
Paradise Playhouse, 155
Paris, 206
Parkcliff Cabins, 75
Parker, Charlie
"Yardbird," 91
Parkville, 168
Parkville Nature
Sanctuary, 170
Parlor Bakery & Café,
The, 150
Patee House, 175
Paxico, 46
Payne's Jailhouse Bed
&Breakfast, 161
Peace Church
Cemetery, 71
Pear Tree, 106
Peculiar, 123
Perryville, 41
Pershing State Park, 204
Persimmon Ridge
Winery, 31
Peters Market, 116

Pickle Springs Natural Wildlife Area, 41
Pickney Bend Distillery, 20
Pierce City, 72
Pilot Knob, 33
Pineville, 72
Pin-Up Bowl, 11
Pirtle's Weston Vineyards Winery, 172
Plain & Fancy B&B, 34
Planters' Seed and Spice Co., 98
Plattdutsch Hadn Tohopa, 127
Platte City, 170
Platte Landing Park, 168
Plattsburg, 179
Pleasant Hill, 136
Pleasant Hill Pool Hall, 136
Pleasant Hill Thrift Store, 136
Pleasant Valley Quilts, 131
Point Lookout, 80
Polished, 97
Polly's Soda Pop Factory, 109
Pomme de Terre State Park, 58
Ponak's Mexican Kitchen, 101
Pony Express Museum, 175
Poplar Bluff, 46
Poppy, 200
Porky's Blazin' BBQ, 125
Posh KC Blow Dry Bar, 97
Powell Gardens, 122
Praying Hands sculpture, 73
Prospero's Books & Media, 103

Q
Q39, 103
Quackers Steakhouse, 177

R
Rainbow Trout and Game Ranch, 67
Randy's Roadkill BBQ and Grill, 27
Ray's Diner, 155
Rayville, 162
Real Hatfield Smokehouse, 71
Red Apron, The, 148
Red Barn Antiques, 22
Reeds Spring, 75
Restless Spirits, 143
Resto 101, 136
R Farm Distilling, 177
Ridgedale, 82
River Ridge Winery, 44
River's Bend Gallery, 168
River's Edge Resort, 64
Riverside Country Club, 151
Roaring River Inn, 74
Roaring River State Park, 74, 75
Robidoux Row Museum, 175
Robyn's, 168
Rocheport, 201
Rockbridge, 66
Rockbridge Mill, 67
Rockcliffe Mansion, 191
Rock Eddy Bluff Farm, 25
Rockin A Distillery, 115
Rolla, 26
Rolling Hills Store, 153
Rotary Jail, 153
Route 66, 9
Route 66 museum, 59
Royal Gorge, 33
R & S Mercantile, 136

Rush Limbaugh tour, 43

S
Salvatore's, 113
Sam's Store, 207
Samuel Berton Distilling, 16
Sandy Creek Covered Bridge, 31
Sandy Valley Brewery, 31
Sara's Ice Creamand Antiques, 39
Scandinavia Place, 109
Schlafly Bankside, 186
School House Bed and Breakfast, 202
Science City, 101
Scott's Kitchen BBQ, 148
Scotty's Trout Dock, 79
Sedalia, 121
Señor Barrigas, 177
Seven Springs Winery, 134
Shakespeare Chateau Inn & Gardens Bed & Breakfast, 176
Shamrock Ranch, 162
Shatto Milk Company, 178
Sheffler Rock Shop and Geode Mine, 192
Shepherd of the Hills Fish Hatchery, 82
Shepherd of the Hills Inspiration Tower, 75
Shepherd of the Hills Theater, 76
Sherwood Quilts and Crafts, 152
Shirley, Myra Belle, 69
Shoal Creek, 144
Shrine of Mary Mother of the Church, 133
Shrine of St. Patrick, 191

Siloam Mountain Park, 159
Silos at Prairie Vale, The, 128
Silver Heart Inn & Cottages, 112
Sip, The, 150
Six-Mile Ordinary, 201
Skullsplitter Spirits, 209
Slice of Pie, A, 27
Slightly Off Broadway, 154
Slivinskis' Bakery, 166
Smallin Civil War Cave, 85
Smithville, 179
Smithville Lake, 180
Smoke House Market, 18
Snow Creek Ski Area, 174
Sorella's Deli, 147
Soulard, 14
Southern Hotel, 40
Spiva Center for the Arts, 71
Spooksville, 72
Springfield, 53
Springfield Art Museum, 56
Springfield Conservation Nature Center, 56
Square One Brewing, Distillery and Restaurant, 16
Squeez Inn, The, 137
St. Albans, 19
St. Ambrose Church, 12
Stanton, 29
St. Charles, 14, 185
Steamboat Arabia Museum, 97
Ste. Genevieve, 38
Ste. Genevieve Museum, 38
St. George Hotel, 173
Still 630 Distillery, 8

St. James, 27
St. James Winery, 27
St. John's Episcopal Church, 187
St. Joseph, 174
St. Louis, 3
St. Louis Cathedral, 7
St. Louis Distillery, 185
St. Louis Iron Mountain & Southern Railway, 42
St. Louis Loop, 11
St. Louis Mercantile Library Association Art Museum, 8
St. Louis Walk of Fame, 10
St. Mary of the Barrens Church, 41
St. Mary's Episcopal Church, 100
St. Mary's ghost, 100
Stockton, 137
Stockton State Park, 58
Stockyards Brewing Company, 89
Stone Canyon Pizza, 169
Stone Hill Winery, 23
Stover, 134
St. Patrick, 191
St. Patrick's Catholic Church, 133
St. Roberts, 61
Stroud's Restaurant, 106
Stuff, 106
Sugar Creek, 113
Sugar Creek Vineyards & Winery, 194
Sugar Leaf Bakery Café, 77
Sugar Whipped Bakery, 179
Sullivan, 29
Sundance Ranch KC, 162
Sweet Expression, A, 136

Sweet Things, 40
Swiss Meats and Sausage, 22
Switchgrass Spirits, 16
Swope Park, 89

T
Table Rock State Park, 75
Taboo Ice Cream & Grill, 133
Tall Pines Distillery, 72
Taum Sauk Mountain, 36
Taylor Family Orchard, 147
Ted Drewes Frozen Custard, 9
Ten Mile, 206
Thespian Hall, 118
Thousand Hills State Park, 205
Tightwad, 135
Tipton, 120
Tom Sawyer Riverboat, 30
Tony's, 47
Top of the Rock, 82
Top of the Rock Chapel, 82
Touring Cyclist, 186
Tower Grove House, 3
Tower Rock, 41
Towosahgy State Historic Site, 48
Toy and Miniature Museum, 105
Trail Through Time Path, 41
Trash & Treasure, 166
Trenton, 151
Trenton Cemetery Prairie, 150
Triple Creek Golf Course, 128
Truman Presidential Library, 107

Tryst Falls Park, 164
TWA Museum, 143
Twelve Mile Creek
    Emporium, 35
Ty Lechyd Da
    Distillery, 57

U
Union, 16
Union Covered
    Bridge, 207
Union Station, 4, 101
Unity Village, 126
University of Central
    Missouri., 126
University of
    Missouri, 198
Urbana, 58
US Army Engineer
    Museum, 61

V
Vaile Mansion, 111
Van Buren, 65
Van Till's Winery, 162
Ventana Gourmet
    Grill, 155
Versailles, 128
Victorian House, 78
Vienna, 25
Vietnam Cafe, 100
Villa Antonio Winery, 31
Villainous Grounds, 41
Ville Escape Room &
    Axe Throwing, 204
Vintage 1847
    Restaurant, 23
Visitation Catholic
    Church, 25
Vivilore, 108
Volpi's, 12

W
Wabash BBQ, 158
Wallace State Park, 167
Walnut Creek
    Winery, 179

Walnut Street Inn Bed
    and Breakfast, 55
Warm Springs
    Ranch, 118
Warrensburg, 126
Washington, 19
Watercress Park, 63
Watkins Woolen Mill
    State Historic
    Site, 163
Waverly, 116
Waynesville, 60
Weathervane
    Antiques, 206
Weavers' Market, 132
Webb City, 73
Webster House, 95
Weston, 170
Weston Bend State
    Park, 173
Weston Historical
    Museum, 170
Weston Tobacco, 171
West Plains, 66
W. F. Norman, 137
Where Pigs Fly Farm
    and Pigs Aloft
    Museum, 119
Whirlwind Ranch, 60
Whiskey Mansion, 176
White House Hotel, 22
Whiteman Air Force
    Base, 127
Wilderness Lodge, 34
William Jewell
    College, 147
Williamsburg, 213
Willow Boutique, 136
Willow Springs
    Mercantile, 159
Windy's Canoe
    Rental, 61
winemaking, 194
Wines by Jennifer, 169
Winston Churchill
    Memorial and
    Library, 209

Wok N Roll, 133
Wonderland, 105
Wood Chux Axe
    Throwing, 161
Wood Hat Spirits, 212
Woodhenge, 180
Woodlock Cemetery, 37
Woodsmen
    Distilling, 201
Woodstock Inn Bed &
    Breakfast, 111
World Craft and Thrift
    Shop, 129
World Sheep and Wool
    Festival, 193
World's Largest Fork, 56
Wurstfest in March,
    Maifest, 22
Wyoming Street Wine
    Shop, 136

Z
Zanoni Mill, 66
Zona Rosa, 107